SAUDI ARABIA
AND THE
UNITED STATES

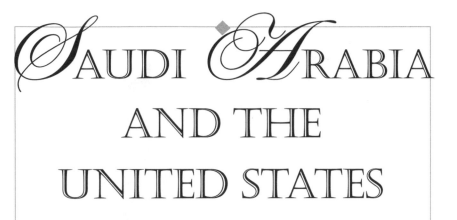

SAUDI ARABIA AND THE UNITED STATES

Birth of a Security Partnership

Parker T. Hart

AN ADST–DACOR DIPLOMATS AND DIPLOMACY BOOK

INDIANA UNIVERSITY PRESS   BLOOMINGTON & INDIANAPOLIS

This book is a publication of

Indiana University Press
601 North Morton Street
Bloomington, Indiana 47404-3797 USA

www.indiana.edu/~iupress

Telephone orders   800-842-6796
Fax orders   812-855-7931
Orders by e-mail   iuporder@indiana.edu

The paper used in this publication meets the minimum
requirements of American National Standard for Information
Sciences—Permanence of Paper for Printed Library
Materials, ANSI Z39.48-1984.

Manufactured in the United States of America

Library of Congress Cataloging-in-Publication Data

Hart, Parker T.
Saudi Arabia and the United States : birth of a security
partnership / Parker T. Hart.
p.   cm.
"An ADST-DACOR diplomats and diplomacy book."
Includes bibliographical references (p.   ) and index.
ISBN 0-253-33460-8 (cl : alk. paper)
1. United States—Foreign relations—Saudi Arabia.
2. Saudi Arabia—Foreign relations—United States. 3. United
States—Foreign relations—1945–1989. 4. United States—
Foreign relations—1989–   5. National security—United States—
History—20th century.   I. Title
E183.8.S25H37   1998
327.730538—dc21   98-35841

1   2   3   4   5   03   02   01   00   99   98

To JANE, MY GREAT TROUPER AND LOVING ADVISOR.
To MEG, OUR FIRSTBORN (IN DHAHRAN), WHO

HAS NEVER CEASED TO LOVE THE DESERT.

To JUDY, WHOSE LIVELY NATURE HAS BRIGHTENED

MANY A DISMAL INTERNATIONAL SCENE.

AND TO THOSE ARABS AND AMERICANS WITH A PATIENT

INTEREST IN DIPLOMACY-AT-WORK.

CONTENTS

CONTENTS

THE ADST-DACOR DIPLOMATS AND DIPLOMACY SERIES

For more than 220 years, extraordinary men and women have represented the United States abroad under all kinds of circumstances. What they did and how and why they did it remain little known to their compatriots. In 1995 the Association for Diplomatic Studies and Training (ADST) and Diplomatic and Consular Officers, Retired (DACOR) created a book series to increase public knowledge and appreciation of the involvement of American diplomats in world history. The series seeks to demystify diplomacy by telling the story of those who have conducted our foreign relations, as they saw them and lived them.

Parker ("Pete") Hart, a career minister in the United States Foreign Service, was widely regarded as a consummate diplomatic professional. Fluent in five languages and determined to know each host country in depth, he concluded his service, appropriately, as director of the Foreign Service Institute. As one of the State Department's most eminent authorities on the Middle East, Hart held important posts at crucial junctures in the tumultuous history of the region. In 1968–1969 he served as assistant secretary of state for Near Eastern and South Asian affairs. While ambassador to Turkey in 1965–1968, he played a leading role in successful US efforts to prevent war between Turkey and Greece over Cyprus, the subject of his 1990 book *Two NATO Allies at the Threshold of War*.

His three tours of duty in Saudi Arabia gave Pete Hart a unique appreciation of that desert kingdom's culture and people. He watched it develop, he once wrote, from "a newly united collection of illiterate tribes deprived of almost all the resources needed to cope with modern statehood" into an enormous economic power and important ally of the United States. Helping forge that critical security partnership engaged all his accumulated diplomatic skill, as revealed in this scrupulously researched account, written over five years and accepted for publication just months before his death in October 1997.

Edward M. Rowell, President, ADST
Joan M. Clark, President, DACOR

FOREWORD

Saudi Arabia, blessed with a quarter of the world's known oil reserves, has been a reliable source of energy upon which the United States and much of the rest of the world rely. The Saudi kingdom, in turn, depends on the United States and the West to help it fend off the predators and potential enemies that inevitably arise in a region plagued by political and economic instability. This formula has proven both workable and durable over the years. Hence, Saudi Arabia's security constitutes a vital interest for both countries and has for decades been at the heart of a remarkably close bilateral relationship.

Historians will long cite the Gulf War of 1990–1991 as a landmark example of successful international action against military aggression. It was also a striking example of remarkable cooperation between the two principal defenders, the United States and Saudi Arabia. Washington's unprecedented military response to Riyadh's call for help at the time of Saddam Hussein's occupation of Kuwait, and the military cooperation that ensued both during and since the Gulf War, attest to the extraordinary strength and mutuality of that partnership.

Most observers at the time viewed US-Saudi collaboration as a logical manifestation of the two countries' strong common interest in protecting the Saudi kingdom and its vast oil resources, as well as the natural outgrowth and culmination of many years of working together in the security domain. As sensible and viable as the oil-for-security tradeoff may appear, however, we should not overlook the obstacles and impediments that have long complicated the partnership and could, if not carefully navigated, recur and adversely affect the bilateral relationship.

Only those familiar with the history of United States–Saudi relations can fully appreciate the extent to which the success of operations Desert Shield and Desert Storm was rooted in long years of intricate, often difficult diplomacy. One such recognized authority is former US ambassador to Saudi Arabia Parker Hart, a career diplomat extensively and personally acquainted with that history. Not only was he present at the creation of much of today's Saudi Arabia; he was intimately involved in the delicate process of building the framework of trust and cooperation that, even now, requires constant and careful nurturing.

Inevitably, religion is prominent among the factors both past and present that complicate the US-Saudi security partnership. Saudi Arabia, as the home of Islam, bears special responsibilities in a Muslim world often beset by fear and suspicion of too close involvement with the "infidel" West. Saudi leaders face the difficult dilemma of working effectively with the United States and other Western powers to assure the country's security while at the same time maintaining credibility as an independent custodian of Islam's holy places. Similarly, as Parker Hart reminds us in recounting the long and sometimes difficult dialogue on the status of the airfield at Dhahran, though the Saudis desire US military assistance, they prefer to minimize domestic and regional criticism of such assistance by keeping it discreetly "over the horizon."

Such dilemmas are a recurring theme throughout the history of the bilateral relationship. They help explain why the issue of Saudi national sovereignty has repeatedly arisen in the context of security cooperation; why neither government has contemplated establishing US military bases in the kingdom or concluding a formal defense treaty; and why such matters as joint investigations following the 1995–1996 truck bombings of US military installations in Saudi Arabia have proved so politically sensitive.

Middle East political rivalries have also contributed to Saudi caution in dealing with the United States and other Western powers. Washington's close identification with Israel, long viewed as the Arab world's paramount enemy, is an obvious case in point. Though progress toward Arab-Israeli peace has served to ameliorate this impediment to closer US-Saudi ties, it remains a sensitive factor in Arab politics and one that Saudi leaders feel obliged to take into account when dealing with Israel's principal sponsor.

Ambassador Hart also reminds us that there have been regional strains other than those involving Israel, as when differences arose in the 1960s between Riyadh and Washington on how best to cope with the revolution in neighboring Yemen and with Egyptian president Nasser's military intervention along Saudi Arabia's southern border. Hart's fascinating insider's account of this threat to the Saudi kingdom—intensely real at the time but largely overshadowed by Cold War developments elsewhere and too often forgotten by observers of the current scene—underscores how skillful diplomacy and overriding mutual interests eventually brought US and Saudi policies into fruitful harmony.

Regional predators such as Iran and Iraq have continued to endanger resource-rich Saudi Arabia. The United States, for its part, has increased its dependence on imported oil. Maintenance of healthy bilateral relations has thus remained of vital importance to both Saudi Arabia and the United States. Cultural, religious, and other significant differences notwithstanding, the partnership draws its strength in no small measure from the pioneering efforts of both countries' statesmen in laying the early foundations of security cooperation.

Parker Hart ranks among the best of those dedicated and determined diplomatic pioneers. His remarkable accomplishments greatly facilitated the work of those of us who succeeded him as envoys to the desert kingdom.

Walter L. Cutler

ABOUT THE AUTHOR

Parker T. Hart was a career minister of the Foreign Service of the United States and former assistant secretary of state for Near Eastern and South Asian affairs. He served as US ambassador to Saudi Arabia, Kuwait, and Turkey, minister to the Yemen, and director of the Foreign Service Institute. From 1969 to 1973 he was president of the Middle East Institute. Years earlier he was detailed to the founding conference of the United Nations in San Francisco. His book *Two NATO Allies at the Threshold of War* was published in 1990 by Duke University Press.

Born in Medford, Massachusetts, Hart graduated from Dartmouth College, received a master's degree from Harvard in 1935, and studied at the Graduate Institute of International Studies in Geneva. In 1952 he also graduated from the National War College. Having entered government service in 1937 as a translator of French with the Department of State, he was commissioned in the Foreign Service the following year. His diplomatic service as a Middle East specialist included the following:

1944	Opened the US consulate in Dhahran, Saudi Arabia
1945–46	Consul, Dhahran
1947–49	Served with the Division of Foreign Service Planning, Department of State
1949–51	Consul general to Saudi Arabia
1952–53	Director of the Office of Near Eastern Affairs
1955–58	Deputy chief of mission, Cairo
1958	Sworn in as ambassador to Jordan, but unable to proceed to post because Jordan had united, briefly, with Iraq
1958	Minister to Syria during the first months of the United Arab Republic
1958–61	Deputy assistant secretary of state for Near Eastern and South Asian affairs
1961–65	Ambassador to Saudi Arabia; concurrently minister to Yemen (1961–62) and ambassador to Kuwait (1962–63)
1965–68	Ambassador to Turkey
1968–69	Assistant secretary of state for Near Eastern and South Asian affairs

PREFACE

In September 1963, I had a long conversation with His Royal Highness Prince Faisal, twenty years after his first visit to the United States. At the time of our discussion, the kingdom he governed—Saudi Arabia—was virtually at war with Egypt over Yemen. As President John Kennedy's ambassador to Saudi Arabia, I had just delivered a message of warm friendship and reassurance intended to defuse this crisis. I remember the prince's words: "Since 1943 I have considered the interests of my country and community to be the same as those of the United States. We differ in nothing basic. . . . After Allah we trust in America."

This book is my personal recollection of the US-Saudi relationship that was put through critical tests during two successive decades, long before Operations Desert Shield and Desert Storm. I witnessed the birth and growing pains of this relationship during three tours of duty in the Saudi kingdom: in Dhahran, when I opened the consulate there, from 1944 to 1946; in Dhahran again, from 1949 to 1951, when the post was upgraded to consulate general to meet the needs of US armed forces during the Cold War; and, finally, in Jeddah, as US ambassador, from 1961 to 1965, when I played a part in the US policy of preserving the independence and territorial integrity of Saudi Arabia as a vital interest of the United States and its allies. In late 1965, I was appointed ambassador to Turkey and ceased to have any direct connection with events in the kingdom. My emphasis here, therefore, is on my firsthand knowledge and recollection of the time of my involvement there, refreshed by consultation of many still classified, and some declassified, materials.

My service as deputy chief of our embassy in Cairo from 1955 to 1958, and as minister in Syria in 1958, heading our consulate general in Damascus after that government voted to join with Egypt in forming the United Arab Republic, enabled me to assess the methods of Egypt's Gamal Abdel Nasser as he sought hegemony in the Arab East and special influence in the world of Islam and in Africa. During my service, I watched and participated as from 1956 to 1961 Nasser generated momentum in an attempt to fill an Arab leadership void, shattering the last vestiges of colonialism and moving the Arab world closer toward unity.

He envisioned a unity, led by himself and by Egypt, that also involved his commanding the vast oil resources being discovered in the most isolated and economically undeveloped Arab countries. Nasser's interest in these resources was only natural; possessed or controlled by Egypt, they would enshrine his image throughout the Middle East and much of the developing world. That he intended to make a serious play for them is beyond doubt, as evidenced by a bungled February 1963 Egyptian airdrop on the Saudi coast of weapons and ammunition intended for use in the overthrow of the Saud regime.

In the face of this and earlier threats, Saudi Arabia had no friends it could rely upon in the Arab world or elsewhere in the Middle East. When I first went there in 1944, its population, informally estimated today at sixteen million, was possibly two million and desperately poor. Saudi oil reserves at the time were roughly estimated at 10 billion barrels and were considered gigantic. Today, despite the high level of production during the past forty-seven years, Saudi Arabia presides over oil reserves estimated at well above 300 billion barrels, and new sources continue to be found. Nowhere else on this globe does so much energy lie under one flag. A sure defender of this vital deposit and of Saudi territorial integrity has been the United States, alongside the kingdom's small and increasingly improved armed forces.

The original 1933 concession to "mine" Saudi oil was signed at a time of stiff international competition and required that the concessionaire— Standard Oil of California (SOCAL)—educate Saudis so they could replace foreign nationals at every level as soon as this could be accomplished with no loss of efficiency. This task absorbed the company for the sixty-three years of the concession because it proved necessary to establish, with the Saudis, a solid educational base in science and technology previously nonexistent. Only recently has the policy of preferential use of Saudi labor at all levels been brought to realization. Oil in commercially valuable quantity was not available until 1938 after millions of dollars and much stubborn work over five years.

The Arabian American Oil Company (ARAMCO) has always been independent of US government supervision, raised its own capital, and been a true partner of the kingdom.[1] To the company's early pioneers goes credit for a harmonious relationship with its Arab hosts, quite at variance with the turbulent oil-company-versus-government scenarios that characterized twenty years of oil history in Iran and Iraq. Because their motivations meshed, and because Washington refrained from meddling, the Saudi government and ARAMCO achieved enormous transformations in the Saudis' national infrastructure, their educational system (including education for women), and the general quality of Arab life.

The official US connection has been to play a vital role in Saudi security; but a far greater, if less spectacular, role has been chalked up by

ARAMCO. It has been the economic heart, the pump that drove the society and that made possible a foreign policy independent of those collective Arab pressures that might otherwise impede Saudi Arabia's development as a modernizing but temperate Islamic society.[2]

Gradually formed from an amalgamation of indigenous tribes and possessing both wealth and a small population, Saudi Arabia needed help primarily against external physical attack. Early in the relationship, the United States was asked by the modern state's founder, King Abd al-Aziz Al Saud, or Ibn Saud (who ruled from 1902 to 1953), to supply such external protection, and over the years the United States has done so. In return, the United States has benefited economically beyond calculation, as have many of Saudi Arabia's neighbors and those beyond the seas. It is not simply a matter of oil; Iraq, too, has oil in great abundance. The difference is that Saudi Arabia has so far been able to preserve its rationality in a sometimes irrational Middle East. This is evidenced by Saudi Arabia's use of its oil windfall: the many aid programs the kingdom has established in the Third World; its huge infrastructural development, most of it planned in five-year programs and carried out with foreign technological assistance; and its establishment of joint US-Saudi advisory committees on agricultural and industrial-technological manpower, meeting regularly in Riyadh.

Behind all this is a diplomatic history of which most Saudis and Americans are barely aware. It dates back to 1933. As I wrote these pages, many recollections of half a century came flooding back. The roots of US-Saudi common interests are many. Their exposure in detail may surprise, but they should offend none but the most hypersensitive. In this the ninth decade of my life, I have undertaken to make of these memories a gift to Saudis and Americans of goodwill, hoping that in a recounting of the facts will come a better understanding of a remarkably durable and productive friendship.

ACKNOWLEDGMENTS

This book, begun six years ago and written in almost monastic seclusion, was brought to reality by the dedicated labors of a few people who encouraged my belief that a valuable story was mine alone to tell. No other US government servant now active had participated in or observed at such close hand these three decades of the mutual security policies of Saudi Arabia and the United States.

It gives me pleasure to record my gratitude for the outstanding cooperation extended to me in my research by Frank M. Machak, Jr., the State Department's chief of Foreign Affairs Information Management, and several of his staff, notably Joyce A. Mabray, a cheerful and tireless researcher. At the end of the day, Mr. Machak obtained a most expeditious official clearance for which I am also deeply grateful.

Thanks go to the Association for Diplomatic Studies and Training and its then president, Ambassador Stephen Low, for helping bring the book to publication. Thanks are also due to the former book publishing program of Georgetown University's School of Foreign Service and its Institute for the Study of Diplomacy, in particular to Margery Boichel Thompson, former ISD director of publications. She encouraged my efforts from the start, stayed with the project even after the book program ended, and subsequently, as ADST publishing coordinator, facilitated the book's adoption by the ADST-DACOR Diplomats and Diplomacy Series. Her deep experience and skill as an editor are all beyond adequate words of thanks.

I am also most grateful to Brian Lepak, a former graduate student at Georgetown, for putting the first draft onto the computer; to the many students who followed in his electronic footsteps; to former Foreign Service officer and Georgetown professor G. Harvey Summ for his insightful editorial suggestions; and especially to Robin Surratt for her thorough and meticulous editing.

Lastly and of paramount importance has been the encouragement of my wife Jane and our two daughters, Judy and Meg, who grew up in the Middle East and maintain an interest in the dynamic changes taking place there.

ACRONYMS AND ABBREVIATIONS

ARAMCO	Arabian American Oil Co. (renamed from CASOC after Texaco became equal partner with SOCAL in the Saudi concession)
CALTEX	Equal partnership of SOCAL and Texaco
CASOC	California Arabian Standard Oil Co. (operative arm of SOCAL in early period of exploration and development of concession in Saudi Arabia)
COMMIDEASFOR	Commander, Middle East Force
FSO	Foreign Service Officer
SAUDI ARAMCO	Official full name of the now Saudi government-owned ARAMCO
SOCAL	Standard Oil of California (parent of CASOC)
STRICOM	Strike Command (Tampa, Florida)
UAR	United Arab Republic (Egypt and Syria, 1958–1961)
UAS	United Arab States (Egypt, Syria, and the Mutawwakilite Kingdom of the Yemen, 1958–1962)
UN	United Nations
UNGA	United Nations General Assembly
UNSC	United Nations Security Council
UNTSO	United Nations Truce Supervision Organization
UNYOM	United Nations Yemen Observation Mission
USMTM	US Military Training Mission
YAR	Yemen Arab Republic

SAUDI ARABIA
AND THE
UNITED STATES

Saudi Arabia, Yemen, and Neighboring Countries

$\mathscr{P}$ROLOGUE

HISTORY IN THE MAKING: A PORTRAIT OF KING ABD AL-AZIZ AL SAUD

 Khalid al-Sudairi, emir of Dammam, looked up from his notes of our weekly exchange of Arabic-English lessons. "His Majesty has invited Your Excellency to Riyadh. We shall leave together in three days." There were no particulars. Like most Saudi princes I had met, Khalid was sparing of words. On royal request a C-47 loaned from the US Army Air Corps, bucket seats and all, would take us from Dhahran to Riyadh, at a formative moment in the US-Saudi relationship.

I was thrilled but at the same time a bit worried. I had cooked up this invitation with Khalid a month earlier at one of our lesson exchanges, and I had not cleared it with my boss, our minister plenipotentiary at Jeddah, eight hundred miles to the west. Consuls did not, of their own accord, call on heads of state; that was the domain of chiefs of mission, in this case former Marine Corps Colonel William A. Eddy, then US minister to Saudi Arabia, a soldier-diplomat sensitive to the recent accumulation of "courtesy" visits by US officialdom.

The monarch's hospitality had been great, and it had been abused. "Sword collectors" was the term Eddy used in protesting to the Department of State the gathering wave of officials with dubious job descriptions who had wired ahead for arrangements to "pay respects." It was

1

getting to be more than the relationship could bear, and in no uncertain terms Eddy had demanded a screening of such visitors in Washington or he would do it arbitrarily from Jeddah. It had gone against the grain but the matter was now out of my hands and even those of Eddy. The king's invitation was an overriding command. But did I have cause to visit and talk with him?

It was March 1946. I had been in Saudi Arabia for two years and knew that, according to usual Department of State practice, my time would shortly be up. The odds were that I would never return and would therefore never have another chance to meet a towering figure of Bedouin history—King Abd al-Aziz ibn Abd al-Rahman Al Faisal Al Saud, or Ibn Saud, a self-made king who had created and consolidated a desert realm the size of the United States east of the Mississippi.[1] I felt sure that the US legation in Jeddah would not "fit me in" to one of its numerous desert field trips to communicate with the king, although that was how all serious business was done. The king was in close touch with the tribes of his country and was frequently on the move, camping with his retinue in the desert. He made all the basic decisions, and telegraph and telephone facilities were so primitive as to be almost nonexistent.

From my post at Dhahran on the Saudi east coast, I had been giving assistance, as US consul, to the US Army's Cairo-based African and Middle East Theater (AMET), which was under the local command of two able officers of the US Corps of Engineers, Lieutenant Colonel N. Shumate and Major E. Wenge. They had built at Dhahran, from scratch, Saudi Arabia's first airfield, the most modern in the Arabian Peninsula; almost operational, after seven months of backbreaking work, its long runway and limestone buildings were quarried from an adjacent hill. Although it was a US Army air base, the facility was the gift of the US government. It was the posthumous investment of the friendship between President Franklin D. Roosevelt and King Abd al-Aziz, a follow-on to their years of correspondence and to their remarkable meeting on Great Bitter Lake at the Suez Canal on February 14, 1945. But it was the US Army Air Corps that had formally asked the Department of State, in 1944, to obtain the monarch's permission to build the airfield as an urgent wartime measure. Permission had been given only after much royal hesitation, but at this time, March 1946, I was unaware of these complications; I knew only that the job had been done with amazing speed and skill by very competent young Americans who, World War II being over just as their labors began, resented having their demobilization delayed in order to provide, at US taxpayers' expense, a gesture to a remote desert ruler.

Many were the GI letters of complaint to Capitol Hill. Why not a private contractor paid for by the king? Or by the oil company, since "oil and profits were what it was all about"? I had a hard time answering these questions as I monitored the project, which I did frequently on consular business and in order to be as helpful as I could for the sake of morale. I could not, however, compensate for the lack of normal social life, and I possessed no remedy for the heat and the attentiveness of billions of flies. I told the men that the US government had made a promise to the king while the war was very much on and that only AMET had the ready-to-go resources in men, experience, and equipment to do the job promptly and well. Shumate would then chime in, "Get the goddamn thing done fast, but right, and we'll all be home!"

I had wanted to take Shumate with me to Riyadh, but he had been "demobbed" and had lost no time departing by US military aircraft, leaving in command Wenge, his deputy, to clean up details. Wenge, also a first-class engineer, had a few snapshots he had taken of the job site and was glad to be making the journey with me. He could answer the king's questions, which, I rationalized, would be numerous. His Majesty had not yet seen this, his first airport, or for that matter any other modern airport. Indeed, my records showed that he had left his country only twice, the last time in 1945 to meet FDR at the Suez Canal. Along with Wenge, I selected to accompany me Vice Consul Larry Winter Roeder of my office and our Bahraini interpreter, Mahmoud Yusuf. We were all dressed in Arab garb, by the king's command and at his expense. The king was sensitive to Islamic extremism in his country's interior, especially in the highland north, the Nejd. Foreigners traveled to Riyadh and elsewhere in the kingdom, outside the oil fields, only at the king's invitation (which, however, could be in response to one's own request) and under his protection. A tailor visited every prospective and official foreign traveler and outfitted him in one hour with a measured woolen robe (*mishlah* or *aba*), a cotton head cloth (*ghutrah*), a cotton undershirt (*thob*) of ankle length, and a head rope (*aqal*) of black, tightly woven goat's hair.

THE KING AT RIYADH

The flight, my first to Riyadh, took about three hours and was not entirely uneventful. A teenage relative of Khalid al-Sudairi became restless and began to finger an emergency window exit. It flew open and banged against the rudder before dropping some two thousand feet to the desert below. None of the princes aboard was the least bit disturbed; they did not even reprimand the boy, who was simply told to fasten his seat belt and remain quiet. The pilot came back to inspect. He pronounced the rudder damage to be insignificant and went back to his seat. The C-47 was, of course, not pressurized. In the cool early morning air, we continued on course then banked for our descent toward what appeared to be an uninhabited, featureless terrain. The heat came up to meet us. The "landing strip" was desert hardpan; there were no buildings. We taxied toward a windsock and tent.

As we pulled up to the tent, there emerged from the flap to greet us a distinguished figure in Arab attire whom I recognized from an earlier acquaintance as Sheikh Hafiz Wahba, the Egyptian-born private counselor to the king and Saudi minister to Great Britain. He invited us into the tent, picked up a World War I field telephone powered by a dry-cell battery, gave it a crank, and was at once in a brief conversation with the king. Upon hanging up, he announced that the king wished us to come at once to the palace. Several cars and drivers were waiting, and we were driven rapidly in clouds of dust over a washboard track for some fifteen to twenty minutes. We approached a citadel of tawny baked mud with crenellated towers and turned into a wide, open gate guarded by several uniformed, bearded soldiers of fierce and determined mien. They snapped to attention as we slowed to identify ourselves. From a large inner court we were escorted to a shaded veranda, and then I discovered that I was "alone" with only three other passengers from our flight: Roeder, Wenge, and Yusuf. The remainder of the passengers had vanished: Emir Khalid al-Sudairi, his elder brother Abd al-Aziz al-Sudairi, Emir of Jauf, Abd al-Rahman al-Sudairi, and Emir Muhammad al-Sudairi. I construed the sudden absence of these men to be a matter of royal protocol; I was the guest, as was my party. The Sudairis would make their call when the king so directed. Sheikh Hafiz Wahba did not accompany us into the palace, but had informed us that it was the king's command that we come to dinner and spend the night in the Badia guest house.

As I led the way around an L-shaped turn into the great *majlis* (public sitting room) of the Qasr al-Murrabba, the bulky frame of Ibn Saud, seated near the far corner beyond a sea of overlapping Persian carpets, rose. Giving a kind of salute, he beckoned us to come forward. I was surprised to see that the king stood only a bit taller than I (at my 5' 10"), for he had been said to be 6' 4" in his youth. (I was later to learn that the king had suffered extensively from spinal problems in his later years.)

Mahmoud Yusuf, knowing Bedouin protocol in manners of address toward a paramount chief, knelt on one knee before the king to preserve eye-level subordination. I was gestured to take a chair on the king's immediate right, Wenge to his left, Roeder to the seat on my right. Around the walls were gilt-framed armchairs, and I estimated that easily eighty visitors could be accommodated.

At first, it appeared that we were alone. Then I saw two tall Arabs seated far away to the right, one of whom I at once recognized as Faisal, second prince of the realm, beside whom in San Francisco's Opera House in April 1945 I had stood as Department of State monitor while he signed documents relating to his country's membership in the United Nations. The other, taller figure I knew must be his elder brother Crown Prince Saud. The king introduced them both, and I stepped over to shake their hands. Saud, like his father, was informal, jolly, and outgoing; Faisal was friendly but reserved and of the two bore easily the more princely demeanor. It was a meaningful contrast that never dissipated in the years that followed. They were half-brothers. Shortly after the introduction, they quietly left with their father's permission.

As I sat down, the king reached for my hand, enveloping it in his huge palm. Radiating an indefinable fatherliness, he welcomed me in a manner that reassured me that my maneuver to visit him was understood and by no means taken amiss. I thanked him for affording me the honor of meeting him and asked Wenge to show the king snapshots of his airport at Dhahran. The king went through them quickly. He asked no questions but remarked, "A good thing for both of us." And there it was, the end of my excuse for business with the king! We were served, in alternation, Arab cardamon coffee and mint tea, whereupon the king suggested we rest. He would see us at dinner in the palace.

Along with our pilot and copilot, we were driven to the Badia guest house, a large two-story, mud-brick building with an extensive vegetable garden, situated on the edge of the desert well outside the tiny walled city of Riyadh. The property was fully owned by Sheikh Abd Allah Sulaiman al-Hamdan, the king's minister of finance, but at the time used by the king for foreign guests. We were ushered into a courtyard surrounded by two-story colonnaded passageways that shaded the bedrooms against the intense outside heat. Accommodations were comfortable, simply furnished, very clean, and shuttered against the desert glare. An utter quiet was broken only by the sound of doves and the squeak of wooden wheels as leather well buckets were raised by harnessed camels walking up and down a tread path. We were served lunch and retired for the customary siesta.

Two hours after sundown, we returned to Qasr al-Murrabba, where I found no less than the new British minister at Jeddah, Arabic-speaking Sir Laurence B. Grafftey-Smith, dressed in Arab clothes, the black and gold *aqal* customarily worn by a prince of the blood adorning his head. He was quite at home with his excellent Arabic and was asked by Arab attendants to lead the guests to the king. Wearing the monarch's colors on his head symbolized customary adoption as a royal "son," and Grafftey-Smith bowed and kissed the king's hand. I decided as an American not governed by traditions of royalty to simply do an emphatic handshake and give a respectful verbal salutation. The king accepted it cordially.

Inside the dining room we joined two lanes of some forty Arab guests and sons of the king crouched before the food in two rows, Bedouin-style, right sleeves rolled above the elbow. Between these lanes was an array of huge trays of whole roasted lamb on rice and, on separate plates, chickens, vegetables, camel's milk (from a single large bowl, passed around), a sweet milky gelatine called *mahallabiya*, and fresh fruits. There were no place settings, and etiquette decreed that only the right hand was to carry food to the mouth. Grafftey-Smith was on the king's right, I on his left, and etiquette decreed that only the king and his principal guests were to converse. The Arab guests, including most of the king's sons (minus Saud and Faisal), therefore, ate in silence, as barefooted Arab stewards circulated deftly among the plates and around the great trays, using knives to cut choice pieces of lamb for the king and his guests. The atmosphere was informal.

My Arabic, rudimentary and mainly self-taught, was called upon to do its primitive best, as no interpreter was at hand; Mahmoud Yusuf was being served elsewhere. I decided to exploit the opportunity of a lifetime and settle a question much debated by westerners, namely, how many children did the king have? He appeared slightly taken aback but quickly asked, "Sons or daughters?" I replied, "Both." After a moment's reflection, he said, "By God I do not know exactly, but I know it is above seventy."[2]

According to custom, the king, seeing that his principal guests had eaten their fill, rose and led the way to waiting servants holding ewers of warm water, soap, towels, and basins for washing our hands. We entered a small lounge accommodating about a dozen leading guests. Over Turkish coffee, a free and easy conversation was possible, and an interpreter was included for my benefit. King Abd al-Aziz was in high good humor. Like most Saudis, he joked only with people he liked, and could be ultrapolite and all business with those he did not. The king brought up a favorite topic: the advantage of multiple marriages over Christian monogamy.

"I do not understand you Christians," he said. "You marry only one woman, and as you both age you become older looking at her. Why not a young woman for a second wife?" Slapping the British minister on the knee, the king added, "Look at Sir Laurence here. He has been married for ten years now and he has fever every day! Now I have four wives, always, and never any fever." There was general but respectful merriment, the monarch joshing a visitor who spoke excellent Arabic.[3]

The next morning my three fellow passengers and I bade a brief but grateful farewell to the king's representative and flew back to Dhahran. Minister Eddy not only took no exception to our visit with the king but a few weeks later, while I was visiting in Jeddah, he sent me in an auto convoy as escort to two eminent American agricultural scientists to see Abd al-Aziz.

THE FATHER OF HIS COUNTRY

Abd al-Aziz was a great warrior and a successful military strategist. Furthermore, the state he unified had as its main pillar assiduous respect for the *sharia* (Islamic law), as defined by the independent leaders of the *ulema* (religious scholars). The Saudi *ulema* faithfully follow the teachings of the eighth-century imam Abu Abd Allah ibn Hanbal, founder of the most conservative of the four Sunni, or orthodox, schools of jurisprudence. This school had been revived in Nejd by the eighteenth-century charismatic scholar and preacher Sheikh Muhammad ibn Abd al-Wahhab. The sheikh formed a historic pact of mutual support with Sheikh Muhammad ibn Saud, of al-Diraiyya (near Riyadh), which survives to this day as the cement of an otherwise diverse society and carries the popular label "Wahhabism." It is ultraconservative, a sort of Cromwellian puritanism of Islam, and was the vehicle for the Saudi unification of most of the Arabian Peninsula into a united realm in 1925. Abd al-Aziz, the last unifier and the first Saudi king, was a genuinely religious man. Though he rigorously held to strict Wahhabism, he loved life and had an earthy sense of humor and a profound distrust of the impractical and the extreme. He had set his mind on economic development.

Apart from knitting a vast territory into three political units—Nejd, Hejaz, and al-Hasa (Ahsah)—the huge Saud family, as of the late 1940s, was also a system of social security. Under its leadership, no one in the kingdom, on principle, could be allowed to starve. The size of the Saud clan in the total population could not be accurately estimated at that time, but it was credited as putting an end to intertribal feuding in an age of growing drought. It was *not* "feudal," as was the contemporary imamate of Yemen, for example, since the tribes were no longer completely independent political entities; rather, their leaders were "brothers" under an acknowledged paramount chief, who now had become king. Although he had no scepter, crown, or throne, the king was the most eminent of the single most eminent clan, and was directly accessible in a *majlis* at least once a week. His rule, furthermore, was not arbitrary but by consensus.

Stories by travelers who had met Abd al-Aziz portrayed a strong leader, gracious and hospitable. Two stories I had heard go back to this period. If unverifiable in detail, they bear a degree of apparent authenticity and must have been running through my mind during my visit.

In the unification and political consolidation of the vast landmass from the Red Sea coast to the Persian Gulf, in the period from 1902 until 1927, British recognition of Abd al-Aziz as king of the Hejaz, the Nejd, and Its Dependencies had been of decisive importance. The king's greatest worries had been control over his own Wahhabi extremists and noninterference with his independence by Great Britain. His brotherhood in Islam, the Ikhwan, was fearless in battle and essential to a desert victory, but, being unyielding, it was of negative value in diplomacy and at times almost impossible for Abd al-Aziz to restrain.[4] The Ikhwan also resisted modernization, which it regarded with tunnel vision as the work of Satan through Western infidels.

A deputation of the brotherhood called on Abd al-Aziz, following his political unification of the tribes into a kingdom, to denounce his use of radio and telephone. Omitting purposefully the appellation "Your Majesty" (as reserved, in any case, for God), they demanded that these two instruments of corruption be destroyed. The king looked at his clock and, seeing that prayer time had arrived, he tuned in to Cairo's broadcast from a radio receiver he kept near his chair. Suddenly, it gave the call to midday devotions. He watched the faces of the delegation, then demanded in thunderous tones to be told what was being said. After a silence the reply came that it was the call to prayer. When he pressed further to know the person behind that voice, he received a shamefaced reply that it was that of a *muezzin* in Cairo. Then came the clincher: "Can you supposedly great scholars maintain that the words of the Holy Quran can be pronounced by Satan!" With no response forthcoming, the king denounced his visitors as "hypocrites," a deadly sin to Muslims. Be aware, he told them, that not only the radio but other instruments, such as the telegraph and telephone—wherever they came from mattered not a whit—would be used in his kingdom henceforth as widely as possible to spread the Holy Book and its Truth to all his people. They had best stop their agitation if they knew what was good for them.

The end of this encounter, however, was not the end of this problem. On July 7, 1933, Abd al-Aziz ratified a concession with Standard Oil of California to find, develop, produce, and market internationally any oil that could be found in the larger part of his kingdom. Almost immediately Western men began to arrive, dressed in Arab clothes as the king commanded and wearing full beards. In the eyes of the people, they were, nonetheless, infidels. They roamed the desert in devilish vehicles and used all kinds of instruments never before seen. "Give them courtesy," the word spread, "they are the guests of Abd al-Aziz."

One sheikh high up in the Ikhwan had had enough. When he demanded to see the king, he was admitted at once. Standing before the monarch he shook his finger under the nose that tradition prescribed he should have respectfully kissed. "You, Abd al-Aziz, are a traitor to your people and to Islam! You are unworthy to rule or to lead in prayers as our imam; you must get out!"

The king let him rant on without interruption, then summoned an aide and ordered him to ask (with due respect) the highest judge (*qadi*) available to proceed in all haste to his presence to judge a matter of highest religious importance.[5] Upon the *qadi*'s arrival, the king stood to greet him and to offer him his seat, which the high cleric took. The king then removed his own *aqal* and cast it on the carpet. In the prescribed fashion he stood beside his accuser facing the *qadi*, who now demanded to know who was the complainant and what was the complaint. Apprised, the *qadi* ordered the sheikh to state his charge, following which he ordered Abd al-Aziz to make his reply. Clarifications and specifics ensued during which each side invoked the Quran to support his points. Abd al-Aziz held his own in holy writ and after several hours, the *qadi* delivered his judgment. He exonerated the king from deadly sin, whereupon Abd al-Aziz put on his royal *aqal* and turned on his adversary, warning him of dire consequences if he made further trouble. The sheikh left the room.

Rounding the corner of the L-shaped *majlis* of Qasr al-Murrabba and passing a door to the veranda, the plaintiff was suddenly seized by a powerful hand grasping his neck from behind and propelled into and across a windowless room, through an equally dark second room, and into a third that was well lit. The rough escort then let go and disappeared. Squinting in the light to get his bearings, the *Ikhwani* saw a brazier and a large coffeepot and, cross-legged before it, Abd al-Aziz. "Come, sit here," the king commanded in a soft voice. "Have coffee. I want to talk to you."

The *Ikhwani* obeyed and for several hours the king, who had traveled hardly at all outside his great realm, spoke of that wider outside world with familiarity. How, he asked, was Saudi Arabia to live beside that world and keep its integrity? To do so required strength that could come only through modernization and a powerful friend, preferably one deeply interested for sound economic reasons in a Saudi relationship, but uninterested in usurping its government. Nonetheless, that friendly state must be powerful enough to be an effective ally in a world of conflict. The sheikh asked many questions, raised many objections, was not intimidated, but in the end was convinced. He became a lifetime supporter of the monarch.

Little did I realize at the time of my meeting with Abd al-Aziz that I had elbowed my way into the beginnings of a long-term relationship of mutual security between the United States and Saudi Arabia, which was to become a fulcrum of US policy toward Southwest Asia and the Arab East. Nor could I have known that it would eventually involve both countries in an alliance of armed force to protect responsible custody of the world's single greatest source of oil.

PART ONE

DIPLOMACY OF AN AIR BASE

1

TROUBLED US-BRITISH COOPERATION

Three years into World War II, the government of Winston Churchill in war-battered London might have been expected to welcome an economic as well as a military partner in the Middle East, especially one with so little political ambition or concern in the area. Such was not the case. While the motivation of the United States centered on winning the war, England's preoccupation was first and foremost with survival. Following closely on that objective was survival of its empire and the country's special privileges as reward for its costly responsibilities. US and British policies clashed because Washington's attitude, particularly regarding the Middle East, would deny long-standing British rights that ensured pro-British commercial activities and monopolies. (At times conflicts had to be settled in London, sometimes at the highest level, to preserve the alliance.)

Meanwhile, Ibn Saud sought to avoid the ire of either party, as he struggled to keep his country of perhaps two million fed and clothed. He also feared for his country's independence. To him, the threat came not from the Germans but from the British, who had ties to his old rivals who ruled in Iraq and Jordan to his north. Additionally, the British were entrenched in the areas rimming Saudi Arabia to the south. The United States soon became embroiled in these complexities.

GENESIS OF THE DHAHRAN AIRFIELD

The construction of Dhahran Airfield materialized not as the result of a request from the Saudi government but from urgent US requirements in 1942 and 1944, originating in the Military Air Transport Command (MATS). Most compelling for the United States was a strategic requirement for the fastest, cheapest, and most secure transit of its aircraft carrying personnel and war equipment eastward from Cairo. Washington also feared the depletion of its domestic oil supplies undergirding this transit; the war was going to be fought on fossil fuels as much as anything else. The United States needed overflight, refueling, and landing rights. Ibn Saud needed just about everything, but specifically food and consumer goods that had been cut off by the war, silver coinage for payrolls, subventions to keep the tribes in line, and cash income from whatever source.

US generalized planning for air routes across South Asia to the Far Eastern theater began in February 1942,[1] barely three months after the bombing of Pearl Harbor. The United States and Britain wanted to obtain overflight rights and airfields to shorten their eastward air route between Cairo and Karachi by some 212 miles and to avoid expensive landings and takeoffs at Habaniyya in Iraq and Abadan in Iran.

When the British North African campaign against Nazi forces under Field Marshal Rommel was at its height in mid-1942, an alternative route via Khartoum and across Saudi Arabia was tentatively explored with Saudi officials by both US and British officers. Direct overflight of unpopulated areas was quickly obtained from Ibn Saud in 1942. MATS, however, still wanted fueling, maintenance, and emergency landing bases. The British already had secure bases at Muharraq in Bahrain and in Sharja on the Trucial Coast, where, by long-standing treaties, they fully managed the foreign relations of the seven tribal rulers.[2] However, Muharraq's runways in Bahrain were salt marsh and soft, and Washington needed runways capable of sustaining heavy loads. The alternative of crossing Saudi Arabia would require the building of one or more airfields in Saudi Arabia's Eastern Province.

Although Ibn Saud was formally neutral, his sympathies were clearly with the Allied nations. At the time, US President Franklin Roosevelt considered most of the Middle East, except for certain French-dominated areas such as Syria and Lebanon, to be a British sphere of influence and a British responsibility. British military planners, too, were interested in the shorter Saudi air route and would enjoy its use with MATS.

Selection of the routes would require on-the-spot investigation by a qualified US officer from the Cairo US command. Protocol and policy moved with deliberation, as Washington's war planners had not yet reached a consensus. Cairo-based Minister Alexander C. Kirk had presented his letters of credence in Riyadh on May 11, 1942,[3] as the second nonresident US envoy to the kingdom. After the formalities, he had conversed with the finance minister, Sheikh Abd Allah Sulaiman, the senior official closest to the king. Kirk led the minister into a discussion of wartime airfield needs without any implied US commitment. To his surprise, he found the sheikh ready to come at once to the point. He saw no objection to overflights or even to the US building of airports on coastal areas.[4]

Kirk was not as yet authorized to initiate negotiations, but he reported fully to Washington and informed his colleague, British minister Francis H. W. Stonehower Bird, who told Kirk he had already discussed this matter with the finance minister and had received much the same reaction. Both agreed that the next step was for the US and British governments to be precise about their needs. No instructions were forthcoming, however, until the end of June 1942, when the War Department suggested to the Department of State that efforts be made to obtain Saudi government nonstop ferry command routes across central Arabia from Khartoum to Bahrain and from Khartoum to Basra and to include the right to forced landings. The War Department also suggested that State explore the possibility of landing fields for short-range aircraft.

State asked Kirk for his advice regarding compensation for Ibn Saud in the form of financial assistance or protection from German reprisals. Kirk, in turn, asked the advice of Chargé James Sayle Moose Jr. in Jeddah and was told that overflight rights should be obtainable but that airfields would be more difficult. Moose recommended that no compensation be offered at the start on the basis that the airfields would be part of the common war effort, but he also suggested that the US government consider supplementing the £750,000 shortfall between the British government's subvention and Ibn Saud's estimated needs. Kirk recommended that Moose sound out the Saudis through Finance Minister Abd Allah Sulaiman, and State so instructed Moose in July 1942. The finance minister referred Moose's request to the king.

Abd Allah Sulaiman counseled Bird and Moose not to raise the issue of landing fields at the time. Moose was therefore instructed to make a joint approach with Bird to the Saudi government asking only for specific overflight rights. Ibn Saud replied verbally to the British in a statement directed to both London and Washington. He granted the British routes for nonstop flights from Khartoum to Bahrain, passing north of Birka, and from Khartoum to Basra, passing north of Dhiba. He would not object if the US planes used the same routes. He insisted on utmost secrecy, having not yet declared war on Germany. The flights could begin at once.

There was no further pressure at this time for permission to build an air base,[5] perhaps because of the turn of the tide in North Africa. The threat by Rommel to Britain and its allies in Egypt and the Near East was approaching its apogee at al-Alamein. In the great battle that began October 23, 1942, Rommel's mangled forces were in full retreat by November. The most immediate danger to Egypt and the neighboring Near East had passed, but it was not yet certain that Axis forces were gone for good.[6]

A significant augmentation in the US official presence in the British-controlled Persian Gulf was delayed not by the British but by Ibn Saud's personal hesitation, which for months held up approval of the establishment of a US consulate at Dhahran. The most urgent need for a consulate in Saudi Arabia's Eastern Province arose from the expanding requirement of documentation and general consular protection for resident US personnel. Dhahran promised to be the hub of a rapidly growing oil community. Also, transient construction personnel required passport services.

To meet passport renewal requests, it was necessary to send US passports by safe-hand to the US consul in Basra. US shipping operations and seamen also needed help in processing visas to Iraq and other countries of transit. Such trips required the better part of a week, and sometimes more. Not only was Jeddah too far away, there was no transportation over those thousands of miles of worn desert tracks except by occasional company caravan, in very old and battered trucks. Bahrain was not satisfactory either; the British would not permit resident foreign consulates, as such institutions would implicitly derogate from exclusive British treaty rights in the gulf sheikhdoms. (But London had no objection to business visits by nonresident US consular officers, provided British political agents were in control of all contacts with the Arab rulers).

All such requirements had been beyond satisfactory handling when only a hundred men, without families, kept the concession of the California Arabian Standard Oil Company (CASOC) alive between 1941 and late 1943.[7] After the failure of Rommel to conquer British forces in Egypt's western desert, however, Washington agreed to assist in sponsoring a major development by CASOC of oil refining and shipping in the Persian Gulf. That meant shipments of massive infrastructure and a return to Arabia of hundreds of employees, plus construction teams from Bechtel, McCone, and Parsons, the consortium destined from 1943 to build a 50,000-barrel-per-day refinery and oil pier at Ras Tanura on the gulf.

The US government, as a war measure, encouraged this project and released steel for fabrication of the refinery and ships to bring it to Saudi Arabia's first oil pier. Meanwhile CASOC had begun to accelerate its discovery program and was finding new oil deposits of great promise at Abqaiq, fifty miles south of Dhahran, and at Abu Hadhriyah in the north.

It was clear that the US presence in eastern Saudi Arabia would geometrically increase as the war in the Pacific intensified. The Department of State by 1943 was convinced that it had to have a resident consular officer at Dhahran and made a secret decision that once the king's permission was obtained, it would ask British approval for allowing the US consul at Dhahran also to handle US needs in the gulf, outside Saudi Arabia and without office or flag, as an informal consular district. In Jeddah, Minister Moose was instructed to seek Saudi permission for a resident consular mission and did so on August 23, 1943.

The royal reaction was sharply and surprisingly negative. To the king and his advisors, it was a matter of setting a precedent, of opening a Pandora's box, and of jeopardizing Saudi security. To Moose's practiced eye it was obvious that neither the king nor his principal counselors had any notion of what a modern consul's duties were. Ibn Saud seems to have feared a revival of Ottoman-style capitulations and a US extraterritorial authority over his courts of law, as exercised by the British in Bahrain and the gulf. Most of all, he clearly feared a precedent into which Britain and Iraq, Jordan, and other Arab states would leap, demanding equivalent privileges. Not all of these would be friendly to him. In this he was vulnerable. Iraq and Britain had already applied for consulates, and in Basra there was already a Saudi consulate. However, both British and Iraqi requests had been refused. The king, while not flatly refusing the US request, strongly urged that an alternative be found. He sent two of his most trusted counselors, Khalid Bey al-Gargani and Bashir Bey al-Sadawi, to Moose to help find that alternative.

When the king's counselors arrived, Moose explained that Dhahran was an urgent but very special US case, most unlikely to be repeated by others in eastern Saudi Arabia inasmuch as the Dhahran and other oil deposits were located in an almost totally unpopulated area. Al-Gargani pointed out that Iraq had centered its request on the village of Qatif, at that time a desperately poor, squalid, and trachoma-ridden Shiite oasis with insignificant commerce. Iraq had also applied for permission to establish a consular office in Riyadh, which Ibn Saud wanted to keep free from resident foreigners who might run afoul of the Wahhabi religious police, the *Mutawwa'in*. The two counselors revealed to Moose that the Saudi government had applied for permission to establish a resident consulate in Bahrain and been refused by the British government. (Such an office would have gone against a century of British control over Bahrain's foreign relations.) Instead, later, a resident Saudi trade representative would be permitted.

On further instructions, Moose, on October 3, went to Riyadh to clear up the issue with the king. Ibn Saud was greatly troubled. He said that approaches to open a consulate at an unspecified location had also been made by the Iranian government, but he had refused. As the US government was being very insistent, he would not flatly say "no," but he would discuss the matter further with his advisors.

In retrospect, it is my belief that, among other considerations, Ibn Saud feared embarrassing diplomatic incidents involving any foreign presence, but especially with Iranian, Iraqi, or British officials living in Riyadh. Riyadh at that time was a most sensitive stronghold of the Hanbali school of law; the *sharia* would ordinarily be applicable in all its severity to any Muslim without compromise, and to non-Muslims to a degree not yet tested. This situation obviously worried the king. Its testing was certainly on the minds of informed Arabists, such as Moose and Eddy and of experienced Arabists in Washington.[8] One brutal punishment could trigger a large exodus of American oil personnel, with a disastrous reduction in Saudi economic development. The request was therefore put on ice until Prince Faisal made his first trip to the United States in late 1943, accompanied by his half-brother, Prince Khalid ibn Abd al-Aziz, and Sheikh Hafiz Wahba, the Saudi minister to Great Britain.

President Roosevelt's written invitation of 1943, addressed to the king, had invited him or a member of his family, if he could not accept, to visit Roosevelt in Washington. The king, who suffered infirmities, felt the trip to be too long. Crown Prince Saud eagerly accepted, then was obliged to regret when his father decided he needed him to assist in tribal problems. The king thus selected Faisal, the second prince of the realm and titular foreign minister.[9]

On this, his first visit to the United States, in October/November 1943, Faisal displayed great caution but also understanding of the wartime problems facing the United States. In one of several discussions at the Department of State, he was asked by Wallace Murray, head of the Near East division, to accept the need for a US consulate at Dhahran, since a very large refinery and oil pier were to be built near Dhahran at Ras Tanura. An influx of several hundred Americans for the construction and operation of these facilities would therefore soon begin. Murray told Faisal that the argument that such an office would set an unfortunate precedent and create pressures for consulates of other countries could, in the US view, be readily rebutted. The Saudi government could explain that no countries other than the United States and Saudi Arabia had a natural interest, or a share, in the development of this area. Faisal did not argue the point, but rather appeared sympathetic. He would take the matter up with his father on his return home. Later, back in Riyadh, he persuaded his father not to further oppose the establishment of an American consulate in Dhahran.

Finally, on March 2, 1944, the answer came, and it was positive. In due course, the British Foreign Office registered their nonobjection and also accepted the US-proposed arrangement for a visiting US consul to the gulf. By June 1, 1944, while I was stationed temporarily in Jeddah, the way was cleared for me to proceed to Dhahran, there to be joined by a most capable junior colleague from the legation, Vice Consul Clarence J. McIntosh. In July 1944, I proceeded from Jeddah to Dhahran via the British supply route of Cairo[10] to Baghdad, Basra, and Bahrain, under instructions to open the first and only consulate ever established at Dhahran.[11]

About a month and a half after the formal flag raising at the new consulate on September 1, 1944, I reported a visit to Dhahran by Benjamin F. Giles, the commanding major general of US Forces in the Middle East (USFIME), headquartered at Cairo. Giles informed me that he had recently been told by a "high British authority" at Cairo that the British were opposing the granting of an airfield at Dhahran to the United States on the grounds that it was unnecessary to the war effort. Giles found this to be against British expert opinion, since the existing Bahraini airfield could not satisfy Allied requirements for heavy aircraft.

Against this background, Giles had been informed by the US minister to Saudi Arabia, Colonel Eddy, then visiting in Cairo, of a report by me that two British officers had recently made a survey visit to Dhahran in search of a British airport site. Eddy had reported that a "most authentic confidential source" confirmed that the British had "told the Saudi Government" to refuse US permission to build an airport at Dhahran and that the Royal Air Force chief in Cairo had stated to the same source that the Air Ministry in London would not concur in the US Army request for the Dhahran airport. It was shortly confirmed that two British officers had indeed visited Dhahran to find a site for a British air base. It was also confirmed that the king would not grant the United States permission to build the airport unless the British indicated their "no-objection" in writing.

In Washington, Eddy's report on the matter, borne out by corroborative information, was acted upon quickly and emphatically by Assistant Secretary of State Adolf A. Berle. He called in British deputy chief of mission Michael Wright on October 9, 1944, and bluntly informed him that we knew for certain that Ibn Saud had declined, on official British demand, the US request to build the airport. The king had, therefore, suggested that the United States consult the British. Angrily, Berle informed Wright of Eddy's report and added, "There is no law in heaven or earth which entitles anybody to interfere with our building an airfield for legitimate purposes in Saudi Arabia."[12] Wright agreed that such back-channel activity should not continue and that it was entirely contrary to the spirit of overarching US-British wartime "arrangements" regarding the Middle East.[13] He said he would make inquiries to London and report the results to Berle.

Secretary of State Cordell Hull reinforced Berle's protest by directing

John Winant, US ambassador to Britain, to point out to British foreign secretary Anthony Eden that this matter had made a "most painful impression" in Washington, the more so because it was not the first instance of such "dog-eat-dog" policy vis-à-vis US interests. It would complicate the forthcoming international civil aviation conference in Chicago and could affect what had been a generally nonexclusive, cooperative "live-and-let-live" US attitude toward British and US aviation traffic, which "might otherwise lead to closer cooperation." The British saw that their own broader interest of landing rights in the United States could be jeopardized. On further US prodding, they made clear in May 1945 to Ibn Saud that the United Kingdom approved of the US project to acquire and construct a US military air base at Dhahran.[14]

The way was now open not only to negotiate the air base, but also to achieve better Anglo-American cooperation in the area. This required paying attention to the most urgent needs of the king, which would be the *quid* for Ibn Saud's *quo* before a Dhahran airport agreement could be negotiated. Also to be negotiated with the king would be a commercial airport agreement. After a survey, Dhahran's level area just east of the Jabal Dhahran[15] was selected and later approved by the king. It had a deep, hard surface with a limestone quarry site nearby. It could take any aircraft load.

These and other matters had hardly been ironed out with the king by June 1945 when the War Department, taking note of the end of the war in Europe and the need to redeploy forces westward to the Pacific, made a determination that there was "a diminishing military necessity for construction of an airfield at Dhahran." The Department of State was notified that the War Department could no longer, by law, take military responsibility for the costs of the airfield project. Therefore, the War Department stated, since a promise had been made to the Arab sovereign and his permission given, State would have to consider whether to ask the president to take political responsibility as a matter of "national interest." State did not linger. Together with the War and Navy Departments, it so recommended to President Harry Truman, who at once accepted political responsibility and allowed the project to go forward as of June 25, 1945.[16] Following the signing of an agreement of construction on August 6, 1945, by Saudi officials and Lieutenant Colonel Shumate, the project was launched.

By the terms of the US-Saudi agreement, the Japanese surrender on September 2, 1945, triggered the conversion of the unfinished Dhahran air base to the fully owned property of the Saudi government. The United States, however, had a three-year right of occupancy and use, intended for wide-ranging military postwar cleanup and repatriation of personnel and equipment.[17] There was much confusion in Washington, and some in London, over whether civil use of the airport would be allowed and, therefore, permit broadened landing rights, known as Fifth Freedom rights, by US commercial aircraft. This originated in mistaken rumors that Transcontinental and Western Airlines (TWA), in its drive to pick up the leading role in the founding and piloting of a Saudi airline and in the development of Dhahran airport, was about to conclude an accord with the Saudi government granting it a monopoly. Minister Eddy, through his direct contacts, was able to put this rumor to rest, but the evidence of international opposition to the principle of Fifth Freedom rights and the concern in the US Congress over spending taxpayers' money without obtaining this international right at Dhahran almost brought construction to a halt. What abandonment at this juncture would have done to Saudi-US relations would be hard to exaggerate.

Early May 1946 brought about completion of the basic work on the base. Where nothing but a windsock had marked the site, Saudi Arabia in eight months obtained residual ownership of a 10,000-foot hard-surface runway, a terminal building of cut limestone, a large repair hangar, barracks, a mess hall, an auditorium, and various accessory limestone structures, fully equipped with all utilities. A US Air Force (USAF) custodial crew of seventy-five men was later authorized, all at US expense. The airfield, more than any other tangible achievement in US-Saudi relations, was, and remained for fifteen years, a touchstone of the quality and durability of the US connection—a concrete symbol of official US interest in Saudi security. To obtain this relationship the United States planned and executed a variety of projects of assistance intended to show goodwill, to protect the US-based oil concession, and to raise the level of personal cordiality between the two heads of state and their peoples.

SOME STICKY US-SAUDI-BRITISH NEGOTIATIONS

In the Arab East, or *Mashriq*, undertakings such as the Dhahran airport depended for success in the early war period upon cooperation with the British. In April 1942, Under Secretary (and Acting Secretary) of State Sumner Welles had expressed President Roosevelt's previously noted deference to Britain in a message to Minister Kirk in Cairo (then accredited also to Saudi Arabia): Washington "[feels] that any agreement with the Saudi Arabian Government for installation, defense, and operation of airfields should be negotiated by the United Kingdom," since Saudi Arabia lay within the area of "British military responsibility.... Therefore it is proposed to request British Chiefs of Staff to take the necessary action."[18] During the next two years, Kirk and his successor, William Eddy, were to argue, with gradual effect in Washington, against such total abandonment of US interests to Britain. It took until May 1944, however, for London and Washington to establish a mechanism whereby their respective heads of foreign affairs could and would move quickly to resolve problems found to be damaging to relations at the local level in the Middle East.[19]

In the interim, Britain was already lining up preferential treatment for British postwar trade. The highest levels of government in London and in Washington were naturally concerned that overarching US-British agreement take wartime precedence over local differences. The Middle East was recognized early on as a particularly sensitive region where the grinding exigencies of war could sometimes be overlooked in assertion of local prerogatives. Those prerogatives were mainly British, but the United States was sensitive to British discrimination in matters of trade and access to oil, a sensitivity that had shown itself in US policy since World War I. Without any express intent to do so, the US presence in the area by 1944 was developing its own dynamic and threatened the leadership image of resident British political agents. Not all those agents felt as strongly about US-British harmony in wartime as they did about maintaining existing treaties of preference and defending, for postwar advantage, British commercial opportunities. This outlook is instructive when viewed over the long-term course of US-British and US-Saudi relations.

In Cairo in the earliest days of World War II, no great antagonism had existed. US minister Kirk and his opposite number, British minister Bird, shared information and advice freely with respect to Arab affairs. Nevertheless, in 1943 Kirk reported to Washington an "increasingly discernible tendency toward British economic entrenchment in this area under war impact to a degree which might materially negate the best-intentioned postwar agreements for equality of opportunity."[20]

Britain's position in the Middle East was that of an imperial, commercial power. British officials, and especially political agents in the Persian Gulf, carried with them into the war years a deep indoctrination in the defense of traditional privilege. In 1943, the newly appointed minister of Great Britain in Jeddah, Stanley R. Jordan, a career diplomat and specialist in Arab affairs, regarded relations with US colleagues in a different light than had Bird in Egypt (where British suzerainty in the Middle East was being daily threatened with extinction by one of the most brilliant commanders of Hitler's panzer divisions). Jordan, who had served at the legation in Jeddah in the late 1920s, could see a creeping, then a galloping, increase in the US presence in a country that, to be sure, was not a British protectorate, but in which, up to then, no outside influence had appeared to challenge the weight of Britain's seniority.

In 1942, a US diplomatic mission had moved into Jeddah. James Moose had been assigned as second secretary, heading the operation when Kirk was out of the country. Although not fluent in Arabic and dependent on an interpreter, Moose was well qualified by experience and study to undertake the sensitive task of opening and conducting a legation in difficult and spartan circumstances. He handled it skillfully, as I was able to observe when I was sent there in May 1944 to relieve his deputy, J. Harold Shullaw, who was ill. Roosevelt by then had given Moose the exceptional rank of minister resident, a temporary promotion reflecting a desire to upgrade the mission. Vis-à-vis the British presence, however, this was only a half measure, since Jordan was senior in age and diplomatic precedence to Moose and was not a temporary minister but a full minister plenipotentiary.

A US-UK diplomatic chill became apparent in 1944 when William Eddy was "superimposed" above Moose. Eddy, a native speaker of Arabic from his childhood in Sidon, Lebanon, had served under the direction of William J. Donovan in the Office of Strategic Services (OSS), preparing in Tangier (under cover of the US legation) for the North African landings commanded by General Mark Clark. Eddy had met and briefed Clark after Clark's arrival by submarine at a lonely site on the Moroccan coast. When that mission was completed, Donovan directed Eddy to proceed to Saudi Arabia where, under Jeddah legation cover, he was to visit and become friendly with Ibn Saud. His orders were to report directly to Donovan in Washington rather than to Minister Resident Moose. In view of poor communications, this required frequent visits to Cairo to transmit encoded reports and await answers.

Eddy had already met with the king more than once by the time I was posted to Jeddah in May 1944. His total fluency in the king's mother tongue and his quick sense of humor made him instantly a most welcome guest. From my perspective, he contributed vastly to the overall mission. The king and Eddy were two old warriors getting together, and their meetings at royal encampments as the king moved among the tribes were lively. Eddy's special and preferred status was more than a bit rough on Moose, however, compounding his discomfort at having lost his post to Eddy, his apparent subordinate, whom Roosevelt suddenly appointed to higher rank as the first US minister plenipotentiary to the kingdom.[21]

While Moose and Eddy were both on cordial terms with Ibn Saud, British minister Jordan was not. The king, speaking privately to Eddy, had characterized Jordan as "our enemy," that is, of Saudi Arabia and of the United States.[22] He also told Eddy that he had privately discovered that Jordan was going beyond his instructions in his unfriendly behavior. The king's information was substantially accurate. Eddy confirmed that Jordan was discussing US-Saudi relations privately with the king, and without informing the US government. The Department of State made clear its unhappiness with Jordan to the Foreign Office in London,[23] telling the ministry informally that, this being Jordan's method of operation, the US minister in Jeddah was now under instructions not to share department business with him. Instead, Washington would deal directly with London on sensitive matters. In Washington, British ambassador Lord Halifax, apprised of the problem, promised to take it on. He asked, however, that

State leave to him exclusively the approach to be used with London. Halifax had the connections and the influence. Whatever Jordan may have said or done, his further behavior toward the king, according to Eddy, proved damaging enough to destroy most of his usefulness to the US-British alliance.[24]

Jordan's troubles dated back to 1926, when, as a young second secretary and chargé in the British Diplomatic Service posted in Jeddah, he had had a hand in negotiating with Ibn Saud an agreement whereby Cable and Wireless Limited became the first and sole electronic link between Saudi Arabia—then called the Sultanate of the Hejaz, Nejd, and Its Dependencies—and the outside world. This monopoly provided overseas service, but none directly to the United States or to most of the world outside the British Empire. The agreement was renewable automatically at five-year intervals unless notice was given before December 1 preceding a year divisible by five. After notice, modifications would be made within the next six months.

Ibn Saud, then the unifier of a poverty-stricken realm, had faced a hard choice. In 1925 he had conquered the Hejaz, defeating and sending into exile a foremost Arab friend of Britain, the *sharif* Hussein ibn Ali, descendant of the prophet and hereditary custodian of the two holiest places in Islam, Mecca and Medina. It would not have been wise for Ibn Saud, now sultan, to have refused to grant this first British concession, which produced much-needed telegraph communication for local merchants. Nor would it have been good diplomacy to antagonize London when he had no external friends to come to his assistance. Thus, he swallowed the monopoly features insisted upon by Chargé Jordan. Over the years the contract provided undistinguished international service, largely through London, so as to favor British interests. Rates were exorbitant and delays frequent.

By 1944, Saudi requirements had changed, and Jordan was back as minister. There were urgent civilian and impending military demands (especially at Dhahran) for rapid direct telegraph service to the United States and its allies. The Cable and Wireless station at Jeddah was the only one in the kingdom, and it could not efficiently handle the new workload. As all US traffic had to be retransmitted from London, US minister Eddy preferred to take frequent flights on US Army aircraft to Cairo to use the legation's cryptographic facility.

Getting around the Cable and Wireless wartime code restrictions proved expensive and cumbersome. In Dhahran, ARAMCO chartered a tugboat, fitted it with radio equipment, and took it beyond territorial waters in the Persian Gulf to avoid having the British government read all its traffic (and possibly pass it on to British oil companies). Cable and Wireless had refused to transmit any messages for a non-British civilian organization in code, demanding either that the message be sent in the

clear or that the codebook be provided to them. (There was no mechani-
cal or electronic encryption available even to the US legation at that
time.) Standard Oil of California (SOCAL), ARAMCO's parent company, thus set up an arrangement with the New York branch of the US
Coast Guard to furnish ARAMCO with codes whereby the Coast Guard
decoded ARAMCO's messages in New York before forwarding them to
SOCAL and provided special codes for decryption, on the ARAMCO
tugboat, of confidential messages from SOCAL.

The king responded favorably when ARAMCO's top management
recommended in July 1944 that he authorize construction of a Saudi
wireless station to service the kingdom's worldwide needs, with direct
connections to the United States and such other overseas stations as the
king might wish. ARAMCO was ready to assist in design and construction
of such a facility and in training its operatives. The company would have
permission to use it when and if it were built, but did not seek to own it.
To avoid violating the Cable and Wireless concession, ARAMCO pointed
out, the Saudi government would have to give formal notice before
December 1, 1944, of its desire to change the contract .

Ibn Saud decided that the Saudi government would negotiate the
construction and operation of such a station through ARAMCO, but
wanted a specific written no-objection from the British. He also implied
that the matter should be settled between the US and British governments. Not surprisingly, the British objected.

Cable and Wireless had received reports of the US démarche and
objected vehemently to a prospective notice of intent to modify the 1926
agreement. Jordan raised the matter with the king. As the deadline for
notification approached, Eddy reported that Jordan's protest to the
Saudi government had been "violent." Washington refused to accept
such behavior, and by lengthy instructions both to Eddy in Jeddah and to
Ambassador Winant in London made two points for delivery by Eddy to
the Saudi government: The issuing of notice before December 1, 1944,
was not a matter for settlement between the United States and Britain,
nor was a British withdrawal of its objection before that date a necessary
precondition to the Saudi government's giving notice. The giving of
notice was entirely legal and by no means irrevocable, whereas failure to
give notice on time offered no assurance of any improvement in the
radio-telegraph service for another five years.

As discussions ate up time, the US tone became tougher. Stressing that
this was an urgent matter for both the United States and Saudi Arabia,
Eddy reminded the king that the US government "has supported the
economy of Saudi Arabia by furnishing many millions of dollars' worth of
goods and services [an allusion to lend-lease silver currency for internal
Saudi payments] and is giving consideration to means by which the
extent of this aid may be broadened."[25] To Winant in London, Secretary

of State Edward Stettinius sent instructions to obtain a direct and personal audience with Anthony Eden in which the foreign secretary should be told that the United States hoped that from now on there would be no further difficulty with regard to this matter and that "we may confidently expect the closest cooperation between our two governments, which can only redound to our mutual advantage."[26]

On November 21, 1944, Eddy relayed to Washington a message from Sheikh Yusuf Yassin, Saudi deputy foreign minister: Cable and Wireless had been notified that day, in writing and by confirming telegraph, that the king had decided to reserve his right to modify the agreement of 1926 as he might wish. In response, Eddy had told Yassin that now he need not deliver the message to Ibn Saud that he had in his pocket. (It was a copy of a letter of protest from President Roosevelt to Prime Minister Churchill.) Minister Jordan, reacting to the news with anger, argued with Yassin that this had been an unnecessary and an "unfriendly act." Since the United States and the United Kingdom were in full discussion on the matter, said he, the renewal question could be reopened at any time. This, of course, was not correct and did not end the matter. As might be expected, the Saudi government was leaving this aspect up to the United States and to its ongoing discussion with the British, taking the position that British and US agreement on the terms of the modification should govern any further Saudi action.

Correspondence between Washington and London went nowhere. Washington found the British position dilatory and deliberately time-consuming, intended to let the June 1 date for modification pass and the Cable and Wireless contract be preserved intact as an "important British interest." Cable and Wireless appeared to be drafting all British Foreign Office messages on this subject to the United States. Washington, therefore, prepared and sent to Eddy on April 30, 1945, for transmission to the Saudi government the text of a suggested amendment to the Cable and Wireless contract of 1926. It stated that nothing in the text of the 1926 agreement "shall be construed to limit the right of the Saudi government to use or to permit the use of a radio station in Saudi Arabia for the establishment and operation of direct radio communications circuits with other countries when, in the opinion of the Saudi Government, the use of such channels would be in the interest of Saudi Arabia."[27] The Saudi government was urged to send such a statement to Cable and Wireless before June 1.

Eddy reported the following surprise: The Saudi deputy foreign minister had advised him on May 13 that the British minister would be providing him with a written message saying that the Saudi government had already secured the right to modify the agreement at any time. In Eddy's opinion, the Saudi government would now welcome a definite proposal to build a radio station for its ownership. The British minister who had been instructed to write such a message to the Saudis was not Stanley Jordan but Laurence Grafftey-Smith, who had replaced Jordan effective February 22, 1945.[28]

Following clarification of the record between London and Washington, technical representatives of both sides got together on a protocol, dated December 4, 1945, by which the British government undertook to inform the Saudi government that it would not stand in the latter's way if it should wish to accept the construction of a radio-telegraph station by a US company. That station would be the property of the Saudi government for the purpose of operating a direct circuit between Saudi Arabia and the United States, and it would be up to the Saudi government to decide whether it desired further modifications of the Cable and Wireless agreement to permit the operation of additional circuits. On October 10, 1946, it was announced that the US-based Mackay Radio and Telegraph Company had entered into an agreement whereby the company would build a radio-telegraph station for the Saudi government and operate it for at least two years. Saudi Arabia thus came into full authority over its external electronic communications, and a milestone was passed in US assistance to the king in asserting his right to exercise it.

The communication crisis passed, and with it a highly preferential British position in a domain central to Ibn Saud's exercise of sovereign powers. The agreement on a US-built station was a landmark in the king's selection of the United States as a partner in his security system. It was also symptomatic of the rapid fading of Britain's ability to use financial aid to maintain spheres of influence. The trouble at this period of the 1940s was that, except for urgently needed foodstuffs and supplies allocated to the kingdom by the Middle East Supply Center in Cairo (a British-led organization in which the United States participated on a fifty-fifty basis), the shipments of coinage from India, and other Churchill-directed wartime assistance, British economic aid to friendly states was fast running down. Promised road construction and training programs were abandoned; few Saudi officers were British-trained.

In the mid-1940s, when British budgetary aid to Ibn Saud had begun to decline due to catastrophic British financial conditions, Minister Jordan had sought persistently to have the United States pace that decline with a diminution of its assistance, thereby to dilute US political damage to British interests in Arabia. He tried to persuade Minister Eddy to agree that Ibn Saud now needed less aid. Pointing to the dramatic rise in Saudi oil exports that had resulted from ARAMCO's rapid completion of oil extraction and export facilities, he argued for a reduction in the US contribution to what had been since the early days of World War II a joint US-British program of budgetary financial assistance. Eddy demurred. Ibn Saud had enormous bills to pay and ARAMCO's major advances against royalties to redeem. Jordan's political strategy was transparent. On economic grounds, Eddy recommended abandonment of the previous fifty-fifty US-British formula. Washington backed him, and London was so informed.

In one of the first acts of US bilateral assistance, Assistant Secretary of State Dean Acheson, on January 9, 1943, had approached Edward Stettinius, then the lend-lease administrator, asking for prompt action to make Saudi Arabia eligible for lend-lease aid. Stettinius did so by memorandum to President Roosevelt, recommending that he make a "finding" that the defense of Saudi Arabia was "vital to the United States," thus making it eligible for direct assistance under the Lend-Lease Act of 1941.[29] Roosevelt made the finding on February 18, 1943, and thus established a wartime source of many millions of specially minted silver coins—in the basic denominations of one riyal (then worth about $0.40), one-half riyal, and one-quarter riyal, all with silver fineness of 0.916⅔— and made policy of the principle that Saudi Arabia's defense was an integral part of US defense. Being war-related, the finding technically expired with lend-lease in 1946, but the record shows that its purpose continued, however changeable the phraseology. Thus by 1946, US and British programming for Ibn Saud, previously joint and roughly equal, had ceased to be joint, with the US contribution compensating for the British shortfall.

While trying not to antagonize the British government, Ibn Saud turned increasingly to the United States for special help not otherwise available. The king was also motivated by a strong desire to lessen his full dependence on Britain, whose territories, as stated earlier, flanked the kingdom on three sides—in the gulf, in south Arabia, and at Aden. A solid relationship with the United States, for Ibn Saud, provided the only counterpoise and way out. President Roosevelt, without benefit of congressional aid legislation other than wartime lend-lease, gradually found ways to pick up the tab. One was in agricultural demonstration.

US AGRICULTURAL MISSIONS TO IBN SAUD

In view of Ibn Saud's 1933 award of the oil concession to a US firm, President Roosevelt owed the king his attention and gave it in a personal letter. Ibn Saud hoped the contact would extend to US financial aid. The king and the president had not as yet met face-to-face, but before the US diplomatic mission in Jeddah was established, Roosevelt had sent the king two personal emissaries of goodwill, Colonel Harold B. Hoskins and Brigadier General Patrick Hurley. Both had exchanged friendly greetings with the king in the late 1930s, just as war became imminent.

In April 1941, Roosevelt received and studied an urgent appeal by James A. Moffett, representing the concessionaire in Saudi Arabia,

CASOC. Moffett urged an advance to the king of $6 million yearly for five years against that value of oil to be purchased by the US government. Roosevelt rejected the request on the ground that the British held the greater stake in this distant area.

By February 1942, however, Roosevelt's initial reluctance to be taken "far afield"[30] had largely evaporated, clearly due to US entry into the war. Instead of leaving the area to the British, the United States now became an active partner. Therefore, when the king sent Roosevelt an urgent request for a mission of experts to advise on agricultural development, Roosevelt concurred. At US expense, he dispatched a study team headed by geologist-businessman Karl S. Twitchell, well known to the king and introduced to Roosevelt by William Donovan of the OSS. The team's two experts were Albert L. Wathen, acting chief of the engineering branch of the Department of the Interior's Indian Bureau, and James G. Hamilton, regional agronomist in Albuquerque, New Mexico, for the Soil Conservation Service of the Department of Agriculture. The mission arrived in Saudi Arabia on May 11, 1942, and traveled 10,793 miles, completing its survey on December 5, 1942.[31] The team provided the king with an extensive report.

As a follow-up to the Twitchell agricultural mission and its report to the king, Roosevelt found a direct way, through his Foreign Economic Administration (FEA), to hire a remarkable three-man demonstration team. FEA employed the team for eighteen months of service at the Saudi finance minister's 3,500-acre farm, used by the king, near al-Kharj, fifty-four miles south of Riyadh.[32] The mission of highly educated graduate farmers, all from Skull Valley, Arizona, was led by David A. Rogers. He and his associates, Karl Quast and Rahleigh Sanderson, were old personal friends, and all three were soil scientists, agronomists, and horticulturalists. Added to maintain, repair, and even invent new equipment was a resourceful mechanic named Ernest Chambers. They arrived via Dhahran in midsummer 1944 at approximately the time I opened the consulate there. Added soon to their ranks was Glen F. Brown, of the US Geological Survey (USGS), whose primary duty was to reconnoiter and report to USGS on surface geology, at the time unmapped, with special attention to water resources and minerals. The mission automatically fell under my consular protection and assistance, but ARAMCO provided the most practical backup in the form of logistical and radio communication support. At regular intervals, I delivered mail and supplies to the Rogers team in a truck, covering some 250 miles of desert track, much of it of great scenic beauty and affording occasional contact with Bedouin tribes.

The king had requested this mission and, from the start, took a personal interest in its progress. Water was to be drawn from two natural limestone sinkholes that were interconnected but not yet in effective use.

They were equipped with pumps, but earlier efforts to activate the system with good crop yield had failed. If the project could be made to succeed using their two wells, named Ain Dhila and Ain Samha, there was a neighboring area containing a major sinkhole, Khafs Dughara, also to be developed. All three contained large reservoirs of usable ground water and measured at least 300 feet in diameter with up to 420 feet in water depth. The water surface was about 100 feet below ground level. To see such reservoirs in the Arabian desert was to invite their use, but the pumps were silent. The mission repaired the wells and linked them to new irrigation channels, where they had planted crops.

The mission worked hard in extremely primitive conditions, doing great credit to the US image in Saudi Arabia. It successfully produced excellent wheat and a variety of vegetables without artificial fertilizers. (A 1945 locust infestation wiped out the crops completely, but the team began again and succeeded again.) From the king on down, enthusiasm for the mission spread. Oasis farmers came to inspect the irrigation and to learn how to avoid overirrigation. The quality of the crops impressed them. They also admired the toughness and resilience of the Americans and their hands-on, but scientific, farming methods.

The Saudis insisted that the mission not leave without replacements, so the responsibility fell on ARAMCO of finding men who could carry on the farm and train the delegations of Saudi oasis farmers sent by the king to be instructed. During frequent visits the king distributed silver coinage freely to the Arab populace, thus guaranteeing the ready cooperation of al-Kharj villagers in meeting the manpower and construction needs of the US demonstration team. Also cooperating was Finance Minister Abd Allah Sulaiman al-Hamdan, who had conceived the idea on his own land.

Given the isolation and the fact that the US team had left families at home in Arizona, it is not surprising that when the eighteen-month contract with the FEA expired well after war's end, in December 1945, no one on the team wanted to renew it. Glen Brown, however, was a special case. Pursuant to the king's express wish, Brown stayed on, not in al-Kharj but in Jeddah, seconded from the USGS. He was joined by his wife and a fellow geologist, US Army Captain Roy O. Jackson, to undertake for the Saudi government, ARAMCO, and the USGS complete geographic and geologic mapping of the Saudi realm on a scale of 1:500,000, place-named in Arabic and Latin script.[33]

One must not discount the political impact of the Rogers mission. It was President Roosevelt's penultimate gift to Ibn Saud. His practitioners of desert farming had taken up their mission during the war as a patriotic duty, and in Washington they had been briefed by an FEA bureaucracy totally ignorant of conditions in Arabia. Their contract had been signed with urgency. Only on arrival in Arabia did they learn that their pay was for a five-day week; this being totally unrealistic, it was corrected by authorizing *per diem* for a sixty-hour week. On top of this, the members of the mission had been advised to rent hotel rooms at al-Kharj until they could find "permanent quarters to lease."[34]

Arab hospitality is resourceful anywhere, however, and the men were quickly sheltered in the mud-brick homes of Saudi villagers until a five-room, one-story adobe structure, Nejdi-style, was built for them and leased. Rooms were "desert air-conditioned," meaning that water was brought by pipes and hoses (supplied by ARAMCO) to wet-drip dense screens of brush jammed into window apertures. This system of air-conditioning, with more sophisticated screening equipment, was widely adopted by ARAMCO and even by the US embassy residence in Baghdad at that time.

The king, who loved the desert and camped in it often with hundreds of his entourage, was a keen farmer and took an admiring interest in the energy, endurance, and wisdom of these Americans of desert upbringing. He not only reassured them that their labors were appreciated, he treated them like his sons. It was a great adventure for the team, and because news in Arabia traveled with astonishing rapidity by human grapevine, word of the success of the American al-Kharj demonstration farm spread far and wide.

THE DHAHRAN CONSULATE

Together, on September 1, 1944, Clarence McIntosh and I had opened the consulate for business in one-half of a CASOC prefabricated duplex house near an oil rig. Coming from Jeddah, we were in heaven. There was air-conditioning. The company was hard put for office and living space, but it found us two tiny rooms in a one-story shack not far from the discovery well number 7. CASOC also installed a flagpole in a thick concrete base beside the office entrance.

When the Stars and Stripes was hoisted for the first time in eastern Arabia, the enthusiasm of CASOC's wartime nucleus of a hundred home-sick men was irrepressible. They wanted the flag raised every day and were annoyed when consular regulations were cited spelling out flag days. Less than enthusiastic was the reaction of the Saudi government. Over CASOC's in-country voice radio from Jeddah came the company's representative, Clark Cypher, relaying from Minister Eddy Saudi Arabia's complaint: the anchoring in the ground of a flagpole from which to fly a non-Saudi banner implied a foreign sovereignty claim over the adjacent land, something quite unacceptable. Eddy, as a Marine, had the solution: remove the flagpole from its base and grapple it to the building (as did foreign legations at Jeddah). There was some astonishment and a little grousing by those who had just completed the pole's installation, but the job was redone quickly, and the problem of flag emplacement did not recur until years later when what was by then the consulate general had built its own walled compound and enjoyed a degree of inviolability in its leased premises.

In Washington, Secretary of the Interior Harold Ickes had had his own ideas on sovereignty. In 1943, while conferring at the Department of State, Prince Faisal had been officially informed that the US government was considering an equity participation in CASOC to protect the exceptionally large cash advances it would have to make to the company in order to finance the Ras Tanura refinery. Faisal made no comment whatsoever, leaving State uncertain as to whether his government would disapprove or not.[35]

A strong objection came instead from US minister Kirk. He was annoyed to have been informed belatedly of these important discussions. In the masterful craftsmanship characteristic of his despatches, he threw abundant cold water on the concept of US sovereignty over Saudi Arabia's chief resource, citing the superb record of CASOC in handling its contacts with the Saudi government and the Arab population. He particularly attacked the assumption that the US government could match the flexibility and sensitivity to local customs so well demonstrated by CASOC. He stressed also that Ibn Saud had awarded the oil concession to an American rather than a European firm in large part because CASOC represented only itself, an oil entrepreneur, developer, and marketer, not a government with ulterior political motives. Kirk saw no good reason for the US nationalization of CASOC unless the company proved unequal to meeting wartime production needs, an unlikely event.

Kirk's message no doubt had an impact in the Near East division; nonetheless, after consultation between State and Ickes, CASOC was ordered to advise the king that a US equity was being studied. Parallel notification to Ibn Saud by the US government would then follow. The order stressed the wartime need for a major area refinery, the size of the investment, and the consequent need for US government sponsorship of the project. If it seemed best to locate such a major refinery in Saudi Arabia, Standard Oil of California's concession terms with the king would be strictly observed, and the refinery, which would be constructed and operated by CASOC, would produce a great increase in the revenues available to the king.

The order to notify was carried out sequentially first by CASOC and then by Minister Moose. To general surprise, Ibn Saud, far from being concerned, appeared pleased. The idea that the US government would own a controlling interest in the controlling share of his nation's entire gross domestic product seemed not to worry him at all. He apparently was sure it would benefit Saudi Arabia as well as the United States, and since the history of oil concessions in the Middle East had usually involved controlling shares in the hands of the British or French governments, there was nothing new in a US equity and something to be said for ensuring an abiding US interest in Saudi Arabia's welfare. As matters developed, however, Standard Oil of California and Texaco ultimately decided to finance the refinery themselves.[36]

2

EARLY PRESIDENTIAL ASSURANCES
AND THE ARAB CALL TO UNITY

When Prince Faisal went to Washington for discussions in October/November 1943, he had more on his mind than an American consular office at Dhahran. Much of the world was at war, and war could spread anywhere, but a threat more imminent than that of a renewed German offensive in the Middle East worried King Ibn Saud. Faisal had missed seeing President Roosevelt, who was abroad, and met instead with Under Secretary of State Edward Stettinius and his deputy, Adolf A. Berle, on November 1.

Faisal explained that Ibn Saud was particularly concerned about reports that the Hashemites—the British-installed rulers of Transjordan and Iraq—were working to expand their domain toward a union of Palestine, Jordan, Iraq, and Syria, essentially trying to surround Saudi Arabia and strangle it.[1] The king did not know the policy of the Allies toward such expansion. If they favored it, he could do nothing to prevent it, but would look upon it with deep regret.

At this point, Stettinius excused himself for a previous engagement and turned the meeting over to his deputy. Berle made it clear that the United States had no interest in aggressive designs and would have no part in an encirclement of Saudi Arabia. What the United States had at

34

heart was a "Good Neighbor" policy not only between the United States and countries near Saudi Arabia, but also between those countries themselves. At this point Berle read to the prince a message on Arab union from Minister Kirk to Deputy Foreign Minister Yusuf Yassin dated October 26, spelling out the general US attitude:

> [W]e desire to see the independent Near Eastern countries retain their liberties and strengthen their economic and social condition. The aspirations of other Near Eastern countries for full independence have our complete sympathy. It naturally follows that if those peoples find it advantageous to unite of their own free will, we would view such a development with sympathy, always on the understanding that it takes place in accord with the principles set forth in the Atlantic Charter. . . .
>
> You may also say that while of course the countries concerned will shape their own decision, it seems to us that the events and problems of the last few years have shown that the Near Eastern countries need a great deal more strength in the economic, social, and cultural domains and that first steps toward unity might well have these ends primarily in view.[2]

Faisal asked for a paraphrase to take with him. The most pertinent clauses of the Atlantic Charter agreed upon between President Roosevelt and Prime Minister Winston Churchill on August 14, 1941, were, "First, their countries [the Allies] seek no aggrandizement, territorial or other; Second, they desire to see no territorial changes that do not accord with the freely expressed wishes of the peoples concerned."[3]

Berle's paraphrase mirrored Kirk's message. It was US policy that each people should have a government of its own choosing and any Arab union, whether social, cultural, or political, should take place only with the entire agreement of the peoples concerned and in accordance with the terms of the Atlantic Charter. Faisal said he now understood US policy and hoped that the US government would continue to keep his father and him informed of any changes in its views. Berle agreed and recommended that Faisal keep in regular touch with the US minister to his country, but make contact with Berle whenever his questions were not sufficiently answered.

Lodged at Blair House and given a White House dinner, Faisal and his brother Khalid, obviously pleased, were above all reassured. Faisal expressed his satisfaction to Minister Kirk in Cairo, during a stopover on December 31, on his return home.

EAST MEETS WEST ON GREAT BITTER LAKE

The Franklin D. Roosevelt Library at Hyde Park, New York, has correspondence going back to an exchange of pleasantries, attendant on the May 1931 US recognition of Ibn Saud, who in 1927 had proclaimed himself king of the Hejaz, Nejd, and Its Dependencies. Full diplomatic relations between the United States and Saudi Arabia were not established until February 4, 1940. Given the fact that a US company had been awarded an oil concession in mid-1933 for the greater part of this huge desert country, one might well ask why this diplomatic action took so long. The answer, apparently, lay in the economic considerations prevalent at that time. That Saudi Arabia had oil in commercial quantities was not discovered until March 1938. Before that, the country was rock-bottom poor. Its foreign exchange budget totaled in the neighborhood of $6 million per annum, derived for the most part from official pilgrimage assessments at 100 gold sovereigns per *hajji*, a levy intended to cover all necessary local pilgrimage costs. No real budget existed, and no paper currency was acceptable for internal payments. In short, the economy was undeveloped and traditional.

In Washington, the Depression had reduced government salaries 10 percent across the board in the 1930s. Simple recognition of a new country, by itself, was cheap enough. It opened the way for possible negotiation of a provisional executive agreement ensuring equal and fair treatment in consular and commercial matters. Such an agreement, being executive, did not require congressional action and was therefore preferred by Secretary of State Cordell Hull, the father of reciprocal trade. He and Roosevelt sought to shape commercial ties in such a way as to neutralize those discriminatory practices that were common in areas under British or French influence. Such an agreement was sought by the United States and agreed to in principle by Ibn Saud soon after US recognition in 1931.

However, given the lack of any diplomatic establishment by either country in the other's territory, negotiations were carried on *ad referendum* by their respective missions to Great Britain, namely, for the United States by Ambassador Robert Worth Bingham and for the king by Minister Hafiz Wahba. Although it was a standard piece of diplomatic craftsmanship, it was not simple. A full two years were required to complete and approve the text, largely owing to slow communications, unfamiliarity on the Arab side with Western legalisms, and the well-known preference of Ibn Saud for agreement by handshake as opposed to a complicated written document. There was an additional factor on the US side: Was it worth the expense to set up a resident American diplomatic establishment to monitor performance? In 1936 Leland B. Morris, US consul general at Alexandria and one of very few veteran specialists in the Near East, was finally sent on a temporary detail to Jeddah to survey the need for an on-site legation. A no-nonsense type, Morris determined that there was no persuasive need for a legation in Jeddah and recommended against its establishment.

By March 1938, when Americans working for CASOC in Arabia numbered more than 300, the United States had a convincing reason to acknowledge a national US interest in Ibn Saud, but the wheels moved with deliberation. On another front, however, consultations accelerated between the US chiefs of mission in Cairo and Baghdad and with policy-makers in the Department of State when it was learned that the Japanese minister to Egypt and the German minister to Iraq were co-accredited to Saudi Arabia and planning visits. Together the chiefs of mission developed a recommendation to the president that, like the Japanese and German envoys, our minister in Egypt be co-accredited to Saudi Arabia. By custom, the US minister would present to Ibn Saud his letters of credence and meet the monarch's principal aides, then return from time to time as important business might warrant. The king made it his practice to receive such visitors in Jeddah during the *hajj*, when he formally welcomed Muslim pilgrims. This practice sharply limited the king's accessibility to foreign diplomats, and by auto the trip to Riyadh required at least five days on rough desert tracks. There was no air service.

From 1940 to 1942, Standard Oil of California (SOCAL) waged a campaign at high levels in the Department of State to have a resident minister stationed in Saudi Arabia to lend support to the American presence following the 1938 oil discovery. On June 30, 1939, Secretary Hull was sufficiently impressed by a report from the American consulate in Cairo on the growth of the American oil community to 325 in the Dhahran area and by reports of German and Japanese diplomatic efforts to win oil concessions from Ibn Saud to recommend, with FDR's immediate acceptance, that American ministers to Egypt be co-accredited to Saudi Arabia, without incurring the cost of the rental or building of a legation structure or hiring a resident staff. On August 10, 1939, he appointed Bert Fish, US minister to Egypt, to carry out the mission. Fish made a single journey to Jeddah on February 4, 1940, and met with the king, after which he resigned both positions and left Cairo.[4] So much for the earliest of face-to-face contacts of American officials with Ibn Saud.

These penny-pinching, arm's-length contacts between rulers and presidents contrasted with the live-together–work-together melding of Americans and Arabs in the Dhahran area and with the inherent need they recognized each had for the other. Ibn Saud's selection of SOCAL for a sixty-year concession over what was then believed to represent virtually all of the oil-bearing structures of the country placed the two peoples in fateful, but surprisingly cordial, partnership. The concession document had been signed May 29, 1933, and ratified on July 7, 1933. It covered 360,000 square miles of a thinly populated area. Geology finally won over State's penny-pinching myopia, but not easily. By early 1938, Max Steineke, CASOC's head geologist, and his men had found no oil in commercial quantities. Six dry holes had been drilled in the Bahrain Zone, a formation in eastern Saudi Arabia that had earlier yielded success in Awali. Failures in drill tests were costly, and CASOC had spent $50 million already. Though the cost of trying for a still deeper deposit—then estimated at an average of $1 million per hole—was great, Steineke nonetheless wired his strong recommendation to CASOC headquarters in San Francisco urging authority to drill for a deeper zone (henceforth called the Arab Zone). Dammam Number 7 rewarded the gamble, yielding commercial grade oil at 4,727 feet in March 1938.

In later years Ibn Saud enjoyed entertaining American visitors with the following reasons for choosing an American firm over one from Great Britain, France, Germany, or Japan, despite the offer of much better terms for a smaller concession. "First," he said, "because you are good oil men. You found it in Bahrain when others said it was not there.[5] Second," said the king, "you treat your Arab employees as equals. Bahrainis are our brothers. We like what we hear.[6] Third," said the king, "yours is a big and powerful country with lots of space and a democratic system; and, furthermore, you are more interested in business than in acquiring political advantage.[7] Fourth and lastly," concluded the king, "you are very far away!"

President Roosevelt took the initiative of inviting Ibn Saud to meet with him for the first time in February 1945 on board the USS *Quincy* on Great Bitter Lake in the Suez Canal.[8] At the meeting, following warm pleasantries and evidence of mutual goodwill (including Roosevelt's gift to the king of one of his wheelchairs), the entire meeting became a vigorous exchange on the Palestine question. This had been the central theme of earlier correspondence between the two leaders, beginning with a letter from Ibn Saud to the president dated November 29, 1938, and the president's reply of January 2, 1939.[9]

In July 1943, Roosevelt had ordered Harold Hoskins, the son of American missionaries and a speaker of Arabic, to Saudi Arabia to determine by personal contact with Ibn Saud whether the king would be willing to meet with Chaim Weizman or other representatives of the Jewish Agency. The purpose would be to seek a "solution of basic problems affecting Palestine acceptable to both Arabs and Jews."

Hoskins was personally well received. His report to Roosevelt recounted a weeklong visit to Riyadh, where he held frequent sessions alone with Ibn Saud. The king was appreciative of the opportunity Hoskins offered to speak frankly on many sensitive topics without an interpreter.[10] The subjects dealt with were many, but Palestine was the main concern. The king chose his words to the president with the utmost care. He said he could neither enter into such talks himself nor authorize a representative to do so. He feared a stage-by-stage wipeout of the Palestinian Arab population; also, he revealed a personal hatred of Weizman, based on Weizman's alleged attempt to bribe him with 20 million pounds sterling, to be "guaranteed" by President Roosevelt. The king later told me that Weizman's proposed intermediary was H. St. John Philby.[11]

Hoskins made his report to Roosevelt in person in a one-hour breakfast talk on September 27, 1943, only a few days before the scheduled arrival in Washington of Princes Faisal and Khalid. To Hoskins, Roosevelt expressed full understanding of the reason for the king's refusal to meet with Weizman, and the president also showed irritation that his name had been mentioned as a guarantor, for which, he said, there was no basis in fact. The nearest he ever came to bordering on a discussion of this subject, Roosevelt said, was a suggestion he made several years earlier to Stephen Wise, chairman of the American Zionist Emergency Council, that if the Jews wanted to get more land in Palestine, they might well think of buying arable land outside of Palestine and assisting Arabs financially to move from Palestine to such areas. Roosevelt also told Hoskins that he favored an international trusteeship for Palestine, as recommended by the Department of State.[12]

In a February 10, 1944, letter thanking Ibn Saud for a set of Saudi postage stamps the king had sent him, Roosevelt expressed regret that he had been unable to meet with the king during a recently concluded trip to Cairo and Tehran. While flying over a portion of the kingdom, however, Roosevelt had seen enough, he said, to make him wish they could meet. He felt sure that the country had a great future if more irrigation and the growing of trees to hold soil were brought to bear. He mentioned his pleasure in having met two of Ibn Saud's sons and concluded: "It is, of course, possible that I may visit the Near East again for conferences and if that happens I count on seeing you. There are many things I want to talk with you about." Thus had Roosevelt prepared the way for the February 14, 1945, meeting aboard the *Quincy*.

On that historic occasion, Roosevelt reiterated an earlier written promise to the king, as reported by William Eddy (who served as interpreter):

> In very simple language, such as he must often have used in cementing alliances with tribal chiefs, Ibn Saud then asked F.D.R. for friendship.
>
> The president then gave Ibn Saud double assurance, repeated just one week before his death in his letter to Ibn Saud, dated April 5, 1945: (1) He personally, as president, would never do anything which might prove hostile to the Arabs; and (2) the US Government would make no change in its basic policy in Palestine without full and prior consultation with both Jews and Arabs.[13]

THE TRUMAN YEARS

It was a 1945 finding by President Harry S Truman that held that the national interest of the United States called for the urgent construction of the airport at Dhahran. One of the key obligations undertaken by the United States in the August 1945 airport agreement was that of training Saudis to operate and maintain the base consistent with internationally accepted aviation standards. This training obligation was, at first, poorly discharged, occasioning much irritation in US-Saudi relations. The US War Department neglected its duty of supervision, being more concerned with demobilization and other matters.

By the agreement's terms, seventy-five US Army officers and men were to be posted at Dhahran and were to discharge their mandate while operating and maintaining the field at standards conforming to those of the International Civil Aviation Organization (ICAO). My own observation was that, in 1945, teachable Saudi candidates with an adequate knowledge of English were extremely scarce, as was Arabic-language competence among the Americans posted there. Officers assigned to Dhahran—the highest rank was initially that of major—were fine men; but most were posted for one year or less, without interest in their assignments—and without their families. They showed little interest in an organized effort to master the communication problem. Only one American on the staff knew any Arabic. Pedagogy was not their field, and the students sent by the Saudi army knew little or no English.

Arab student discontent finally reached the ears of the king, who complained vigorously and with justification. The effect was immediate. The War and State Departments sent out a team to investigate under the command of Lieutenant Colonel Harry O. Snyder, a scholar who had been a War Department liaison at the Department of State, where he had been centrally involved in Saudi Arabian affairs during the last years of the war. Snyder's report was a blockbuster. It implied a likelihood that the United States might well lose the base to the British or others waiting eagerly for a key role in developing the fledgling Saudi civil air service.

The result was the assignment to Dhahran for a minimum of two years (with family) of US Air Force Lt. Colonel Dale S. Seeds, an officer of broad experience who had helped negotiate the base agreement. He came with management qualifications, interest in the job, empathy for the Arabs, and a tremendous store of goodwill and good humor. Best of all, he had backup in Washington, where eagerness to assist was now organized and in place. Henceforth, the Pentagon did not neglect its team in Dhahran, nor for that matter the rank and competence of its small naval unit, the new Middle East Force, based at Jufair, Bahrain.

One might ask at this point, where was Colonel Eddy, US minister to Saudi Arabia, an officer of all-around competence who most certainly had the ear of the king? He had resigned in May 1946, giving no public reason for his action, other than the health of his wife (which was excellent). But he explained to me what had prompted his departure: it was the position taken by President Truman with respect to Palestine. Truman was about to issue an open appeal to Britain to immediately admit 100,000 refugee Jews into Palestine (in the face of the known attitude of Ibn Saud). Truman's public appeal came over the air waves shortly after Eddy's resignation.

Eddy probably knew in advance of Truman's plan and at once concluded that his own credibility with Ibn Saud was thereby undermined. The two had enjoyed an informal, open, fraternal relationship—insofar as one could use that expression between a king and a foreign diplomat—and it was now gone. As for Truman, Eddy told me privately that he could not feel the same *personal* loyalty to Truman as before, but would find other than policy grounds for use with the public in order not to disparage his chief, the president, whom, as a Marine and a minister, he felt honor-bound to respect, even after resigning.

Regarding the Palestine question, Eddy felt a deep conviction that domestic political forces had triumphed over the right of self-determination. He never changed his opinion that President Truman had betrayed Roosevelt's original pledge, which Truman reiterated several times to Ibn Saud, that it was the policy of the United States that no action be taken in Palestine to change the basic situation without advance consultation with both Arabs and Jews.

Eddy informed me of a contributing factor in his decision, namely, a special briefing given to Truman on November 10, 1945, at the White House by a group of US ministers to Near Eastern countries, assembled for the purpose of clarifying issues facing them in their respective countries. The group was escorted by Loy W. Henderson, director of the Office of Near Eastern and African Affairs, and included George Wadsworth, minister to Syria and Lebanon; S. Pinkney Tuck, minister to Egypt; Minister Eddy; and Lowell C. Pinkerton, consul general in Jerusalem (at that time the headquarters of the British governor of Mandate Palestine). All except Eddy were Foreign Service career officers with extensive experience in the Middle East. Their senior was Wadsworth, who acted as spokesman to save the president time. According to Eddy's account (omitted from the published record in *Foreign Relations of the United States, 1945*, pp. 10–18, but related to close friends orally at the time and here taken from the book he later wrote):

> The spokesman for the group, George Wadsworth, presented orally an agreed statement in about twenty minutes. There was little discussion and the president asked few questions in the meeting whose Minutes have been carefully guarded in the Department of State. Finally, Mr. Truman summed up his position with the utmost candor: "I'm sorry, gentlemen, but I have to answer to hundreds of thousands who are

serious for the success of Zionism; I do not have hundreds of thousands of Arabs among my constituents." [14]

Both Ibn Saud and Harry Truman were men of decision. The king could not convince Truman of his position on Palestine nor could the latter change the opinion of the king. Furthermore, both were on record for pronouncements that could not be disavowed, retracted, or even modified, so each took his own road toward what he regarded to be the highest state interest. Truman, without qualification or apology, flatly denied that in supporting the creation of a Jewish homeland in Palestine he was acting in such a way as to harm Arab interests. At the same time, he stated that he agreed with the undertaking given at Great Bitter Lake by Roosevelt to Ibn Saud.[15] Of decisive importance in Arabia, Truman readily accepted measures brought to his attention by the Department of State that would serve to reemphasize the unqualified support of the United States for the independence and territorial integrity of the Saudi kingdom and his high personal regard for the king himself. This put the monarch in a position where, except with extreme provocation, he could not take a line hostile toward Truman as a person or perhaps even cancel the US oil concession as Iraq and Jordan had begun to urge upon him. Such was not his line of conduct, nor was it in his interest.[16]

Meanwhile, the king's reliance on a friendly US presence in the Eastern Province had begun to yield concrete results. On October 5, 1945, I was called by Garry Owen, a vice president of ARAMCO, to inform Ibn Saud officially that the first tanker load of stabilized crude had just been loaded in Ras Tanura.[17] The king then pronounced his policy line: disagreement with Washington regarding Palestine was deep and regrettable, but it had no influence on his friendship with President Truman.

After Prince Faisal had signed the United Nations Charter in San Francisco in 1945, he made his second visit to Washington, from July 31 to August 1, to call on President Truman, as instructed by his father. The president, however, was detained in Berlin at the Potsdam Conference. Faisal and his entourage thus met with Joseph C. Grew, acting secretary of state, attended by Loy Henderson. Faisal made two appeals: first, that the United States understand the king's cautious approach to economic development programs of special interest to his old friends, the British government; second, that it reconsider carefully the US position on the Palestine question and recognize in its policy the ancient rights of the Palestinian people. Grew reassured Faisal that so far as he knew there had been no change in the US policy on Palestine as stated and reaffirmed by President Roosevelt to the king. Faisal returned home enthusiastic over his reception in Washington.

STRAINS IN US-SAUDI RELATIONS:
INTER-ARAB CONFLICT AND PALESTINE

Both Ibn Saud and Faisal were due for a severe disappointment within two years, when the United States voted at the United Nations for the partition of Palestine into separate Jewish and Arab states. Truman's position on the Palestine question in 1947 was a major blow. While the king could hardly maintain that there had not been consultation between himself and Roosevelt, there was less with Truman, and he was immeasurably disappointed with the overall result.

Ibn Saud's position, as an independent Arab ruler amid other Arab communities just beginning their last and final struggles to be free of European tutelage, had become preeminent. He had been an effective spokesman for Arab self-determination, but now his following could diminish, leaving him isolated. Isolation was dangerous in the Arab East, especially when one had a huge subsoil resource to protect and little population with which to defend it. No census had ever been taken, but the Saudi population, chiefly nomads and oasis farmers, appeared vulnerable. From personal observation I found its better-armed northern neighbors exceedingly envious and very disparaging toward the kingdom, whose oil reserves were rising geometrically. The king distrusted the intentions of the monarchs of Iraq and Jordan, sons of Hussein ibn Ali, whom Ibn Saud had defeated in 1925. The tiny Saudi army was poorly armed and untrained in modern military science, whereas Britain had trained and equipped forces in Iraq and Jordan in World War II.

Saudi Arabia needed a powerful patron, disinterested politically but ready for a vigorous partnership in development. The king decided once again to send a high-level emissary to Washington.

Crown Prince Saud ibn Abd al-Aziz arrived in Washington January 13, 1947, as the guest of the US government. Notwithstanding the economic element in his mission—a request for a $50 million loan for development—its main target was reassurance by the president of his willingness to support the independence and integrity of Saudi Arabia against Hashemite "plots" for a Greater Syria. Since the Hashemites were believed in Riyadh to be basically hostile toward the House of Saud, the combined Arab political forces presented immediate danger to Saudi Arabia. Furthermore, Ibn Saud continued to fear that the British might support a Greater Syria, a possibility strengthened by what the king felt to be a cooling of Saudi-British relations as the result of closer Saudi economic ties with the United States.[18]

Secretary of State James F. Byrnes received the crown prince and his entourage on January 13 and reassured them on several issues: "One of the basic policies of the United States in the Near East was *unqualifiedly* to support the territorial integrity and political independence of Saudi Arabia. Another basic policy was *energetically* to make sure that the principles of the United Nations Charter be fully applied to the countries of the Near East, including Saudi Arabia. King Ibn Saud could therefore depend upon the full active support of the United States in the United Nations in case any outside forces were to threaten or endeavor to undermine the integrity and independence of Saudi Arabia. Furthermore, the United States would support in the United Nations the independence of other countries such as Syria and Lebanon or Iraq in the event these countries should be threatened by aggression."[19]

Pressing on, Byrnes emphasized that the United States had scrupulously refrained from injecting itself into inter-Arab struggles and intrigues. It had no information causing it to believe that the British government was supporting a Greater Syria. On the contrary, the US government believed that the British would not at the time desire developments that might disturb the status quo in the Near and Middle East. Byrnes invited Ibn Saud, through the crown prince, to get in touch immediately if he should receive specific information of a threat to Saudi Arabia. This was a step up from earlier expressions of interest.

The Greater Syria movement had emerged as a natural expression of ambition from the fertile brain of Emir Abd Allah ibn al-Hussein of Transjordan (later king of the Hashemite Kingdom of Jordan). His Greater Syria included Palestine (including present-day Israel), Jordan, northern Saudi Arabia as far south as Tabuk, all of Iraq and modern Syria. Emir Abd Allah, son of the former *sharif* of Mecca and Medina, had accompanied his father into exile after the elder's defeat in battle by Ibn Saud. A man of great qualities of leadership, he echoed the post–World War II restlessness of those Arabs who saw new vistas for Arab glory after years of subordination.

The Arab world, except for Saudi Arabia, Oman, and the Yemen, had never known real independence in modern times; Arab states had had enough of mandates, the protection of foreign privileges, and all other disguises of colonialism. No Arab politician could expect popular domestic support without making absolutely clear his position that subordination to British, French, or other non-Arab authority was at an end. Only in Arab unity would be found the strength to escape this bondage. They aspired not only to full political independence, but also to unity as a visionary source of collective power. The idea of a Greater Syria, as far as it went, fitted into this unity concept.[20] Power could spring quickly from oil, so eyes turned toward the oil producers—Iraq, Kuwait, and Saudi Arabia.

The Department of State did, indeed, receive disquieting information in early 1947 centering on the inferred complicity of the British government in Abd Allah's project.[21] It was serious enough that the department sent a circular message to a number of posts, to London for action and to others for comment. In the House of Commons the government's position was for neutrality. It evidenced strong reluctance to respond positively to Abd Allah's persistent pleas for outright support and at the same time was loath to slap the project down at a time of great sensitivity in Transjordan over the British handling of the Palestine question. Nonetheless, the Foreign Office insisted that it was neither for nor against a Greater Syria.

In Washington, Secretary of State George Marshall asserted in a followup circular that State had received "numerous reports from throughout the Near East" that the subject was fostering disturbances. Rumors were widespread that Britain would support the establishment of a unified Arab political entity by force, if necessary, and that under the cover of official neutrality British agents were secretly encouraging Hashemite agents. Abd Allah's project, said Marshall, had introduced a discordant and troubling element in an otherwise encouraging spirit of cooperation in Arab League[22] activity.

From Jeddah, US minister J. Rives Childs (successor to William Eddy) reported that Ibn Saud believed that the British intended to "appoint" King Abd Allah of Jordan as ruler of Syria, while the British Foreign Office was being pressed by the Government of Syria to announce that it did not favor a Greater Syria. To retain a posture of total neutrality, however, the Foreign Office had refused to declare this position.

On May 8, 1947, Abd Allah issued a "white paper," some 300 pages long, purporting to show the "natural ties" between Transjordan, Syria, and Palestine within the framework of an Arab league. To this the government of Syria responded with a 100-page "White Book" attacking "agents" for destroying relations between sister Arab countries "to achieve private ambitions." Iraq was left out of Abd Allah's 1947 white paper but not out of his plan, or that of Nuri (Pasha) al-Said, mover and shaker of Iraqi governments for decades. Nuri and the Iraqi regent, Abd al-Ilah, were said to be in favor of a Greater Syria, a "Fertile Crescent"— Syria, Iraq, and Lebanon—while Iraqi prime minister Salih Jabr was strongly opposed to it.

Ibn Saud wrote to British foreign secretary Ernest Bevin, asking him to reconsider Britain's stance of neutrality and make known to all the Arab world that the British government would never agree to "any change in the Middle East." Bevin replied that a Greater Syria was not a matter in which the United Kingdom was an "interested party"; it was a topic for the Arabs to discuss and decide. But collective pressures finally brought Britain's minister of state, on July 14, 1947, to answer a House of Commons inquiry unequivocally that the British government did not favor the Greater Syria movement, that it considered the matter to be one between

Arabs, and that the British attitude was strictly neutral. Iraq finally resolved its internal division of opinion in favor of a public statement of neutrality on September 29, 1947, five days after Abd Allah made it known that he had "agreed to participate no further, for the present, in the Greater Syria controversy."[23]

A separate project for a partial "Fertile Crescent" union between Iraq and Syria, to be ruled by King Faisal II of Iraq, brother of Abd Allah, surfaced in September 1949 as an alternative to a Greater Syria under Jordanian auspices. The governments of Iraq and Syria approached the British government to assist them in negotiating a political union on the basis of reconciling two clearly parallel plans. The differences were thought to be resolvable by a mixed commission of experts, and London relayed this news at the end of September to Washington for comment. The Department of State said it would respond only after study.

The resulting study featured a reassertion of the US standing position of opposing force or outside intervention, but of no objection to a union peacefully formed. However, the department expressed great doubt that this would find popular Arab acceptance and remarked that it could presage a Hashemite plan to restore its rule in the Hejaz. The department's soundings also revealed opposition in Lebanon (which feared Muslim pressures by a greater Islamic state), in Jordan (where Abd Allah was already excluded from a "Fertile Crescent," a concept rivaling his own), in Egypt (where King Farouk opposed the creation of any large rival state), and in Israel (where there was fear of any growth of Arab power).

The US position, as explained to London and relayed to the Syrian and Iraqi governments, was that, in advance of a constitutional move toward unity by Iraq and Syria, the US government should not express any opinion that might influence decisions by the parties or consultations with other interested governments. The United States therefore reserved judgment and would expect assurances by Syria and Iraq that the proposed union would safeguard US interests, carry out existing obligations, and respect the independence and territorial integrity of neighboring states. Saudi Arabia and Kuwait had undemarcated frontiers with Iraq, and Washington had the long-range welfare of Saudi Arabia very much in mind.

The goal of Arab unity, subscribed to by virtually all Arab leaders (as a theoretical means of marshaling power to gain full independence from Great Power tutelage), cropped up again and again in various sponsorships and forms over the decades. The period of the late 1940s was one of great disquiet to King Ibn Saud, who made persistent efforts to obtain reassurances of US support. At one point, on December 2, 1947, seeking to obtain this reassurance from President Truman and Secretary of State

Marshall, Ibn Saud summoned Minister Childs to a private audience in Riyadh. He wanted specific answers to three questions:

1. Putting aside the Palestine question on which the United States and he disagreed painfully, in what manner could he rely on the United States?

2. A British confidante and friend of the king since the days of Sir Percy Cox had informed him that the United States and the United Kingdom had a secret agreement that Saudi Arabia belonged in the British sphere of influence. Was this true?

3. Would the United States supply arms to protect a trans-Arabian pipeline? Ibn Saud regarded his borders with Transjordan and Iraq as among the most sensitive of his kingdom and yet through them the trans-Arabian pipeline, known as TAPLINE, would pass. TAPLINE was already under threat, as demonstrated by violence in Transjordan against the operation—the TAPLINE camp had been razed and the workers evacuated to Beirut. There was also popular anger being expressed over the November 1947 US vote in the UN General Assembly favoring the partition of Palestine into Jewish and Arab states. Ibn Saud stated that he was determined to protect the pipeline and had the men to do so, but he needed arms.[24]

Acting Secretary of State Robert A. Lovett replied quickly through Minister Childs in Jeddah, restating points made earlier in the year to Crown Prince Saud by then Secretary of State Byrnes. Lovett made the additional point that the US government could "not conceive of a situation arising under which Hashemite states would attack Saudi Arabia merely because King Ibn Saud continued to be friendly to the United States" and that the US government, "after careful consideration, recently decided that broad interests of peace [could] best be served if, in existing circumstances, [the] US should for the time being refrain from exporting arms and munitions to Palestine and neighboring countries," especially while the United Nations was considering the security aspects of the situation. "One of the basic policies of the US in the Near East" is unqualifiedly to support the territorial integrity and political independence of Saudi Arabia. If Saudi Arabia should be attacked or be under threat of attack, the United States, through the United Nations, would take "energetic measures to ward off such aggression."[25]

Crown Prince Saud, who received this message by hand from Childs, obviously put the greatest weight on the US pledge of "unqualified" and "energetic" support in the face of unlikely attack, rather than on the US refusal to supply weaponry. Indeed, the prince was gratified. Saud told Childs that at an Arab League meeting just held, the ministers of Iraq and Transjordan had asked that Saudi Arabia show its displeasure with the US vote at the United Nations for the division of Palestine by breaking relations with the United States and canceling the 1933 oil conces-sion. Saud had replied, he told Childs, that his country opposed this recommendation, that it saw no reason to undermine Saudi interests by such measures, and that if Iraq and Transjordan persisted, Saudi Arabia would break relations not with the United States but with them.

The king's own written reply in this sequence of messages, while ex-pressing regret over the US refusal to supply arms and ammunition to defend the trans-Arabian pipeline, stated that he intended to request a US special mission to supervise the training of a Saudi northern defense force and preparation of such bases as would be required. This was the second test to which President Truman was put by the interjection of the Palestine issue into US-Saudi relations.

A STRENGTHENED PARTNERSHIP

Truman became engaged in the Palestine issue, along with innumer-able other matters of high urgency, immediately after taking office on the death of President Roosevelt on April 12, 1945. Among spokesmen await-ing their turns to call on April 20 was Stephen Wise of the American Zionist Emergency Council. Prior to seeing Wise, the president had reviewed a memorandum from the secretary of state that set forth depart-ment thinking on Palestine. It advised caution in responding to what the department expected would be an urgent plea to the president to com-mit himself in favor of the Zionist program. The department reported rising tensions in the area where the United States nurtured long-range interests. The president, however, was already deeply affected by what he had learned of the condition of tens of thousands of displaced persons, particularly Jews; they were without homes to which they could return. Most Jews, he found, were unwilling to return to their countries of origin or citizenship.

Truman's *Memoirs* show that he was skeptical about the attitudes of what he termed the "striped-pants boys" in the Department of State, who, he felt, "didn't care enough about what happened to the thousands of displaced persons who were involved." "It was my feeling," said Truman, "that it would be possible for us to watch out for the long-range interest of our country while at the same time helping these unfortunate victims of persecution to find a home."[26] After attending the Potsdam Conference, Truman had held a press conference at which he answered a question on the US stand with respect to Palestine by stating, "The American view on Palestine is that we want to let as many of the Jews into Palestine as it is possible to let into that country. Then the matter will have to be worked out diplomatically with the British and the Arabs, so that if a state can be set up there they may be able to set it up on a peaceful

48

basis. I have no desire to send 500,000 American soldiers there to make peace in Palestine."[27]

As seen from the 1990s, in thus publicly backing the establishment of a Jewish state in Palestine, Truman violated the spirit and expectations of what the Arabs, including Ibn Saud, regarded as the pledge given to them in February 1945 by President Roosevelt at Great Bitter Lake and reaffirmed by Truman within weeks after Roosevelt's death[28]—that the United States would take no steps in the Arab-Jewish quarrel to alter the basic situation in Palestine without first consulting Arabs and Jews. Official Department of State records and Truman's memoirs are replete with US correspondence on this matter with Arabs and with Jewish leaders. In initiating new investigations of the problem, such as the Anglo-US Committee of Inquiry, the records also show, Truman was concerned chiefly with the quick settlement of displaced Jews.

Based on the press conference cited above and his reflections, it is clear that Truman long favored a Jewish state but was less interested in how to work it out than in pressing the British for emergency realization of the Balfour Declaration of 1917. He was determined, first, to remove the intolerable spectacle of further mass suffering by 100,000 stranded Jews. By invoking the Balfour Declaration and pushing the British to open Palestine to unlimited immigration, he placated the powerful Zionist political feelings in the US electorate. At the same time he "consulted" Ibn Saud and other Arab leaders by letters, in which he reassured the monarch of his unwavering support for his country's integrity and independence. With Saudi Arabia, this reassurance was increasingly specific. Truman organized his priorities and then accepted the consequences of his actions. While he supported independence for all Arabs, he focused his attention and maximum effort on the one truly independent Arab leader with whom the United States had a close bond. The deep aspirations of Iraq and Egypt for full independence could be satisfied only by negotiation with Britain, the protecting power.

As a seasoned politician, Truman concluded that if he played his cards right Ibn Saud would not cancel the agreements on the Dhahran Airfield or the oil concession. He proved right, against the honest advice of the dedicated area-competent "striped-pants boys." He had in his favor the magic of the Roosevelt–Ibn Saud friendship and the drama of their historic meeting. Truman knew that Roosevelt had touched the king's heart and created a bond when he gave him, aboard the USS *Quincy*, one of his two wheelchairs—a very personal possession.

On two occasions—April 18, 1950, and August 15, 1952—Truman responded to Ibn Saud's private requests for medical attention by dispatching his personal White House physician, Major General Wallace H. Graham, USAF, with a planeload of specialists, nurses, and technicians armed with advanced equipment, including X-ray machines, generators, and medicines. Graham had been the physician not only of Truman but also of Truman's mother.[29] My colleague and old friend Fred H. Awalt accompanied both missions as Department of State officer-in-charge for Arabian Peninsula affairs. He made the now declassified reports on both missions.[30]

Awalt did not divulge medical records but made clear that the king had greatly failed since Awalt had last seen him in 1945. He did not rise from his seat and had lost his exuberance and fire. However, the king reacted positively and quickly to Graham's schedule of daily treatments. He was most grateful, and in conversation referred to President Truman as "brother." Apart from the lavish hospitality he had ordered shown to the medical team, the king permitted them unprecedented run of the palace and grounds, where soccer matches were held with Saudi students. Graham responded wholeheartedly, authorizing treatment to the entire household as well as to senior Arab and non-Arab counselors. In writing his thanks to President Truman for the Graham mission, Ibn Saud showed no reserve or nuance in his form of address or warmth. He praised the doctor's "superb abilities" as well as his geniality. "Through his [Graham's] genuine love of the Arab world he imparts your own feelings."[31]

Truman thus did not hesitate an instant in dispatching the Graham team for its second visit in 1951, when Secretary of State Dean Acheson advised him on August 9 that the Saudi chargé in Washington had called urgently at the department to say that the king was experiencing "severe pains and convulsions in the lower abdomen"and "would greatly appreciate it if the president would make General Graham again available, along with American specialists to go to Riyadh." The chargé added that the political situation in the Near East was such that secrecy regarding the king's health was desirable. Acheson strongly recommended that Graham be allowed to make the trip, stating that Ibn Saud was the "best friend the United States has in the Middle East" and that the alacrity of the president's action in 1950 "was not only a deeply appreciated personal gesture but also a diplomatic stroke which paved the way for the recent signature of an extremely favorable United States–Saudi Arabia agreement for the use of Dhahran Airfield."[32] On August 14, 1951, the president suddenly appeared at a White House preparatory briefing session for General Graham with Awalt and others and told the group "that they were going on an important mission to a great man." [33]

Unfortunately, the best US medicine had to offer could not stem Ibn Saud's decline. In November 1953, he died, deeply mourned as a king who had for so long inspired pride, confidence, and hope for the future.

PART TWO

THE RESTLESS SEARCH
FOR BOUNDARIES

3

COLD WAR AND REGIONAL PRESSURES
AND THE REIGN OF KING SAUD

During the Truman-Eisenhower era, the United States sought to bolster anticommunist forces all along the southern perimeter of the Soviet Union and communist China. It was a matter of top priority. However, while understandable in the aftermath of the Soviet takeover in Eastern Europe; Soviet threats to the independence of Greece, Turkey, and Iran; and the Korean War, the US policy did not dovetail comfortably with realities in the Middle East. It pleased Nuri al-Said's prerevolutionary Iraq; it did not please Greece; and it infuriated Egypt's Revolutionary Command Council, which would brook no competition to its leadership of the cause of Arab unity. If it was congenial to Saudi Arabia, it was anathema to Ba'thist Syria. In short, US Cold War policy hit too many crosscurrents of local importance that escaped early detection in Washington.

The Soviet Union was never a palpable threat, for example, to the independence of Egypt, Syria, Jordan, Saudi Arabia, Kuwait, post-1963 Iraq, or the Yemen, although it was trying with indifferent success to woo them all. Egypt under Nasser exploited Washington's tunnel vision for its own ends. Nasser took military aid from the Soviet Union, paid for with a pro-Soviet stance at the United Nations, but countenanced no

Soviet guardianship of infant domestic Egyptian communism. At the same time, Nasser sought major economic assistance from the United States, explicitly inviting it "to compete" with the Soviet Union. The Yemen, dependent on Egypt as a counterweight to Saudi Arabia, followed Egypt's example until interrupted by revolution and war.

Of the Arab states with which Secretary of State John Foster Dulles sought to form a "second tier" of containment, only Jordan and Saudi Arabia at that time maintained a degree of meaningful solidarity with US policy. They were recipients of military grant aid and, more important, of American strategic and political support. They were highly vulnerable, and they knew it; the enemy to their independence, whom they knew, was Nasser. The Soviet Union was more distant, but as its shadow approached them through Nasser's brokerage of Soviet arms, or behind the ideology of the Syrian Ba'th, Jordan and Saudi Arabia felt common cause with the Dulles-Eisenhower defense program and were able to relegate (as others could not) the Palestinian-Israeli issue to second place in their priorities.

DULLES INTRODUCES HIMSELF, AND US STRATEGIC THINKING, INTO A SKEPTICAL MIDDLE EAST

Upon taking office in January 1953 in the new Republican administration of President Dwight D. Eisenhower, Secretary of State Dulles was filled with energy and motivation to develop strong points for the United States in the Middle East and South Asia, and to organize as much as possible of the "Free World" under the containment policy. He accepted the December 17, 1952, recommendation of his Bureau of Near Eastern, South Asian, and African Affairs (NEA) to include in his early months of office a comprehensive tour of the Middle East. The purpose was to become personally familiar with key personalities and issues of concern to the United States in this volatile and unsettled region.

The journey was accomplished May 9 through 29, 1953. The secretary's official entourage included Harold E. Stassen, director of the Mutual Security Administration, Henry A. Byroade, NEA assistant secretary of state, and Douglas MacArthur II, counselor of the Department of State. I was then director of the Office of Near Eastern Affairs, having left Dhahran in 1952, and preparations for the Arab and Israeli portions of the journey were assigned to my office. These took the form of informational reports, drafts of remarks for the secretary's recommended use on all arrivals and departures, comments to the local and world press for all occasions, classified talking points to be used in official discussions, highly private biographical sketches of all the political leaders in countries to be visited, policy studies, recommendations on every issue likely to surface in any situation during official exchanges, and condensed background materials. The result, inevitably filling a footlocker, promised to far exceed the capacity of several persons to absorb, even though this was still the propeller age and flights took twice the time they would a decade later.

The secretary's traveling staff, Byroade and MacArthur in particular, made it a point to cover as much background and analytical material as would be possible to pass on to Dulles during in-flight sessions.[1] MacArthur, a fast reader and quick study but not an expert on the Middle East, proved to be as near equal to the task as anyone could be, finding that extra velocity that comes from unfamiliarity with details and a compelling opportunity to organize and synthesize for the secretary's benefit. Byroade was up to the minute on all substantive Middle Eastern developments and on personalities and issues. It would require a separate volume to go into these details, but it is worth noting that Dulles was the only secretary of state ever to make a comprehensive tour of the Middle East. He was directed to do so by President Eisenhower, if indeed he needed such a push. He was certainly the best informed on the area of all secretaries of state since World War II.

Dulles's journey was billed as one based on information gathering, but it was much more. Dulles was a headstrong secretary of deep convictions, more than a bit oversure of his judgment, and he possessed a mandate from his chief to build or preserve strategic barriers against communist expansion, such as the extensive British-operated Suez base complex. Dulles carried a policy basket of strong biases and notions built up during his years of service. He was to learn the hard way that, from the perspective of most Middle Eastern and South Asian countries, local issues decisively took precedence over the world struggle between the Soviet Union and the United States—unless the cards from that titanic encounter could be exploited so as to further one's own ends.

Following visits to Tel Aviv, Amman, Damascus, Beirut, and Baghdad, Dulles arrived May 18, 1953, in Riyadh, where he met in the evening with King Ibn Saud. The experience was evidently vivid and baffling. The king lost no time in rehashing fundamentals of the Saudi-US diplomatic equation. He stated that his friendship with the United States had received a "heavy blow." Asked by the secretary for an explanation, the king implied rather clearly that the United States had failed to support him as a friend. Pressed further, he stated that his old friend the British government had turned against him because of his closer friendship with the United States, to which he had awarded the oil concession. Now Britain had begun to "chase Saudi subjects from their own country,"[2] by which he was referring to Buraimi.

Ibn Saud's son Faisal had informed Dulles fully about the Buraimi boundary dispute[3] and had expected help from the United States, which never materialized. The king wanted execution of the "promises given in the letter sent to him by President Truman and confirmed by President Eisenhower."[4] Because of the massive amount of briefing materials compiled for this trip, Dulles had not yet become familiar with the letter nor with the Eisenhower confirmation. Americans generally were not aware of the letter or of the dispute over Buraimi, which for at least the next five years would be a major impediment to good US-Saudi and US-British relations.

BURAIMI: SAUDI ARABIA'S COLD WAR WITH THE UNITED KINGDOM

While living as I did in the Dhahran oil camp on my two tours of duty in Saudi Arabia, I came to have a close personal relationship with Saud bin Jilewi, the hereditary emir and viceroy of the Eastern Province, and with the top management of ARAMCO. In particular, I met informally but often with members of the exploration department, the organization that carried out the reconnaissance and seismic testing required to indicate structural conditions favoring the entrapment of oil and gas. By 1949 I had begun to hear about some of ARAMCO's responsibilities under the terms of the 1933 concession, which included using "due diligence" and advising the king regarding the geology of border areas. In these still nomadic years, boundary markers were nonexistent, but oil was likely over an especially wide area of the kingdom's eastern desert south of Dhahran. What these hard-working experts had to tell me became steadily more mind-boggling as estimates of petroleum reserves rocketed, particularly so after seismic tests well south of Abqaiq in the northern limits of the Empty Quarter, central Arabia's mostly uninhabitable great dunes region. Anticipating counterclaims by British political agents acting on behalf of the seminomadic Trucial sheikhdoms that were British protectorates,[5] ARAMCO had sought royal guidance. It came quickly from Ibn Saud and, later, from his son. Their response was, in essence, "You tell me the areas that interest you, and I will tell you if it is mine and you can develop it."

It was a prescription for collision and therefore disturbing to Washington. ARAMCO management thus sought the counsel of legal experts, and in 1950 brought Manley O. Hudson to our embassy and to the Dhahran consulate general (upgraded from consulate status in 1949). Hudson was a renowned professor of international law at the Harvard University Law School and chief editor of the *Journal of International Law*. His advice was sought on a full docket awaiting his attention, notably, the feasibility of an international agreement on a median line in the Persian Gulf; how to strengthen Saudi claims to disputed land areas, marking the sovereign rights of riparian states; and how to support the king's claims of sovereignty over eighteen islands in the gulf. It was not for ARAMCO (or

Hudson) to question claims, but to advise on how to assert them under international law.

Ibn Saud, by 1949, had claimed a land boundary with Abu Dhabi that cut through the oasis of Liwa and anchored in al-Ain, one of the oases of the Buraimi complex, a tiny group of settlements made up of *barrasti* (palm frond) huts, lying about 100 miles east of Abu Dhabi town. ARAMCO's exploration department had, by virtue of "due diligence" in fulfilling the king's command, reported the likelihood of oil and gas deposits at Jabal Hafit, an isolated mountain close to al-Ain.

This looked like a particularly sensitive claim, and in 1949 I made use of one of my periodic social visits to Saud bin Jilewi, resident at Hufuf, to ask him whether Saudi Arabia had sovereignty over Buraimi. As he emphatically denied such a claim, I had to take him seriously. Emir bin Jilewi had become a good personal friend and was a true desert chieftain, more deeply knowledgeable about tribal claims and realities than any official in Jeddah and perhaps even in the palace at Riyadh. The emir was esteemed and not a little feared among Bedouin tribes of the eastern desert, whose boundaries had never been agreed upon, much less delineated. The land at least 100 miles inland from the gulf was disputed territory. On a visit to Muscat during that same year, 1949, I had put a similar question to Sultan Said ibn Taimur, sultan of Muscat and Oman, whose hinterland extended to Buraimi. He responded by drawing a line on a map I had brought showing al-Hamasa, one hamlet of the Buraimi complex, where he maintained a *wali* (representative). Since al-Hamasa was also claimed by Saudi Arabia, all this by 1949 was grist for active disputation, destined to occupy British and American diplomats and international lawyers well beyond the next decade.

Whether acting on the advice of Judge Hudson or not, the Saudi government decided to follow the dictum that sovereignty, in order to become or remain real, must be asserted by actions as well as by words. Such actions can be founded on the right of self-existence and, therefore, of self-defense against a threat; in so doing, however, a state may risk war. The first step taken by the Saudis in 1949 was to permit—authorize or ignore—a small Saudi armed guard to cross into what the British held to be Abu Dhabi territory near the base of the peninsula of Qatar, and possibly into Qatar itself, and set up camp. There they were intercepted by an alert young British political officer, Patrick Stobart, who was commanding a troop detachment of armed Trucial levies. Stobart normally reported to the British political agent at Bahrain, the soon-to-be-knighted Tom Hickinbotham, but in this case he correctly judged time to be of the essence. Although his unit was small, he acted with sensitivity to Bedouin "face" and with remarkable skill. Without a shot being fired, he persuaded the Saudi unit to decamp and leave the disputed area.

On January 28, 1952, a meeting on boundary questions between British, Trucial, and Saudi high officials took place at Dammam.[6] The British did most of the talking for their protected rulers, so the discussions were effectively between them and the Saudis in the presence of two Trucial rulers, Sheikh Abd Allah Al Thani of Qatar and Sheikh Shakbut ibn Sultan of Abu Dhabi. There were indications that the British team needed more time for preparation, since they twice requested adjournment to later dates. The Dammam meeting accomplished little, except to reach a "standstill agreement" that became a negotiating marker, more honored in the breach than in the observance. When complaints from the British side were ignored, British sappers were dispatched to blow up bronze sovereignty tablets mounted by the Saudi government in the king's name. Saudi reaction seemed muted.

Disappointed at the outcome of the Dammam gathering, Ibn Saud sent word to US ambassador Raymond Hare (successor to Ambassador J. Rives Childs) asking that he meet informally in Jeddah with Prince Faisal for a firsthand account of the negotiations, and thereafter with the king himself at Riyadh.[7] The king asked Hare at their meeting to request the US government to intervene with the British. The US and British governments had in fact been in close touch in London and in Washington as a matter of standing postwar policy since 1947. In discussions intended to clarify facts and forestall serious misunderstandings, the United States and the United Kingdom had both come to see the crucial importance of their cooperation in containment, an outlook evolving naturally from their wartime policy.[8]

Because the sultan of Muscat and Oman was (and is) completely independent, the Foreign Office in London sent a note to the Saudi Foreign Ministry asking why the Saudis had dispatched Emir Turki ibn Utaishan, a high-ranking prince, to al-Hamasa as the *wali* of Ibn Saud. The reply being unsatisfactory, the Foreign Office protested to Riyadh that the Saudis had violated the Dammam standstill agreement that permitted only the "usual administrative actions in disputed areas."[9] London advised Washington of its intent to send Trucial levies to occupy villages not yet under Saudi occupation and to overfly al-Hamasa, dropping leaflets containing messages from the sultan to his subjects.

Asad al-Faqih, the Saudi ambassador in Washington, on September 17, 1952, informed the Department of State that Ibn Saud desired a US stand implementing President Truman's letter to the king of October 31, 1950, reaffirming "US interest in the preservation of the independence and territorial integrity of Saudi Arabia" and repeating that "no threat to your Kingdom could occur which would not be a matter of immediate concern to the United States."[10] The ambassador asked that the United States be ready to aid Saudi Arabia in case Britain took the threatened "steps to protect its position" unless Riyadh arranged the immediate withdrawal of

Turki and all his followers. The king, Ambassador al-Faqih said, held that the people of Buraimi were independent and entitled to a settlement on the basis of the principle of self-determination. The Saudi government was considering taking the matter to the UN Security Council.

The October 1950 Truman letter to Ibn Saud had been drafted only a few months after the start of the Korean War, and within the broad framework of the US containment policy. It had been timed so that newly appointed Ambassador Hare could present it to the king along with his credentials.The Saudi government had now invoked it, but not against the Soviet Union or other predatory Middle Eastern neighbors, but against America's close ally, the United Kingdom. This threw the Buraimi question into the highest level of Washington's and London's over-arching policy of friendship. It was a considerable embarrassment to both governments. The Department of State sought at once to persuade the Saudis to keep the dispute within quiet diplomatic channels and to promote the acceptance of a standstill and the mutual avoidance of provocative acts. At the same time, it did not want the United States to be drafted as mediator and made no prompt reply in regard to the letter.

On July 11, 1953, I was called in by Secretary of State Dulles to brief him on the location and background of Buraimi, a dispute he had inherited from his predecessor, Dean Acheson, and an agenda item in the ongoing bilateral talks he was holding with Lord Robert A. J. G. Salisbury, the British foreign secretary. Dulles, who certainly had a head full of major world-shaking problems, found this baffling struggle of tribes in a virtu-ally unknown and isolated desert both incongruous and absurd. None-theless, he sought to share its paradoxes in a lengthy and probing bilat-eral talk with his British counterpart. His lighthearted manner helped the tone of the discussion.

It was obvious that both the United Kingdom and the United States were being more than somewhat pressured toward confrontation by smaller societies bearing old complaints and new ambitions. The inter-Arab dispute had now become a powder keg whose fuse was close to ignition. Turki and his men were being reinforced with supplies, and a sizable Saudi army contingent was reported forming at al-Kharj, near Riyadh. Fire had been exchanged over a roadblock near the coast of Abu Dhabi between tribal elements of the Beni Ka'ab, loyal to the sultan, and others loyal to Ibn Saud.

The sultan, claiming sovereignty over al-Hamasa and other villages split by the crisis, was reported to be mobilizing an army unit. Meanwhile, a British blockade in force against Turki was being challenged. This was no ordinary intertribal squabble. At stake for the British was their 125-year-old position as protector of the gulf sheikhdoms, a position they had not yet decided to terminate. These Arab gulf states were relying on British power in most instances; the sultan of Muscat and Oman had traditionally hired British officers to command his small forces. There was, furthermore, a common Arab-British and American interest in these British security ties. The British-dominated Iraq Petroleum Company oil group in the lower gulf, as in Abu Dhabi—correctly believed to have very large oil deposits—included two major American companies, Standard Oil of New Jersey and Socony-Vacuum. Together the Americans held a total of 23.6 percent of the total IPC equity. IPC offered the promise of real wealth to the still very poor.

In Washington the extraordinary awkwardness of this crisis was obvious in that there were two American companies heavily invested in both sides of a frontier dispute. ARAMCO, at that time, was totally American with a much larger concession area in Saudi Arabia, but the British-dominated IPC group contained two of ARAMCO's owners and was in the position of defending the two companies along with the rest of IPC's investment. Like a background noise to an already discordant theme, the Soviet Union redoubled its unsuccessful efforts to establish diplomatic and commercial ties with the states involved.

By late 1952, with British-officered Trucial levies posted in most of the Buraimi enclaves (on behalf of the sultan and the ruler of Abu Dhabi) and eighty Saudis under Emir Turki occupying al-Hamasa (claimed by Muscat) and other villages, Ibn Saud apparently realized that confrontations could trigger direct Saudi-British hostilities. The United States had yet to respond to the king's demand that the Truman pledge of 1950 be implemented, or even to agree to mediate. On October 6, 1952, Ibn Saud, therefore, stepped away from pursuing US mediation and sought Ambassador Hare's active help. Replying to the king that he had as yet no instructions, Hare said he would personally recommend to Washington the following:

1. to seek termination of RAF [Royal Air Force] overflights of Buraimi and of such other British measures that could be described as punitive or restrictive, and the understanding that the Saudis also desist from provocative acts, restarting normalcy. [Among the Saudis' "provocative acts" was the issuance in Buraimi of Saudi nationality certificates.]

2. that both sides remain in Buraimi for the time being, retaining their present positions.

3. that direct discussions be resumed between the British and Saudis [which had been broken off by the British in February 1952], and that the United States facilitate negotiations.[11]

Ibn Saud at once agreed, and so did the Department of State. Under Secretary of State David K. E. Bruce put the same thoughts to Sir Oliver Franks, the British ambassador, and to his deputy, Bernard A. B. Burrows, the same day, in a meeting that I attended. The British almost simultaneously ceased overflights and offered to resume direct talks with the Saudis. They also announced their readiness to withdraw the Trucial levies from Buraimi if the Saudis would simultaneously withdraw Emir Turki. The Department of State suggested to the British that if direct discussions failed, rather than see Saudi insistence on US mediation or on throwing the issue into the UN Security Council, the United Kingdom might propose arbitration.

During the following weeks the Saudis pressed for a tripartite commission—the United States, United Kingdom, and Saudi Arabia—to visit the area of Buraimi as a fact-finding body, and they began to evidence a desire to postpone or avoid further direct discussions with the British. Through pressure on the United States, they sought to maximize their chances of obtaining a favorable settlement of the dispute.[12]

On a visit to Washington from New York, where he had been leading the Saudi delegation to the UN General Assembly, Prince Faisal now entered the arena. He urged outgoing Secretary of State Acheson to accept the principle that Buraimi had belonged to Saudi Arabia for 100 years and that "any recognition of its now being in dispute would entail grave consequences for King Ibn Saud."[13] He developed the point that Buraimi inhabitants were Sunnis, while surrounding areas varied in religious affiliation, and that this was of major importance. The British had proposed arbitration, which was totally unacceptable, although he had nothing against a plebiscite. His country, he stated, desired US good offices to stop "British interference" in the area and introduce a calmer situation leading to a settlement. It also wanted US help to "protect the rights of Saudi Arabia." Faisal defined such help as US acceptance of membership on a tripartite commission with Saudi Arabia and the United Kingdom. The commission's purpose would be the handling of a plebiscite of the inhabitants of the Buraimi area.

Meanwhile, the Foreign Office in London became increasingly worried over Emir Turki's success with handing out money in Buraimi and the consequent weakening of the British position as time went on. Both Turki and Ibn Saud were convinced that the United Kingdom would not use force to expel Turki.

The Department of State finally decided to agree fully with a proposal by Ambassador Hare that the matter go quickly to arbitration, not because it was a British position, but because the United States was quite unwilling to cast votes between close friends or appear to favor either side. Meanwhile Faisal, in Washington on December 31, 1952, for a special luncheon at Blair House, took the initial position that Buraimi had always been Saudi and, therefore, arbitration was unacceptable.

Taking me privately by the arm, in the manner of an old friend, Faisal said, "I hear you are not with us in the matter of Buraimi!" I replied that this was truly the case. I felt the kingdom had taken a flawed position and that arbitration was the right course. Shortly afterward Faisal canceled, without explanation, the appointment he had made with Secretary Acheson, leaving us the impression that, given the upcoming change of administration in the United States, he had decided not to hear an outgoing official state the US position. As Acheson was sure to reject US participation in a tripartite commission—which would subject us to great Saudi pressures—and would take a firm stand in favor of arbitration, Faisal preferred to await the inauguration and have a go at the Eisenhower administration team, which would not yet have developed an immutable stand. Faisal was indeed thorough.

The department, however, decided not to wait for this development and had Under Secretary Bruce call in the Saudi ambassador and make the same points to him that Acheson would have made to Faisal. This was done on January 8, 1953, twelve days before the inauguration. Bruce asserted that the United States, being an intimate friend of both parties, declined to be involved in a fact-finding commission where settlement machinery could require it to attempt to verify allegiances or otherwise exercise judgments. As Bruce pointed out, it was a time-honored Arab as well as tested world practice that arbitrators would have means to travel freely with interpreters and all manner of facilities to wherever they wished, to talk directly with whomever they might select, and to study all documentation, so as to form the basis for a lasting settlement. Unspoken was the concern that any plebiscite would devolve into a farcical competition of monetary and other inducements.

Prince Faisal came to Washington again in March 1953 and was received by the new secretary of state, Dulles, on March 2 and later that day by President Eisenhower. On March 3, he was received by the new under secretary of state Walter Bedell Smith. The intensity of these meetings progressed from a generalized exchange of good wishes in the White House to fairly specific matters with Dulles, then to a specific and probing session with Bedell Smith, with whom the prince had a follow-up meeting on March 25. At this latter meeting Faisal was clearly informed that, regarding Buraimi, the United States favored arbitration, though it was not willing itself to mediate or arbitrate; that arbitration machinery would cover the present allegiance of inhabitants; and that allegations of aggression could cut both ways. Faisal nodded his concurrence. He now understood the US position, he said, and asked what the United States planned to do to stop British violations of the standstill agreement. Bedell Smith informed him that he had taken up the question with British foreign secretary Eden, visiting from Britain, and with the British ambassador. Both had categorically assured him that the United Kingdom would scrupulously observe the standstill agreement. Though he would be willing to renew the matter, he wished to be able to say he had firm Saudi assurances that they too would respect the agreement. Faisal concurred and gave the assurance.

The obvious disappointment of the prince over certain features of the US stand on Buraimi was mitigated somewhat by presidential action on one of Faisal's complaints—that of US failure to act on a grant of military aid as requested by the king. On March 14, 1953, President Eisenhower, writing to Harold Stassen, director of the Mutual Security Administration, found Saudi Arabia eligible for military assistance under the Mutual Defense Assistance Act of 1951.

The March visit of Faisal with President Eisenhower offered an opportunity for the United States to reaffirm, as one of the first acts of the new administration, the now customary special assurance of US support to the independence and territorial integrity of Saudi Arabia. The assurance was made explicit in a letter dated June 15, 1953, from Eisenhower to Ibn Saud.[14] Tying it to the Truman letter of October 31, 1950, was crucially important to Ibn Saud, because the language was regarded as tighter. Dulles, in his May 1953 visit to Riyadh, made clear in argument with Princes Saud and Faisal that the Saudi government must not interpret Truman's pledge as one that would lead the United States to war against Britain. In various discussions, the United States also made clear its dissatisfaction at being put on the spot by not being forewarned of Saudi territorial claims.

The Buraimi *compromis*—the agreement to arbitrate the Saudi–Abu Dhabi border[15]—was signed on July 30, 1954, by Saudi foreign minister Faisal and British ambassador George Clifton Pelham. Its basis was a proposal by Pelham that had suffered many changes as both ARAMCO and IPC objected to ongoing exploration for oil by the other party in the disputed areas. Pelham finally devised a text acceptable to the Saudi government that defined the "Buraimi Zone" as an area within a 20-kilometer radius from the village of Buraimi, and the "Buraimi disputed areas" as the zone plus all other land claimed by Saudi Arabia and Abu Dhabi between the Saudi claim of October 14, 1949, and the claim put forward on behalf of Abu Dhabi by the United Kingdom at the Dammam conference in 1952. The Omani claim was quietly dropped.

By August 1954 it appeared that the arbitration process had fallen into place. The tribunal consisted of Sheikh Yusuf Yassin, representing Saudi Arabia, Sir Reader William Bullard, minister to Saudi Arabia from 1936 to 1939, representing the principalities of the gulf and of Oman, and three neutral members, Ernesto Dihigo of Cuba, Mahmud Hasan of Pakistan, and Judge Charles de Visscher of Belgium, president of the tribunal. Proceedings opened in Geneva on September 11, 1955. By September 15 hearings were completed and the tribunal had withdrawn to consider its decision. On September 17, Bullard suddenly announced his resignation, charging that Saudi Arabia had violated the arbitration agreement, had attempted a coup d'etat in Abu Dhabi, and had sought to bribe the Abu Dhabi ruling family.

Throughout this protracted controversy, Sir Anthony Eden reported to the British House of Commons that the Saudis continued to violate the arbitration agreement despite the exposure of earlier violations at Geneva. Meanwhile, President Eisenhower had received numerous notes of complaint from King Ibn Saud (until the king's death on November 9, 1953) over British violations of the principles of the 1952 standstill agreement. A new situation arose on October 25, 1955, when British-commanded Trucial levies ejected Saudi police from Buraimi and put them on the Riyadh, or "Ryan's," Line, a British claim of 1935. There had been no forewarning to the United States of this British action ending five years of hard work by the Department of State directed toward holding off a British-Saudi confrontation. Because of the normally close US relations with British officialdom, including the offices of the political resident and the British navy in Bahrain, the Saudis appeared sure to implicate the United States for the British action despite any US disclaimer.

BURAIMI, KING SAUD, AND DHAHRAN

Following Ibn Saud's death in November 1953, Crown Prince Saud ibn Abd al-Aziz, as the eldest living prince in order of succession, had been named by consensus of a council of elders to succeed his father. He had taken over immediately and was widely accepted by tribal leaders and the ulema, as well as by Saudi business circles. The United States hoped to continue its special relationship with Saudi Arabia in new circumstances.

King Saud now, in late 1955, wanted the Buraimi arbitration renewed, but he felt that for him to urge the British to return to arbitration would imply that his government was acknowledging the veracity of at least some of the British charges of Saudi corruption of the arbitration process. None of these charges were made explicit to Riyadh or to Washington. Instead, British accusations were couched in very broad terms, such as the wholesale buying out of tribes with bags of gold on a scale with which Britain could not possibly compete, and which ARAMCO made possible by advances against future royalties. The United States suggested the addition of neutral observers to the tribunal to ensure full compliance with the arbitration board's agreed-upon rules. This was taken under advisement by London but was then rejected. The developing impression was that Britain, win or lose, faced loss of prestige, but it came to this realization late. Arbitration was not resumed.

On June 1, 1954, in the midst of the Buraimi dispute and reflecting the frustration in the top command in Riyadh, Prince Faisal had informed

US ambassador George E. Wadsworth that US Point IV (technical assistance) would not be further needed in the kingdom. He said this was not because the Americans had not done their work well. When then asked by Wadsworth why the kingdom was ending the program, Faisal replied that it was now Saudi policy "not to bother the US Government." This comment had been made as Faisal was reporting to Wadsworth the deep dissatisfaction in Riyadh over the alleged US failure to decisively back the Saudi position on boundary claims, notably Buraimi. Faisal's comment seemed primarily to express anger and signaled the possibility of a reduction of ties with the United States.[16]

At this juncture, the United States began to worry that if the Saudis would cancel Point IV on short notice, might they not do the same with the Dhahran Airfield agreement, soon to be up for renewal or to lapse on June 18, 1956? The Pentagon began to study possible substitutions for the base, but the worst did not materialize. Reflecting deep concern evidenced in Riyadh as well as Washington, King Saud turned to the United States for advice and for further military training and equipment.

Wadsworth advised Dulles that the bargaining over the terms of the Dhahran Airfield agreement renewal would be hard and expensive, but that terms would be easier to agree upon if negotiations were conducted with the king personally. To make this work, he advised that the matter be raised with President Eisenhower, to whom he recommended that the king be invited as a personal guest to Washington. (Although his advice was accepted by the president, the visit did not take place until 1957, under circumstances very changed from 1955.)

The State and Defense Departments' strategic evaluation of the Dhahran air base, meanwhile, concluded that it would be desirable for the United States to retain it, but not at an exorbitant price. The US Air Force at this time unofficially valued the base at $50 million. Civil use was becoming remunerative at three thousand landings per month.

The Soviet Union, acting on good intelligence, embarked on a diplomatic offensive. It informed the Saudi government in late July 1955 of its desire to establish diplomatic relations, offering weapons in unlimited quantity; about the same time communist China issued an invitation to Prince Faisal to visit Beijing. Both approaches were declined by King Saud, and the US reaction toward these decisions was sought ex post facto by members of the royal *diwan* and by the Saudi ambassador in Washington. In a meeting with Wadsworth on November 30, 1955, the king reported the arms offer (as well as offers from Czechoslovakia and Poland). He declared, however, that he wanted the United States to be the sole supplier of arms for Saudi Arabia and to provide guidance in a five-year military training plan (as partial quid pro quo for renewal of the Dhahran air base). He sought further US advice on whether to take the Buraimi question to the UN Security Council[17] and whether to break relations with and boycott the United Kingdom. He added, "Whatever action the US Government advises, I would like guarantee of its support, and I will be guided by its advice."[18]

The period was one of diplomatic groping by each side for signs of reciprocal commitment to security measures and how far they could be made to go. Saud wanted weapons, and he wanted to restore normal ties despite the crisis over Buraimi. He carefully followed the US-Egyptian explosion over the unconditional and sizeable mid-1955 Czech arms credit to Nasser. The Egyptian leader, by December 1955, had received a US offer of grant military aid, which he rejected, being unwilling to accept the safeguards against misuse required by the US Congress of any recipient of such aid. The safeguards were not onerous and had, by this time, been accepted by thirty-five other recipients. King Saud also wanted the grant aid without the safeguard language, but he was by now obtaining oil royalties amounting to $250 million per year; in American political circles it was thus hard to justify any grant assistance whatsoever to King Saud.

Nonetheless, the United States in 1954–1956 was willing to consider grant military assistance for Saudi Arabia (if the standard terms were accepted) as a user's payment for the Dhahran air base. Eisenhower and Dulles's concept of building a "Northern Tier" of defense along the southern perimeter of the Soviet Union as a loose extension of NATO was an elaboration of Truman's containment policy, popularly renamed the Eisenhower Doctrine. Dhahran was of potential value as a strategic backup—a hinterland in the evolving security structure that in 1955 became the Baghdad Pact, comprising Turkey, Iraq, Iran, Pakistan, and the United Kingdom (with the United States as an "observer"). Dulles had sought to encourage Nuri al-Said of Iraq and Adnan Menderes of Turkey, already allied, to build this structure as an indigenous project, a bastion of anticommunist Middle Eastern states.

The Saudi government viewed British membership in the Baghdad Pact as susceptible to Hashemite pressures and plots and was reported to be opposed to the inclusion of Syria, Jordan, and Lebanon in Western-sponsored collective security arrangements.[19] It was not a good moment for a British-Saudi dustup over boundaries in the Persian Gulf, nor for a Saudi break in cordial relations with the United States.

British prime minister Eden, in preparing for a state visit to Washington on January 30–February 1, 1956, was briefed by Charles A. E. Shuckburgh, the British Foreign Office's expert on the Persian Gulf. In paving the way for Eden's visit, Shuckburgh consulted with his own foreign affairs and defense offices. He was a hard-liner on Buraimi, and British policy was now firm in its refusal to return to arbitration. The ensuing Eisenhower-Eden exchange served to clarify US and British positions, but was inconclusive, and high-level talks with the British subsequently continued in Washington, London, and Paris.

The British position, however tightly embraced by the Eden government, suffered from built-in rigidity and was getting nowhere with the United States. Dulles and Eisenhower fully agreed with Eden and Foreign Secretary Selwyn Lloyd on just about every aspect of the Middle East situation except Buraimi and Saudi Arabia: Washington refused to commit itself to a coordinated position with London in case the Saudis brought the Buraimi dispute to the UN Security Council. It also found to be exaggerated British claims that Saudi money, advanced by ARAMCO, was being spent by the Saudi government in a conspiracy to drive the British out of the gulf and thereby serve Soviet interests and weaken British and US positions in pro-Western Iraq. The United States agreed to Lloyd's proposal that the United Kingdom and United States sit together and compare sources of intelligence on the Middle East, especially the gulf. Subsequently, putting aside Britain's refusal to return to arbitration over Buraimi, Lloyd instituted direct discussions on the gulf with Prince Faisal, after extensive talks with Abd al-Rahman Azzam Pasha, King Saud's trusted trouble-shooter.

Meanwhile, Washington, after a review of what it could justifiably pay to stay at the Dhahran Airfield, stiffened its basic negotiating instructions to Wadsworth regarding renewal of the agreement. As a carrot it offered new proposals on the sale of arms and other US assistance in strengthening the kingdom, giving the Saudis reason to cooperate in achieving a position of strength; at the same time, Washington made it absolutely clear that it would not stay in Dhahran at any price the Saudis might set. The king, talking with Wadsworth, had referred constantly to a need for "justification" (grant aid) for renewing Dhahran. The United States prepared its negotiating stance with a "sweetener," to be introduced at the right moment, to build a much-needed new air terminal at a US cost of $5 million. Negotiations on arms aid and the renewal of the Dhahran Airfield agreement began September 11, 1956.

THE EISENHOWER DECISION TO BUILD UP KING SAUD

On October 29, 1956, the Suez War was touched off by Israel's invasion of Sinai, followed shortly by the intervention of British and French forces. At the United Nations, Dulles condemned this action vigorously, and in the Security Council Britain vetoed the US draft resolution of condemnation. I had been transferred from Washington to Cairo as deputy chief of mission in 1955. From my very busy vantage point there, it was apparent that, as a by-product of the enhancement of the US image in the Third World for its stand at the United Nations, King Saud's moral position before his "external" as well as "internal" critics had been considerably strengthened.

The king had repeatedly raised with Ambassador Wadsworth his vulnerability to Arab attack for having accepted a foreign base on Saudi soil. He gave it as the prime reason for asking the United States for something "special." In return for this something, he could answer his critics in regard to permitting the United States to retain Dhahran. What he wanted, it turned out, were arms in considerable quantity, on a grant basis as the United States had recently offered Nasser.

On November 6, 1956, Saud broke relations with the United Kingdom. He did so to support Egypt, to demonstrate solidarity with the overall Arab condemnation of Britain, France, and Israel, and to register his reprisal for the British action against him in Buraimi. At the same time, via messages through the US embassy in Jeddah, Saud developed contact with President Eisenhower and accepted the president's invitation to visit him in Washington. The time set was January 30 through February 1, 1957.

Just as Saudi-US relations had reached their lowest point in 1953–1954, in 1957–1958 they rode on a crest. Eisenhower and Dulles constituted a team that could rely on the president's unchallenged popularity at home and his vast prestige abroad. Dulles had stood up at the United Nations against America's major and indispensable allies in condemning, and reversing, an aggression on a Third World country. The effect was electric; even Nehru of India was impressed. Dropping his usually caustic attitude toward the US government, he rose in the UN General Assembly to pay eloquent tribute to an America that had at last located its soul. The US image was greatly strengthened around the Arab world (for the time being), making Saudi Arabia's relationship with it defensible. The Eisenhower-Dulles team considered King Saud a most useful counterweight in the Middle East to the pro-Soviet Nasser,[20] an idea that proved to be a miscalculation.

The Saud-Eisenhower meetings in Washington drew on the best talents of both sides and were held against a background of great cordiality and determination to reach a meeting of the minds. The king was an active participant, as was Eisenhower. Cabinet and subcabinet meetings explored military and economic factors in depth. By contrast, the evenings were filled with elaborate dining. When the king reciprocated the presidential hospitality offered him, the scene was lavish in the extreme, with a huge guest list to match and ice sculpture as a centerpiece of the extended banquet hall. It overstepped, by far, the image appropriate for a monarch counting on US grant aid from the many congressmen present as guests.

In the conference rooms, the royal debt in the aftermath of the Suez War was computed at $200 million, including $50 million in lost oil revenues due to closure of the Suez Canal. Estimates were that six months would elapse before the waterway could be reopened. Looking to the future, it was noted that Saudi dollar income from oil revenues would probably double in ten years to $600 million. For its major development projects, the Saudis sought very large "outside" help (grants), but the United States argued that loans were the logical means of financing development. The Saudis announced that they had decided to join the World Bank but were not yet ready to borrow. Eventually, a compromise of loan-versus-grant military aid was reached—a high point in the history of US relations with Saudi Arabia. The solution required the military expertise of all levels of the US government, from President Eisenhower on down. An agreement was reached on February 9, 1957.

Military grant aid to Saudi Arabia included air force development, training, and maintenance; the augmenting of army training, including the Royal Guard; and construction of a new air terminal at Dhahran, not to exceed $5 million—with the cumulative cost to the United States over a five-year period not to exceed $50 million, in consideration of renewal of the Dhahran Airfield agreement. Military sales called for a ground force program of two divisions at $110 million; the immediate sale of eighteen M-47 tanks; reconditioned equipment to fill the gap pending delivery of new equipment ordered; eight T-33 aircraft for training; coastal patrol craft and US training for use; and US credit for sales up to $41 million. As economic aid, the United States offered technical assistance—in principle US funding, at moderate levels, of specific projects, such as the port of Dammam (about $20 million)—and US good offices for the development of projects through commercial institutions, namely the Export-Import Bank and the World Bank.[21]

In Washington on April 2, 1957, an exchange of notes relating to renewal of the Dhahran agreement of June 18, 1951, completed the formal framework of what was certainly a high watermark in relations between the two heads of state. Their personal and official regard for and cooperation with each other reached a zenith in the joint communiqué in which Eisenhower asked Saud to "exert his influence to the greatest extent possible in Syria and Egypt to help prevent them from going Communist," in response to which Saud gave his promise.[22] Eisenhower told Saud that he now considered both these countries to be in "great danger."

KING SAUD AND NASSER

When Secretary of State Dulles had stopped in Cairo May 11–12, 1953, on his comprehensive tour of the Middle East, the Egyptian Revolution, begun July 23, 1952, was still very young, as were the appealing, reform-minded members of the Revolutionary Command Council (RCC). These vigorous young officers, mostly of colonel rank, were physically fit, disciplined, and eager to learn and to raise Egypt out of the degradation and neglect into which it had sunk. They presented an agreeable contrast to the leadership during the reign of King Farouk. They seemed to offer Dulles a strong position against potential Soviet expansion into one of the most strategic water passages of our planet.

Dulles used the carrot generously. He made clear to the new leadership what he believed to be needed at this juncture—namely, his own official encouragement of the concept that Egypt was the natural leader of the Arabic-speaking world and that, in close association with the United States, Egypt would be built up militarily to defend Free World principles over the vast Arabic belt from Morocco to the Persian Gulf.

One man who pondered Dulles's comments carefully was a key participant in the May 12 talks—the actual leader of the RCC, Colonel Gamal Abdel Nasser. Another was Prime Minister Muhammad Naguib, an elderly military figure, highly respected and even beloved by his public. He had accepted the ostensible leadership of the RCC on the night of July 22, 1952. The RCC functioned as a sovereignty council, a sort of politburo of final decisions on all matters of state. The cabinet reported to the RCC through Naguib. The council shunned formal diplomatic contacts, but selectively used private contacts with middle-grade embassy officers, civil or military. It deliberated on and decided all matters raised by the cabinet or by its own members.

For the first two years of the revolution the RCC sought to reexamine all inherited policies, including the most sensitive, to identify all of Egypt's options. During this period Naguib projected a favorable image abroad and at home as a man of warm strength and good sense. He sought means to enlist help from Free World sources and made direct policy recommendations to the RCC, coordinated with those of Foreign Minister Mahmoud Fawzi, a widely respected career diplomat.

Dulles's words of encouragement (now declassified and published) contained expressions most stimulating to Nasser's ambitious and restless turn of mind, to wit: ". . . he [Dulles] would like the Prime Minister to know that when the new US Administration had studied world strategy in the Department of State and in the National Security Council, they had concluded that Egypt is the country in the Middle East which, under the leadership and guidance of the Prime Minister, contains the promise of a great future. . . . So far as arms are concerned there is desperate need for American arms in Laos and other places in the Far East as well as in Europe. It will not be easy for the US to assist Egypt. However, if arms and economic help are justified and if Egypt itself desires these things from the US, the US would be prepared to consider making the Egyptian Army a real force in the world."[23]

This was bound to lead to overexpectations on both sides, but the most serious case of overexpectation was to appear on the side of the RCC. It expected not to become a "chosen instrument" of the United States, but an independent operation at the pinnacle of Middle East affairs, without serious competition. The only other Arab countries that might challenge Cairo's position as a regional arbiter were Syria and Iraq, which separately presented no threat to Egypt's preeminence, although together they might.

The challenge to Egypt came on February 24, 1955, when, to the outrage of the RCC, Iraq (under the government of Nuri al-Said) announced its intention of forming what became the Baghdad Pact with Turkey. Egypt took these developments as a declaration of political war against it and accused the United States of sponsoring a security pact to offset the rising leadership position of Egypt in the Arab world. The general tone suggested a treacherous United States turning its back on Egypt in favor of Cairo's ancient rival, Baghdad, and its pro-Western leader.

The pact between Iraq and Turkey (which was Nuri's idea) was a turn for the worse in US-Egyptian relations. Far from abandoning Egypt and its natural leadership of the Arab world, the United States was conducting protracted negotiations through Assistant Secretary of State Byroade in London and Washington to smooth out British and Egyptian obstacles to a final British evacuation of its huge base complex in the Suez Canal area. Finally a formula was found for custodial-maintenance arrangements using civilian-dressed "technicians" to keep tabs on and maintain supervision over base stores for immediate use in case of aggression against Egypt or Turkey. Begun following the Dulles visit to Cairo, this diplomatic activity by the United States from 1953 to 1956 was intended to foster new and better US relations with Egypt by getting the British forces out of Egypt. Initially it appeared to register some success, despite the Baghdad Pact, but it was not to last.

In 1957 King Saud stopped in Cairo on his way to Washington, apparently to reassure his charismatic and dangerous Egyptian neighbor that his visit to the United States was by no means intended as a plot against Nasser or his image; the delicacy of Saud's position was clear. Very pointedly, the White House had issued no such invitation to Nasser, and Nasser had expressed to Eisenhower and Dulles no thanks whatever for condemning and checking the Israeli, British, and French invasion of Egypt. Relations there were bad and were likely to remain so; Nasser could imagine the worst, because his deputy, Minister of Agriculture Ahmad al-Mahrouki, had approached me in the aftermath of the October Suez War to officially request wheat through Public Law 480.[24] I passed the request on to Dulles, with Ambassador Hare concurring and with my warm endorsement. Dulles's brusque refusal of this request still puzzles me four decades later. To be sure, Nasser was testing the post-Suez waters of his Washington relationship. His rating with Dulles, however, was already low. While it was Dulles who in late spring 1956 had withdrawn on political grounds the offer to provide indispensable financial backing through the World Bank for Nasser's pet project, the Aswan High Dam, it had been Nasser's spectacular retaliatory seizure of control of the Suez Canal on July 23, 1956, that set in motion the crisis that led to the Suez War.

Dulles, more than any other world leader, bore responsibility for overreacting to certain provocative actions of the RCC by withdrawing from the Aswan project. Conversely, Dulles then brought into play his powerful leadership in the United Nations to effect the rescue of Egypt from what would certainly have been a long and indecisive war with Britain and France ranged on the side of Israel in the immense urban labyrinths of the delta. Dulles disagreed radically with British and French official assessments that Nasser's regime would have fallen quickly as a result of the combined attack if the United States had not intervened. From what Ambassador Hare and his staff knew to be Nasser's immense popularity at home and abroad, Dulles was right. The entire operation revealed critically bad judgment in London, Paris, and Jerusalem. All three had plotted in deliberate secrecy from the US government and from the British and French parliaments, knowing that the operation would be vigorously opposed by Washington because it flouted the NATO alliance. The US embassy in Cairo judged that unless the invasion were stopped, guerrilla war in the delta in support of Egypt's popular hero would have gone on indefinitely.

The dramatic but coolheaded defiance by Nasser of demands by what had been two colonial overlords at one stroke greatly boosted Egyptian prestige in Arab, Muslim, and other Third World perspectives. Nasser's boldness provided extraordinary impetus to the Arab unity movement under Egypt's aegis, far outclassing Jordan's and Iraq's earlier attempts to popularize the "Greater Syria" or "Fertile Crescent" concept that had so alarmed Ibn Saud.

Now, in the blockage of the canal with sunken ships and the wreckage of war, an opportunity beckoned for the United States to make a small humanitarian gesture to the Egyptian people. But Dulles's posture was angry and haughty in tone, admitting of no peaceful gesture to the benefit of the Egyptian leader by the US government, which was seeking to repair its damaged relations with Britain and France. Nasser felt the Dulles-Eisenhower sting of hostility, and he brought it to the conference table in 1957 with Saud, who had offered to Nasser his own good offices with Washington. Among other impossibles, Nasser asked him to intervene in Washington to obtain the badly needed PL 480 wheat. Saud agreed to take the matter up.

Saud offered his good offices on other matters as well. Nasser told him to get President Eisenhower to close the Gulf of Aqaba to Israeli ships, especially war vessels. King Saud argued these issues extensively with Dulles, who, as stated, was unwilling to make even the political gesture the sale of wheat would imply. Dulles was also unable to impress Saud with the fact that under international law, Israel, as a riparian state, had full rights with Saudi Arabia, Jordan, and Egypt to navigate and use the waters of the Aqaba gulf. Thus, King Saud, returning through Cairo, came empty-handed to Nasser with only a generalized message of optimism regarding Washington's desire for better relations with the Arab world.

Nasser heard out King Saud—he knew its substance already from his contacts in Washington—and with heavy sarcasm said, "We have the wheat—coming from the Soviet Union. I'll send you a photo of it on arrival." From there on, it was all hostility toward Saud. The powerful voice of Ahmad Said on Cairo's Voice of the Arabs was turned full blast against the king, his extravagance, his wastage of the oil that should belong to "all the Arabs," and other such charges. It was a declaration of radio war on the entire regime, but with attacks on Saud personally as the cutting edge. Saud was in no position to respond, having neither the trained personnel nor the equipment. He was reluctant in any case to pick up the Egyptian challenge, given Nasser's experienced media organization.

When Ahmad Said's messages to the Arab world had zeroed in on incitement to overthrow the "corrupt" Saud clan, however, the king began to search for areas where he could use the one asset ready at hand, money. Dulles encouraged Saud to maintain firmness in the face of Nasser's radio attacks and not seek to appease him, through personal contacts or otherwise, as this would be construed in Egypt and elsewhere as capitulation. Dulles reiterated that US policy toward Egypt would be governed largely by the degree to which Nasser respected the independence of other states in the area.

Meanwhile, the United States declared that it would "firmly encourage" the formation of an Iraq-Jordan Arab federation, under negotiation in March 1958, even suggesting that Saudi Arabia might some day join it.[25] In making this recommendation, Dulles was not unmindful of the historic aversion of the al-Sauds to a Hashemite union on Saudi Arabia's doorstep. It was indeed a time of change. The federation was purely defensive, a reaction to the far more important United Arab Republic formed by Egypt and Syria earlier in the year. It was designed to preempt Nasserite expansionism and the accompanying penetration of Soviet influence. It was to be a confederation of equals, the realms of two Hashemite cousins—King Hussein of Jordan and King Faisal II of Iraq. Finally organized in May 1958, it collapsed in the bloody army coup in Baghdad on July 14 that same year. Had it survived, it would have presented no threat to Saudi Arabia. In fact, cooperation between Jordan and Saudi Arabia was becoming close and cordial, while Iraq (whether royal or republican) was never willing to surrender its independence to

Syria, and certainly not to Egypt. The enemy was not Saud but Nasser—
who would accept only union (*wahda*) and complete subordination.

KUWAIT AND THE SAUDI SECURITY SYSTEM

Blood ties and close geographic proximity link Saudi Arabia intimately
with Kuwait, though the histories and development of the two neighbors
have been markedly different. True Kuwaitis are distantly akin to the
Sauds, among other gulf ruling clans, and their lineage is therefore
believed to be shared. This factor has had its impact in their recent
history of mutual support.

Until oil was found in the late 1930s, the highland region of Nejd,
covering what is now north-central Saudi Arabia, saw little but nomadic
herding and oasis agriculture for centuries. Its economy was based on
hand-dug wells and simple irrigation. Some 250 years ago, according to
tradition related to me by the 1944 ruler of Bahrain, Sheikh Salman bin
Hamad Al Khalifah, there was a devastating drought. The Anizah peoples,
among them the ancestors of Kuwait's governing Al Sabah family, began
to move in a long search for available wells and pastures on the coast of
the Persian Gulf at the base of the Qatar peninsula. The Al Sabah moved
north until it reached the site of what was locally named Kuwait.

In the past Kuwait had at times been under Persian control, but for the
most part it was under Ottoman suzerainty, autonomous in internal
affairs but paying tribute to the Sublime Porte at Istanbul. In 1869–1870
a de facto ruler of Kuwait joined Ottoman sultan Midhat Pasha in a
military campaign into what later became Saudi Arabia, conquering al-
Hasa, which became a Turkish province.[26] As a result, the sheikh of
Kuwait was rewarded by the Porte with the title of de jure ruler of Kuwait.

By the end of the nineteenth century, however, Ottoman decline had
permitted Britain, through its government of India, to build up an almost
complete monopoly of the external affairs of most of the gulf principalities. The British political resident at Bushire, Iran, one Colonel Meade,
was authorized by the British government of India to meet with the ruler
of Kuwait, Sheikh Mubarak Al Sabah, who had been weakened by clashes
with the Rashidis, tribal rivals of the al-Sauds, and the Wahhabis. On
January 23, 1899, admitting to a need for external support against these
forces, Mubarak agreed with the British to a treaty whereby he undertook
not to let or cede any part of his territory to governments or their subjects
other than to the British, and to receive no representatives of foreign
powers without British concurrence. In return, Mubarak received an
annual subsidy and British-Indian military protection as needed. From
1903, a British political agent, with powers of a chief magistrate over cases
involving other than local citizenry and with control over all foreign
affairs, was established in Kuwait. He reported to the British government

74

of India, which in turn answered to London's India Office. At the time of World War I, Britain declared Kuwait an independent kingdom under British protection. On December 26, 1915, Ibn Saud concluded an agreement with the British and the sheikh of Kuwait defining the boundaries between Kuwait and Saudi Nejd.

After termination of the World War I British mandate over Iraq and Iraq's achievement of full independence in 1932, however, Iraq began to press its claim to Kuwait as a subprovince of Ottoman Basra. For the last years of the Iraqi monarchy, the perennial governments of Nuri al-Said nevertheless quietly accepted the status quo and sought good relations with the Al Sabahs, welcoming the frequent visits of the family to properties it had long since acquired in the Basra area. In those years there was much talk of a water pipeline project from the Shatt al-Arab to Kuwait, where virtually no groundwater existed, much less any flowing stream. Nuri revived, rather quietly, the Iraqi claim to Kuwait as a partial fulfillment of the sacred goal of Arab unity, urging the Kuwaiti ruler to join an Iraq-Jordan federation. But this effort ended with Nuri's death at the hands of an Iraqi mob during the revolution of July 14, 1958. Thereafter, Brigadier Abd al-Karim Qasim, front man of that revolution, picked up the Iraqi claim.

Earlier, Iraq's desire to annex Kuwait had increased when oil was discovered in 1938 by the Kuwait Oil Company (KOC).[27] The deposits represented an oil man's dream: the top of the Burgan formation was tapped at a shallow depth and thus easy to drill, and the location was only a few kilometers of flat terrain from a good Persian Gulf anchorage. Profitable commercial export began in June 1946, and by 1961 even an aquifer yielding about 5 million gallons per day of usable water was found, close to the northern border with Iraq.

Between my first visit to Kuwait in 1950 and my second in January 1962, city walls had been destroyed, high-rises proliferated, the population quadrupled, and desalinated water was introduced. But Kuwait, roughly the area of New Jersey and with less than one million native people, now saw itself as weak and vulnerable in an environment of a much larger and predatory Arab "brotherhood." Revolutionary currents in Egypt and Iraq were polarizing the area while exploiting the mystique of Arab unity as the sole means of successfully liberating the Arab world from the humiliation of British and French colonialism and America's sponsorship of Israel in the Arab heartland. This pressure grew as the oil wealth grew.

Like Saudi Arabia, Kuwait felt acutely the need to show its "Arabism," but also to ensure its survival. Reassuring foreign investment was already in place in the form of the joint British and US ownership of the Kuwaiti oil concession. By 1961 the investment of Getty Oil and Japanese-owned Arabian Oil was added in the Neutral Zone, where the combined yield of oil and gas royalties onshore and offshore was shared 50–50 between

Kuwait and Saudi Arabia. The United States in this period bolstered recognition of Kuwait by supporting its applications for admission to the United Nations Educational, Scientific, and Cultural Organization, the International Civil Aviation Organization, the World Health Organization, and other specialized international agencies.

Then, on June 19, 1961, Kuwait and Great Britain signed an important treaty revoking the 1899 pact, and Britain separately undertook to come to Kuwait's defense if so asked. During that summer, Kuwait sent delegations far and wide, seeking membership in the United Nations and an exchange of ambassadorships with Washington, London, and Cairo. Kuwaiti policy was generally to be friendly to Iraq and nonprovocative.

On the evening of June 25, 1961, just six days after the signature of the Anglo-Kuwaiti treaty divesting Britain of its sixty-two-year control of Kuwait's foreign relationships, Qasim held a press conference. He declared invalid both the treaty of 1899 and that of June 19, 1961, and stated that Kuwait was "an indivisible part of Iraq." Kuwaitis were stunned, infuriated, and frightened. Now, it appeared, Qasim really meant to go after Kuwait.

The Iraqi public showed no enthusiasm for Qasim's claim, and the Saudis reacted vigorously. King Saud announced that aggression against Kuwait would be considered aggression against Saudi Arabia, and dispatched his chief of staff, General Ibrahim al-Tassan, to consult on defense with the Kuwaiti ruler, Sheikh Abd Allah al-Salim Al Sabah. The Egyptian government reacted through its government-controlled press, implicitly opposing Qasim's claim, as did Syria, which was still incorporated in the UAR at the time.

By June 27, 1961, unconfirmed reports came to the United States and the United Kingdom that two Iraqi divisions were moving toward the frontier of Kuwait. The British informed the Kuwaiti ruler that they were taking the precaution of sending a commando force by sea to be near Kuwait. Lord Home, the British foreign secretary, advised US secretary of state Dean Rusk that UK forces would be landing soon, if Kuwait's ruler so requested, and asked for, and received at once, US political support for this action. On June 30, 1961, the emir of Kuwait put in writing his request to the British for a landing of forces.

On the next day, July 1, six hundred Marine commandos (British battalion strength) landed from the carrier HMS *Bulwark* in Kuwait Bay, escorted by two frigates and one tank landing ship. They had plenty of firepower and assembled near a new jet airport south of Kuwait City, while a squadron of Hawker Hunter jets from Bahrain thundered overhead. The Arab League also acted. A small Saudi Arabian paratroop battalion moved to Kuwait in parallel with the British on July 1, and were eventually joined by token forces from Egypt, Jordan, and the Sudan.

In New York the same day, Kuwait requested a meeting of the UN Security Council. As Kuwait was not yet a member of the United Nations, the British permanent representative to the UN introduced and supported the complaint and made clear UK backing of Kuwait. He stated that the UK military presence in Kuwait would be withdrawn whenever Sheikh Abd Allah so desired.

In Jordan, King Hussein made clear privately to the United Kingdom and the United States that he saw the dispute as basically between British and Arab interests. His country had historically supported Iraq's claim to Kuwait, and some years previously he personally had joined with then prime minister Nuri al-Said in pressing the Iraqi claim with the UK ambassador. In this case, he had sent Qasim a message supporting the claim, but had emphasized it should be pursued peaceably. Now, assessing outside reactions to the threat of force, Hussein took the position that the moment for Qasim to press the claim had passed. He so informed Qasim, making clear that Jordanian troops would not support an Iraqi move.

The trained battalion that the Saudis deployed constituted a generous share of the manpower the kingdom could put together. Saudi Arabia was then, as today, defensible principally by geography and climate, but especially by the capacity of its people to boldly exploit the home terrain. Command of the air was essential. In 1961 there were, at best, a half-dozen combat-trained pilots, with a few more in basic training. The Saudi air force, featuring F-86s, was an infant service, though enthusiastic, venturesome, and fearless. In numbers, the armed forces of Saudi Arabia were far from equal to the ground, air, and sea strength of Iraq. There was thus no force in the area comparable to that deployable by the British.

In late June 1961, the US chargé d'affaires at Jeddah, Richard Hawkins, was received in Ta'if by King Saud in the presence of his top defense officers, headed by Saud's son Muhammad ibn Saud, minister of defense. The group included the commanders of all Saudi forces. In an exchange of evaluations, Hawkins was informed by the king that he wished to confirm his earlier public statements that his government was determined to do everything possible to defend Kuwait. The Saudi ambassador to Iraq had been instructed to so inform Qasim personally and to urge reflection and moderation. Saudi Arabia would not attack but would defend at all costs.

On July 11, 1961, the United Kingdom made a public statement of intent to immediately withdraw the bulk of its naval and air units from Kuwait, leaving about 2,600 ground troops in place, though it was not believed that Qasim would retract his claim. At the same time, Kuwait sought close relations with its other oil partner and distant friend, the United States. During that July, in a private conversation with Qasim,

John Jernegan, US ambassador to Iraq, stated simply that the United States recognized Kuwait's independence. When Qasim asked whether the United States supported the British action, Jernegan replied it was not a question of support but that the United States did not oppose the moves the British had made. What the United States did oppose was forceful action by any party to the dispute. Any change must be accomplished peacefully and with the consent of the peoples concerned.

As for Iraqis in Kuwait, who numbered an estimated thirty to forty thousand, they had begun a considerable exodus by the end of July. The border was entirely open for their exit, tightly closed against any return. Despite near-unanimous, long-standing sentiment in Iraq for annexing Kuwait, the intensity of alarms from Qasim subsided after a time, and there were no further indicators of an imminent attack. Perhaps Qasim's 1961 shift away from invading Kuwait in the face of immediate and effective challenge led Saddam Hussein in 1990 to his decision that deception, surprise, and overwhelming force should be employed the next time if annexation of Kuwait was to be realized.

The decisive and sophisticated action by King Saud in deploying Saudi troops had put Kuwait's independence, for the first time, squarely into the strategic defense system of Saudi Arabia. It was a move of unqualified Saudi support given one day after Qasim's first reactions to the UK-Kuwaiti treaty. Saudi Arabia's prompt and unequivocal determination in 1961 was stated by the king both publicly and privately to Qasim. By contrast, the US position in 1961 was ambiguous. The United States was reluctant to abandon entirely a decade of effort to encourage democracy and development in Iraq and preferred to regard the situation as an inter-Arab quarrel.

In December 1961 in Jeddah, to which I had been posted as ambassador since July 22 of that year, I received a letter from Assistant Secretary of State Phillips Talbot inviting me to expeditiously take on, in addition to my duties as ambassador to Saudi Arabia and minister to the Yemen, the post of first US ambassador to Kuwait. US policy required a quick demonstration to Iraq of its endorsement of an independent Kuwait. Once the credentials and other papers were received from Washington, I took my oath of office on December 21, 1961, at the embassy in Jeddah.

On January 5, 1962, I presented, according to traditional diplomatic custom, a copy of my credentials to Foreign Minister Sabah al-Salim Al Sabah, brother of the emir. On January 7, with my wife Jane, Isa Sabbagh, and others from the embassy, I proceeded to Basman Palace, to be met by a British-trained Kuwaiti mounted guard of honor and bagpipe band, all attired in brilliant red jackets. Following the brief ceremony came a series of calls and receptions, devoid of discussion of the threat from Iraq.

In a later private audience, I endeavored on my own initiative, but without success, to interest Emir Abd Allah in a program of economic cooperation with the United States to help the Yemen qualify for membership in the International Monetary Fund and the World Bank. "One arranges one's bed by the length of his blanket," replied the emir, "but in any case aid to the Yemen is useless as long as Imam Ahmad rules the country." I left Kuwait following calls on Crown Prince Sa'd Abd Allah al-Salim Al Sabah, son of the emir and then minister of the interior, in charge of all security matters (and destined to be prime minister in the days of Desert Shield, Desert Storm, and thereafter).

My limited mission of January 1962 was largely symbolic. From all evidence available, I did not foresee an early renewal of a serious crisis with Qasim. But the presentation of credentials on June 1, 1962, by Sheikh Abd al-Rahman Atiqi to President Kennedy as the first Kuwaiti ambassador to the United States triggered the partial rupture of US-Iraqi relations. On June 2, Iraqi foreign minister Hashim Jawad summoned Ambassador Jernegan and informed him that Iraq was recalling its ambassador to the United States and must therefore ask Jernegan to leave. There was no further action against the United States, and the embassies in both capitals remained open, fully staffed, and headed by a chargé d'affaires *ad interim*. My own mission to Kuwait had undoubtedly contributed to Jernegan's ill fortune.

To enhance its independence, Kuwait had formed a National Guard in September 1961 not long after the start of the crisis with Iraq and by 1962 had graduated its first 1,400 trainees. By midsummer 1962, Britain's remaining troops had withdrawn, but Kuwait still had on its soil an Arab League–sponsored Jordanian and Saudi protective force. It considered their presence largely symbolic. Iraq's isolation was growing. Though Qasim's threats continued, his options were sharply reduced.

In the middle of these political and military developments exploded the news of the September 1962 revolution in the Yemen. The reactions in Kuwait were instructive. The new officer corps and virtually the entire public, Kuwaiti and foreign, favored the Yemeni revolutionists, suggesting that Kuwait's politically educated public was no longer enthusiastic about Bedouin monarchical institutions, despite the apparent respect enjoyed by the emir.

Feeling more secure by the end of 1962, Kuwait sought reduction of the Arab League force on its territory from 2,290 to a token strength of 300. Kuwait's action was motivated partially by the expense involved— 250,000 Kuwaiti dinars per month. It also reflected a nervousness at having so large a number of Saudi (1,250) and Jordanian (900) soldiers in Kuwait at a time when Kuwait had decided to recognize the Yemen Arab Republic, a decision unpopular with the Saudi and Jordanian leaderships. Saudi Arabia, Jordan, and the Sudan responded by withdrawing their forces completely. This too made the Kuwaiti leadership nervous.

Kuwait relied almost entirely on Britain's security pledges and its ability and will to carry them out. It was the only country Kuwait trusted. The United States had no desire to replace the British or even to supplement its military forces. The Kuwaiti government turned its attention to aid as a weapon. By early November 1962, it announced it was increasing the capitalization of its Arab Development Fund from $50 million to $100 million.

As elections for a Kuwait National Assembly were to take place and the government announced petroleum production averaging 1,843,665 US barrels per day, Qasim's luck ran out in Iraq. On the morning of February 8, 1963, he was cornered and executed in the Iraqi Ministry of Defense, in a Ba'thist-nationalist coup d'état led by Colonel Abd al-Salaam Arif. During the first month after the coup in Baghdad, Iraqi-Kuwaiti relations improved greatly in a practical sense, that is, in the restoration of telecommunications and transborder commercial activity; but the Iraqi government showed no signs of dealing with the issue of Iraq's claim on Kuwait one way or another.

After extensive maneuvering, however, a landmark accord was reached between Iraq and Kuwait on October 4, 1963, issued as a procès-verbal and signed at Baghdad Palace by the respective prime ministers.[28] Neither party signed off on a vital interest or aspiration, but behind it was a new Iraqi government, hard-pressed for money, dedicated to Ba'thist doctrine, and eager to break the isolation of the Qasim period. A high-level Kuwaiti delegation led by Sabah al-Salim Al Sabah, now prime minister, had visited Baghdad October 2–5, 1963. During the talks, Kuwait secretly agreed to give Iraq an interest-free loan of £30 million repayable over twenty-five years, the first payment due after six years; the payment was to be the equivalent current gold value of a sterling loan. The Government of Kuwait made the loan out of a London account but not from the Arab Development Fund.

The Iraqi reception of Sabah al-Salim and his delegation was cordial enough, but a heavy schedule of visits to Iraqi military installations was designed to make the Kuwaitis aware that they were lucky to deal with a government of peaceful intent. The Kuwaitis were taken to army camps around Baghdad and to the Iraqi air force base at Habaniyya. They were given lengthy briefings on the power and range of the Iraqi army and air force.

As a return gesture, an Iraqi delegation led by Prime Minister Bakr and Defense Minister Ammash visited Kuwait October 10–14, 1963, at which time the loan agreement was made public. In response to the heavy demonstration of Iraq's military might to the earlier Kuwaiti delegation, the Kuwait government now laid aside its usual high-level visitors' sightseeing program of central kitchens, kindergartens, and institutes for the blind and gave the Iraqi delegation a dose of new Kuwaiti military installations and equipment. In this way they hoped to show that Kuwait would not be a pushover. One US Foreign Service officer conversant with the area remarked that now Kuwaitis could sleep at night with only one eye open. It was Saudi Arabia, however, that found it difficult to relax. The sharp focus was on Dhahran Airfield.

SAUD BESIEGED: NASSER, DHAHRAN AIRFIELD, AND FAISAL

By June 1960—when I was NEA deputy assistant secretary and a year before my return for a third tour of duty in Saudi Arabia—the Dhahran Airfield had become a prime focus of Arab nationalist political attack, especially from Egypt via the powerful Voice of the Arabs. The motivation in Cairo and in Ba'thist circles was the overthrow of King Saud, and along with him an ancient patriarchal system. This, in theory, would be replaced by a republic responsive to Nasser's guidance, if not by outright incorporation.

The Soviet Union joined the clamor by commenting on the need for "progressive" (read "Arab socialist") forces and steadfast opposition to US or other Western "bases" in Arab countries. The Soviet Union therefore sought to enlarge its influence in the area by identification with Egypt and to enhance its image of solidarity with Arab "anti-imperialist" movements. But the Soviet Union was never warm to the idea of Arab unity, even under Nasser. It also hoped to reinstate its diplomatic ties with Saudi Arabia, broken by Stalin in 1938. It periodically approached the Saudi government to this end, but always without success. It consequently moderated and did not imitate in its own media Nasser's anti-Saud clichés. Overall it saw greater opportunities for Soviet influence in a piecemeal Arab world. It had been bitterly disappointed over the loss of its gains in Iraq when Qasim was killed and replaced by a pro-Nasser, anticommunist Ba'thist regime under Abd al-Salaam Arif in February 1963.

For Nasser, King Saud was an excellent target, and the Dhahran Airfield was not his only point of vulnerability. Saud was greatly concerned over Nasser's ability to label him as the special friend of Western imperialism, whom Egypt's media had also broadcast as the protector of Israel and the profiteer of Arab oil. As stated earlier, Saud had unsuccessfully attempted an entente with Nasser in 1957 when he stopped in Cairo en route to Washington to volunteer a good word for Nasser and for Egypt with President Eisenhower during a time of Washington-Cairo estrangement. The US administration, however, sought to keep its relations with Saudi Arabia quite apart from US-Egyptian problems.

Nasser's political momentum, by February 1958, had brought about the Syrian-Egyptian union known as the United Arab Republic (UAR).[1] A little additional momentum was gained in 1959 with the addition of the Kingdom of Yemen to special treaty status with Egypt, an arrangement called the United Arab States (UAS). Arab unity under Egypt was spreading and taking concrete form, as volatile public opinion took on a life of its own. In varying degrees it threatened the independence of Lebanon, Jordan, and Iraq as well as Saudi Arabia. Secretary of State Dulles urged King Saud to remain firm and refrain from appeasing Nasser.

In the wake of the mid-1958 Nasser-supported civil war in Lebanon, a military crisis in Jordan, and, above all, the July 1958 revolution in Iraq came the fiasco of the "million dollar check" King Saud had allegedly signed to cover Nasser's assassination. It was displayed publicly by its Syrian interceptor, Major Abd al-Hamid Sarraj, Nasser's hatchet man and watchdog against all Syrian opponents of Nasser's Arab unity. Sarraj had fully suppressed all democratic trends in the Syrian "northern sector" of the UAR and had closed its leading paper, *al-Ray al-Am*, on the unsupported ground that it was against the union with Egypt. No proof was submitted that King Saud had ordered payments made to any person, but suspicion traveled faster than caution.

Embarrassed and deeply worried by Saud's battered international image and that of the kingdom, Saud's brothers were reported to have met to consider the adverse political effect this scandal had spread throughout the Arab world. They also discussed Saud's fiscal extravagances and the absence of a serious, well-planned development program. The princes held no brief for Nasser, but if one check or three checks had been drawn to eliminate the Arab world's most popular leader and the galvanizer of Arab unity, the story would be of marginal credibility in a volatile Middle East. Indeed, it was supported by no evidence. The check, or checks, were all payable to "bearer" and signed only by bank officials, but the princes were still said to be deeply upset by the adverse image the Saudi leadership had incurred internationally.[2]

Thus, in March 1958, after tough negotiations, the king was forced by his brothers to turn over management of all government business to Crown Prince Faisal. Under the new arrangement, Faisal was commissioned by Saud to take over control of the entire income from oil sales and set up the first real national budget. He was assisted by a civilian council of ministers drawn primarily from recognized business and professional leaders. Royal emoluments, which had reached at least 60 percent of total oil income, were quickly reduced to around 14 percent, and all of the Saud clan were put on a system of allowances. This caused an immediate outcry by the king's army of dependents but evoked great if quiet satisfaction in business, professional, and intellectual circles.

Saud was far from pleased with all of this, and his jealousy of Faisal's popularity was known to grow apace. Faisal's reforms had cost him an Arab desert monarch's traditional control over public funds and over the customary annual largesse to tribes and supporters. Meanwhile, Ahmad Said, Nasser's talented gadfly on the Voice of the Arabs, avoided attacking Faisal personally, preferring at first to target Saudi tolerance of the "imperialist base" at Dhahran.

In December 1960 the king's exasperation over his fiscal limitations and being sidelined by Faisal's increasingly popular leadership reached a peak. Reportedly, those closest to the king and most dependent on what had been his open purse had urged him repeatedly to exercise his kingship, not watch it vanish. The king was indeed subject to all sorts of advice, much of it not central to Saudi interests. Saud was prone to impulse. Generous to a fault (and wildly extravagant), he also suffered in later years from debilitating ailments and loss of judgment.

On December 21, he acted. He rejected Faisal's budget, which by law required the king's approval before entering into effect in March of the succeeding year. The news of the rejection was carried to Faisal as he presided over a session of his council of ministers. He read the royal note, rose from the table, and walked out. That same day he submitted his resignation as prime minister, which was promptly accepted by the king. Faisal commanded that his gear be packed, and, with a few members of his family and some domestic help, followed his father's practice of camping in the desert. All of his cabinet resigned, and King Saud took over immediately as prime minister and began to put a new slate into place.

In any other circumstance, camping would have been unremarkable. To be a true Saudi Arab is to love the desert, its silence, its moods of serenity or storm, its plants and its animals. It is a place where one renews oneself by rest and contemplation. Faisal, for all his international experience, learned from his father to love this wilderness. But this excursion was an important political circumstance and reflected a top-level split in command; Faisal underscored it by not revealing his whereabouts. He was to be found only by a trusted few, and he rejected all communications seeking his return. By his own decision he was no longer a government official.

The king was on his own, and he soon became worried. After Faisal returned to his summer home in Ta'if, the king called him. What, if anything, was discussed was not known to me, but I was told Faisal did not return the call. He made it clear to his brother that he had not sought the prime ministership and would not accept it again without authority. As time passed, Saud became totally isolated. In March 1961, he arrived in Jeddah for the *umrah*, the little pilgrimage to Mecca, and none of his brothers met him. All efforts by them and by others to achieve a reconciliation between him and Faisal had failed.

Meanwhile, the Voice of the Arabs continued its vitriol over Dhahran Airfield. The king was beset by fears of Nasser. The Dhahran Airfield agreement, renewable every five years, had been extended by King Saud in 1957 to April 1, 1962. In Washington, acting Assistant Secretary of Defense Hayden Williams, by letter to Raymond Hare, then deputy under-secretary of state for political affairs, asserted that the Dhahran Airfield had now been reappraised and was regarded in the Pentagon as no longer a primary strategic facility. It was essential, however, for Middle East regional logistical support, and the Pentagon wanted the agreement renewed in 1962 or an alternative sought elsewhere.

Dhahran Airfield had not been considered by Riyadh or by Washington as a "base" since 1949, when the United States had formally turned over passive ownership of the facility to the Saudi government. For fourteen years, however, the airfield had been under US command, headed by an officer of the Second Air Division, with senior American air force officers rotating in and out of that command. It acted like a base, it looked like a base, and Americans in the area called it a base.

The airfield created irritants in US-Saudi relations, among which were the following: (1) Saudi officials repeatedly attempted to levy fines on US military personnel; (2) the Saudi government wanted no flagpole anchored in the ground except one bearing its own colors; (3) the Saudis refused on grounds of precedent to allow church services in a "chapel" but eventually permitted US air force chaplains to enter the kingdom, without Christian insignia, as "teachers" and hold quiet services in the assembly hall;[3] (4) there was a long-standing regulation against admission of Jews into the country, but the Saudis generally admitted whatever personnel the USAF assigned. These came in on the basis of no questions asked and no detailed scrutiny afforded.

In December 1960, Crown Prince Faisal, while still prime minister, had taken up his concerns over the status of the airfield with my predecessor, Ambassador Donald Heath, characterizing his remarks as "personal." His message—which he was to reaffirm to me a year later—was that Dhahran Airfield had finally become an obstacle to generally good US-Saudi relations. He suggested that the US government take the initiative and terminate the status before the current agreement expired. On December 9, 1960, the Department of State asked Heath's evaluation of the seriousness of Faisal's proposal and whether Faisal might abrogate the airfield agreement before its expiration. On December 25, four days after Faisal's resignation, Heath pointed out to Washington that, although Faisal would have continued to urge the United States to take the initiative, since he was no longer in office there was a fair chance the king might agree to renewal. The king believed US troops in Dhahran—1,332 airmen and ten transport aircraft—could be a deterrent to outside or inside plots to overthrow the Saudi regime. On February 26, 1961, the Saudi finance minister, Prince Talal ibn Abd al-Aziz, had suggested to Heath that it was desirable that the US and Saudi governments set forth their ideas on the future of Dhahran Airfield before negotiations began, as the Saudis would like to receive US proposals.

Shortly thereafter, however, King Saud decided not to renew the Dhahran Airfield agreement, fearing continued Egyptian attacks on his government and its relations with the United States. On March 13 he accepted a US proposal to issue a joint communiqué emphasizing the friendly nature of the change, whereby full ownership and control of the airfield would pass on April 1, 1962, to Saudi Arabia. Three days later, on March 16, 1961 (before Washington had finished negotiating agreed language with Riyadh), Saud instructed Mecca Radio to broadcast a strictly Saudi communiqué announcing that orders had been issued to the foreign minister to inform US ambassador Heath that the Saudi government did not intend to renew the airfield agreement when it expired the following year. The king had given the required one-year notice, but not, as expected, in a joint announcement. A $250 million investment by the US government was thus headed for write-off. With its 10,000-foot concrete runway, hangars, water well and tower, offices, mess halls, commissary, hospital, recreation center, local roads, and power stations, it was a lot for Washington to dismiss, all the more since the Eisenhower administration (just replaced by that of John F. Kennedy) had paid well for the previous base renewal on April 2, 1957.[4]

What came as an unpleasant surprise to Washington, however, was the timing of King Saud's radio communiqué as much as the substance. It was disquieting evidence of the king's basic insecurity in the face of Nasser's attacks and Moscow's threat, following the Soviet shooting down of an American U2 spy plane, to obliterate US overseas bases in case of war.

What is more, the US and Saudi governments had begun talks, if not exactly negotiations, on a revision of the status of the Dhahran Airfield, and the Foreign Ministry had assured Ambassador Heath that any announcement by it would be deferred until the evening of March 18, 1961, in order that it be joint.

The Departments of State and Defense now drafted and issued a press statement that cushioned the impact of the transfer and emphasized continuing Saudi and US interest in close relations and their confidence that these were in no way adversely affected by termination of US base rights.

When I arrived in Saudi Arabia as ambassador in July 1961, I found the higher echelons of authority in Riyadh deeply concerned to ensure that the United States not leave Saudi Arabia alone and virtually defenseless. They were also concerned about how they could replace the US Second Air Division's managerial custody of the airfield, as well as how they would pay for it. The badly mismanaged treasury of the realm was largely depleted. The government had no technicians or specialists in airport operations and services. It was highly distrustful of placing this sensitive facility under the physical control of contract Egyptians, Palestinians, Syrians, Iraqis, or other workmen from neighboring countries. The order of the king to the United States to turn over Dhahran Airfield could not be revoked, for this would invite ridicule and attack by international Arab commentary. But few of the king's advisors wanted a total US military evacuation.

Colonel W. W. Wilson, commander of the Second Air Division's Dhahran contingent and chief of the US Military Training Mission (USMTM), had made clear to State and Defense that the royal notification of March 16, 1961, would leave the USAF without a single military aircraft maintenance facility in the entire Middle East and that the Saudis were as yet without plans to negotiate a commercial maintenance contract. Five US air attaché aircraft were posted in the area, but their use was restricted. Thus, an important service to other US embassies would soon be lost by December 31, 1961, when Dhahran ceased to provide administrative and logistic services. Lost services would include supplying commissaries, hospital facilities, APO privileges, movies, and schooling for children of US consulate general families.

By the end of August 1961, however, the commander at Dhahran had also concluded that the burden of the closeout would fall more heavily on the Saudi government than on the United States. The loss to the United States was partially offset by savings of about $3 million a year, the fee charged by the Vinnell Corporation for their maintenance contract. This did not include USAF tower control costs. Further, the USAF now had aircraft of greater range than when Dhahran was built, decreasing the need for this facility to a degree. Washington was clearly moving toward the conclusion that it could rather painlessly dispense with Dhahran's overhead.

During my presentation of credentials to King Saud at Ta'if in late July 1961, I urged the Saudi government to begin preparing immediately for the takeover on April 1, 1962. The Saudis then set September 15, 1961, as the final date for submission of bids by private contractors. The front-runners were Vinnell and a keen competitor, Commonwealth Services of New York City. Scandinavian Airlines and SwissAir were also reported to be bidding but in the end were dropped. Saudi officials were calculating overhead at $4.4 million per year, plus an initial one-time expense of 3 million riyals. At one point the Saudis attempted to convince the US government that it should continue to bear this cost for an indefinite period. The idea was rejected outright by US officials and was not pressed further.

The original Dhahran Airfield agreement of August 8, 1945 (revised January 2, 1946), had provided not only for joint use by the United States and Saudi Arabia, under US command, but also for training Saudis in its operation and maintenance. In 1951, as negotiations began on the status of forces, it soon became apparent that the Saudis wanted a US training mission as the *quid* for the Dhahran *quo*. This was agreed to by Washington as a reasonable requirement involving a rather small US expense. Saudi Arabia at the time was still an underdeveloped country, with great demands on its oil royalty income. Revenues had just begun to rise from those based on the modest 1933 formula, measured in gold shillings per ton of crude "extracted and saved," to the very large sums based on the 1950 agreement with ARAMCO, whereby the Saudis obtained 50 percent of all profits realized by the company after payment of expenses, royalties, and "other Saud exactions."

The Saudi request for a US training mission had therefore been accepted by Washington. Accordingly, as noted earlier, the Dhahran Airfield agreement of June 18, 1951, granted the United States operational facilities at Dhahran Airfield in return for a military training mission and a civilian training program, paid for by the US government, to train Saudi nationals to organize and operate the technical administration of the airport. The 1951 undertaking became part of the Mutual Defense Assistance Agreement of June 27, 1953.

Following King Saud's March 1961 announcement that the Dhahran Airfield agreement would not be renewed, Saudi authorities had informed American officials of their desire to retain the USMTM, limited, however, to eighty Americans and relocated out of Dhahran. This would avoid the impression among foreign Arab critics that the United States was still operating the airfield under the guise of a new command replacing the Second Air Division. However, no formal Saudi request for this shift was received in Washington and the whole question of the size and location of USMTM was left hanging for the time being, while King Saud's own command relationships were being addressed within the royal Saudi family.

During the summer and fall of 1961, Saud's deteriorating health affected his competence. It was finally decided in the family that the king and his entourage would fly in December to Boston, where he would undergo extensive examination and treatment at Peter Bent Brigham Hospital in nearby Salem. The standoff relationship between the king and his half-brother Faisal had not changed, despite rather frantic interventions of family and business elements to induce Faisal to reconcile with Saud. Faisal had rejected all such pleas, saying that he would not occupy the position of prime minister without the requisite authority, which the king was not prepared to give. Now, however, the king was to go abroad and the heat was on both men to compromise. Faisal finally consented to be a *locum tenens* during what was expected to be a fairly short interval and to handle matters of importance by telegram to the king, if urgent, or bring them to his attention on his return.[5]

At ARAMCO's hospital in Dhahran, where King Saud stopped briefly en route, he gave a bedside farewell to his half-brothers, other family members, and numerous officials. Faisal appeared, gave his brother the formal nose and forehead kiss traditional in salutes to a chieftain, and left without a word.

Officially, Faisal was now acting king, but he refused to be so addressed or to make decisions on any policy matter. He surrounded himself with seasoned advisors and officials, such as Sheikh Yusuf Yassin, who briefed him on every case brought to his attention. When I called on Faisal with a problem, such as the relocation of the USMTM headquarters, he took careful notes but said that he did not have authority to decide such matters and would see to it that the king was fully informed. Sheikh Yusuf, in his advisory role, was often seated near Faisal and was always silent until called upon, whereas with King Saud he had often performed, even taken over, the spokesman role in the king's presence. I explained this to myself as evidence that Sheikh Yusuf feared the king would be too accommodating and generous if left alone on sensitive business with a foreign representative. It was a device to protect the king from an inadvertent misstatement of established policy.

During Saud's US sojourn, his advisors had unintentionally placed protocol roadblocks in the path of a first possible person-to-person contact with President Kennedy. They had insisted to the Department of State's protocol chief that because the king was ill and a guest in the United States, it was for the president to call first on the king. The White House and State disagreed. This deadlock was finally resolved by an ingenious gimmick. A State officer proposed that the king, now recovered and ready to depart, make a "tourist" visit to West Palm Beach, near where the Kennedy family maintained a recreational estate.

In West Palm Beach, the president, in a personal capacity, called on the king and invited him to a meal at the White House for a specific date. The king's reply was "In sha Allah" (if God wills), which, because it was translated literally, struck Kennedy as less than a clear commitment to accept presidential hospitality. No one was at hand to point out to Kennedy that in Bedouin tradition every move anyone makes is predetermined by God, and thus an informed westerner should translate the phrase as "God willing, I'll be there." After a day or two the matter was straightened out, and the White House luncheon took place just prior to the king's departure. King Saud felt it to be a success. Kennedy, however, was not so well-impressed.

According to informed reports I received in Saudi Arabia, the relationship in the president's mind had gotten off to a poor start by the hostile tone of Saud's reply to Kennedy's let's-get-acquainted letter of May 11, 1961, delivered before my arrival. The letter sought a friendly dialogue on Middle Eastern problems and had been carefully designed to elicit friendly exploration of putative differences, as well as convergences, of views on the Arab-Israeli issue. Saud's advisors—I suspect that Ahmad Shukairi, the Palestinian-born Saudi ambassador to the United Nations, was the point man in this case—took over drafting the reply, which in very bitter terms berated US policy favoring Israel. Through an unconfirmed report, I learned that Kennedy's face turned white with anger as he read the long and acerbic response to his thoughtful and balanced message. I never received from the president himself, however, any indication of his reaction. Therefore, when Sheikh Yusuf Yassin asked me pointedly on my arrival in July 1961 what Kennedy's reaction to Saud's letter had been, I felt it best to tell him that I did not know, rather than repeat unconfirmed hearsay that could be damaging to US-Saudi relations. Nor did I offer to ask for the president's reaction.

In retrospect, I believe that Sheikh Yusuf's inquiry was prompted by his desire for ammunition against Palestinian influence. The sheikh was a tough bargainer, but a friend of the US relationship; Ahmad Shukairi was not. He was accustomed at that time to using his office at the United Nations to berate, without restraint, US policy on the Arab-Israeli conflict.

The king returned home from his hospitalization and interviews in February 1962. In Salem, he and his huge entourage of family, servants, and advisors had occupied for a month more than one floor of Peter Bent Brigham, heavily disrupting its organization but generously rewarding the hospital and its staff. Saud now appeared to be in excellent health and was euphoric over his meeting with President Kennedy.

Shortly after his return, Saud consented to my request for a private interview; I wanted to test his willingness to permit US residual use of

Dhahran and continuation of the USMTM. On March 11, 1962, I took along our embassy public affairs counselor, Isa Sabbagh, a cultivated man in both English and Arabic and a superb interpreter. To our surprise, the king received us alone—absent even his own interpreter to assist him. He was in a jolly mood, which clearly reinforced his statement that all had gone well indeed during his time in the hospital and with Kennedy. I asked him if, in turning over to his government the Dhahran Airfield, he would agree to a military air transport turnaround facility for noncombat aircraft. Such a facility would provide for repairs, refueling, and rest for crews.

He immediately consented, saying it should come under the umbrella of the USMTM. I then asked if he would agree to raise the limit of eighty persons that his government had proposed for USMTM, as we had concluded that not much could be accomplished for Saudi training with such a small unit. He responded that the numerical strength of our mission should be whatever the US government considered desirable.[6] Later the Saudi Foreign Ministry asked me for my notes on this meeting, as the king had made none. It had been a very personal decision by the king, without consulting his staff.

We were now back in business on the basics of American needs at Dhahran and did not have to worry too much about where the USMTM headquarters was to be placed. (It was destined to be in Riyadh.) However, we voluntarily (without a request from the Saudi government) shifted the US Navy communications unit out of a Dhahran building to our naval facility at Jufair in Bahrain, a move welcomed by its ruler. With the unit went withdrawal of the hangaring of the plane assigned to Commander, Middle East Force, which had no Saudi permit to be at Dhahran in the first place but had been tolerated by Saudi officials. Thus we removed symbols of US control over the field and reduced the likelihood of a telling Voice of the Arabs attack on the veracity and "Arabism" of the king. We recommended to Washington that the chief of USMTM be a US Army general officer and that the chief of the air force section of USMTM be a full colonel. These proposals were accepted in Washington and Riyadh.

One of the thorniest problems created by withdrawal of the USAF Second Air Division was the fulfillment of a 1957 revision of the Dhahran Airfield agreement. The language of the revision was not altogether clear, but the USAF regulations applying it provided that, in case of the nonrenewal of the agreement of 1951, the United States could withdraw for sale or use elsewhere such items at the field as were "moveable," whereas items that were "fixed" in place, or anchored into the ground, must be left, free, to the Saudi government.

Under instructions, I informed Sheikh Ibrahim al-Suwayyil, minister of foreign affairs, that the United States would leave behind at Dhahran enough equipment to maintain the airport at the standards set by the International Civil Aviation Organization (ICAO). We soon discovered that these promises, without definition of terms, meant trouble. Moreover, while we were discussing items, Europe-based USAF officers were starting to move equipment out of Dhahran before we could monitor their selections. Soon we were involved in arguments, rising in stridency, between Saudi officers and the Second Air Division. The Europe-based officers had maximized the "moveable," while the Saudis sought to have all, or as much as possible, of the equipment remain in place to cut costs under the new contract that they had now signed with Blount-Commonwealth.

At length, in October 1961, I delivered to Deputy Foreign Minister Muhammad I. Mas'oud a long list, approved by the State Department, of equipment to be left behind at Dhahran, valued at more than $879,000. The Saudis were worried and unhappy, because our pullout was moving on schedule with deliberate speed and they had little time before takeover to procure replacements. They were also worried about money.

The list I left with Mas'oud was generous. It included all varieties of office furniture (all "moveable") and supplies, electronic communications, tools, vehicles, television sets, and a complete radio station. The Saudis responded with a considerable enlargement of the list, inviting a US sale. This went back to Washington, but Prince Muhammad ibn Saud, the king's son and defense minister, and General Ibrahim al-Tassan, his chief of staff, were informed that many of the items they wanted had already been shipped out. The US government noted that items the Saudis might wish to purchase could be had without involvement of outside bidders if classified by the USAF as excess, per the 1951 agreement. The price would be "fair," not "nominal," and the Saudis should realize that many items were not in excess but needed for the USAF buildup in Europe.

Frantic over the financial situation and his chances of successfully managing Dhahran Airfield, Prince Muhammad undertook several moves to reinforce Saudi rights, free of cost, to all equipment still at the field. He tried that October to interpret President Kennedy's friendly letter of May 11, 1961, as implying Kennedy's willingness to leave behind all items desired by the Saudi government. When that did not work, he sent word to me in November 1961, via a Dr. Ahmad Fahim, that the king's notice of nonrenewal of Dhahran was a mistake and that the king now agreed with his son that the United States should remain at the field, but with nonuniformed personnel. The number of US personnel was not important; even 2,000 was allowable.

I was naturally skeptical over this indirect approach and the way Prince Muhammad had mounted it, but I replied to Fahim that I would have to submit this proposal to Washington and asked whether renewal would not meet opposition in Saudi Arabia. It would, he said, and that opposition would come from Sheikh Abd Allah al-Turaiqi, the minister of petroleum.[7] Fahim then invited my wife and me to call informally on the minister of defense and his wife Sarah (daughter of Crown Prince Faisal and a Wellesley College graduate) at Fahim's house. The purpose was to become better acquainted. I immediately accepted, as this was a most unusual invitation to receive in Saudi Arabia at that time. Mixing couples was rare and always handled quietly, given the attitude of Wahhabi religious authorities.

I then told Fahim that a firm understanding was imperative if the United States was to keep military personnel at Dhahran, even in civilian clothes and even if the Saudi government intended to continue on the basis of the 1957 airfield agreement. I asked if the views of Prince Faisal could be forecast. Fahim was doubtful. He said that Prince Muhammad was having trouble answering sharp questions on military matters in cabinet meetings. I offered to provide the minister with specific briefing materials prepared by USMTM. Fahim then urged that the minister of defense be invited to the United States, a matter I had endeavored to finesse.

In summarizing the Fahim episode to the Department of State, my staff and I concluded the following:

1. Money was vitally important to the minister of defense, as the Saudi government had never grasped (or had to grasp) the cost of airport maintenance services.

2. The political climate had changed inside and outside Saudi Arabia since the March 16, 1961, royal communiqué on nonrenewal of the airfield agreement: It was now believed that Prince Talal ibn Abd al-Aziz (the minister of finance when I arrived in July but now out of the cabinet) was a prime mover in getting the king to issue the communiqué; Syria had (as of September 28, 1961) withdrawn from the Egyptian-dominated United Arab Republic, a blow to the prestige of Nasser. The new government of Syria, now called the Syrian Arab Republic, was said to have revealed to the Saudi government certain files regarding Syrian director of intelligence Abd al-Hamid Sarraj that suggested, without evidence, undercover activity by the Egyptian government. Saudi Arabia had reacted by dismissing many Egyptian teachers and replacing them by nationals of other Arab states, especially Jordan.

3. The Saudi government was now concerned about the unhesitating readiness of the United States to pull out the Second Air Division, just as it had earlier acted promptly on Sheikh Yusuf Yassin's directive to withdraw Point IV personnel. The Saudis evidently felt that the United States was the only strong and disinterested friend of the kingdom.

4. The king could not reverse his decision to terminate the Dhahran

agreement (despite Fahim's suggestion), but sought an arrangement short of a 180-degree reversal.

5. It seemed desirable that the US government be flexible in using the strength of its position. Expanding the USMTM seemed possible and appeared better in any event than retention of the Second Air Division or its equivalent in civilian attire. A broadened USMTM role could include services now provided by the Second Air Division regarding overflights and landing rights, and USMTM could operate Dhahran on Saudi behalf until the Saudis were fully able to assume the burden.

In reply to my message, State and Defense preferred to delay an invitation to the minister of defense until negotiations over the airport were further along. Since the Saudis had contracted out for maintenance, had found and set aside the necessary funds, and had requested the ICAO's help in obtaining air operations personnel on a reimbursable basis, Washington was pleased and relieved. It would offer, in return for the turnaround permit, modest advisory assistance in air control operations during the period of transfer of authority at the Dhahran International Airport, as the airfield would be called.

As the deadline for US withdrawal from command of Dhahran Airfield approached, the ongoing problem of what equipment would stay for Saudi ownership, what would be declared excess and thus purchasable by the Saudis, and what would be removed became acute, threatening the tone of overall relations between the United States and Saudi Arabia. During a visit to Riyadh on February 13, 1962, by Assistant Secretary of State Phillips Talbot, Prince Muhammad endeavored to convince him that, coming to this meeting direct from his father, he expressed the royal wish that all equipment not already shipped out be left in place for the Saudi government to use, gratis, or at heavily reduced cost. Talbot responded that this could not be accepted. The Saudi government's proposal came too late. The United States had to be out of the airfield completely by April 2, 1962, in response to royal notice of termination eleven months prior. The US government had issued no authority to give such moveable equipment away, only to sell it. In any case, Talbot reminded the prince that the Saudi government was obtaining, free, a working airport worth $250 million and had let eleven months go by. The prince, however, had more cards to play.

On March 15, 1962, Brigadier General Muhammad al-Mutlaq received instructions from the chief of staff, General Tassan, to prevent the further removal from Saudi Arabia of remaining US military equipment. This put an instant halt to shipments ordered by the Pentagon of 65 tons of air cargo and 1,500 tons of sea cargo from Dammam, including ammunition. This elevated what had previously been a dispute over terms into a crisis. I therefore sought an immediate interview with the king and prepared myself to make a vigorous protest.

On March 21, I called on King Saud, accompanied by Colonel Wilson of the Second Air Division. We were received by the king, Crown Prince Faisal, Prince Muhammad, and Sheikh Yusuf. Quite a testimony to the importance of the occasion, I thought.

To my surprise, the atmosphere was very cooperative. The king had already lifted the ban on removals from Dhahran, and, in addition to my intended demarche, I carried instructions to inform the king that the United States authorized transfer to his government, without cost, of items comprising an "ICAO list," which I presented. These were essential to the continued operation of the airfield as defined by ICAO. Where other equipment was also desired by the Saudi government, sale was authorized by Washington at a 25 percent discount from actual cost to the United States. The Saudis thus received, free, a working airfield with ICAO-standard equipment.

As to the troublesome definition of what was "mobile" and what was "fixed," the king announced on the spot that I was to verify these matters for him as his delegate and as emissary of the United States and I was to be accompanied in a personal check by General Tassan![8] Thus, King Saud followed, to a degree, the example of his father, who in 1949 had made USAF Brigadier General Richard J. O'Keefe commander of Dhahran Airfield for him as well as for the United States. It was a gesture of trust in the grand manner, and it imposed, so to speak, a conflict of interest, making it a matter of honor to be generous to the Saudi side. The expression of confidence was hedged by the presence of General Tassan as the royal eyes and ears. I accepted, well aware of the pitfalls.

Tassan and I immediately went through an inspection of airfield shops, hangars, radio facilities, barracks, dining facilities, the hospital, and other working areas. Almost at once he pointed out an embarrassing discovery. In the large machine shop, lathes, table saws, and steel benches had been removed by ripsaws cutting through large steel bolts anchored in the concrete floor. All I could do was agree with his assessment that these items had been "fixed" in the building and should not have been removed. By now, they had been shipped out. I made known and registered with Colonel Wilson my personal embarrassment, which he shared. Fortunately, no other serious problem areas came to light and, overall, the Saudis had received a most generous gift.

On March 31, 1962, at a meeting in the US embassy living room, I delivered to Deputy Foreign Minister Sayyid Umar al-Saqqaf a first-person note transferring to Saudi Arabia's ownership equipment basic to the operation of Dhahran Airfield. General Tassan's and my joint inventory having meanwhile been verified and formally prepared, I gave this also to

Saqqaf. It was signed by Colonel Wilson and civil director at Dhahran Airfield Abd al-Aziz al-Qayn. To compensate for two fire trucks withdrawn earlier by Second Air Division, the United States made additional gifts, including hospital equipment suggested by Wilson.

The next day I received word that Prince Muhammad promised to pay by April 10, 1962, for all surplus items contracted for by the Ministry of Defense. He was as good as his word. A major irritation was over.

SAUD'S DECLINE

In October 1962, King Saud again left the country for medical treatment, this time to Europe instead of the United States, probably because he had become very angry with President Kennedy over Kennedy's policy of seeking common ground with Nasser wherever possible and reasonable. Saud never understood this and became very agitated whenever I attempted to explain the policy to him. Faisal, however, perceiving the isolation of his brother at a critical time and concerned over the questionable caliber of his entourage, had responded to the situation by agreeing to become Saud's closest advisor, without insisting upon restoration of his former position and authority as prime minister. This shielded Saud from much bad advice and behind-the-scenes power plays.

When I was summoned by the king in early summer of 1962 with the request that I place at his service for anti-Nasser propaganda the US Second Air Division's audio broadcasting equipment at Dhahran—which would have been at best a feeble answer to Cairo's Voice of the Arabs—I was glad to find that Faisal was the only other person in the room. As I endeavored to explain to the king that (1) the air force radio at Dhahran could not, under US laws, be used for such purposes and (2) in any case it had too weak a signal to be serviceable over the required listening area, it was Faisal who attenuated Saud's restless and petulant reactions. Saud understood only that President Kennedy was refusing to help his friend Saud in his direst need.

Faisal, with dignified but respectful demeanor, addressed his brother in terms used by a subject to his sovereign, namely, "Jalalatkum" (Your Majesty), and to me he spoke as if he were a junior figure in the scenario addressing an elder, using "Tawwil amrak" ([May God] Prolong Your Life). This ancient Arab formula lent formality to a discussion among only three participants, and it helped prevent the king from yielding to impulse. Over and over, with a patience I found touching and admirable, Faisal undertook to explain such details as a circuit to an ill-educated and harassed mind. It worked, and the United States was ultimately forgiven for begging off becoming a mouthpiece in an inter-Arab war of invective that Saud was bound to lose.

During the months that followed, the king's health worsened. As he prepared to leave for a protracted period, he designated Faisal as his full alter ego, that is, to act for him in all matters in his absence and in his presence. It was an act of statesmanship for which Saud and Faisal both deserved credit, and it was widely approved.

The late King Ibn Saud, in his last years, had already come to distrust his son Saud's judgment. Two instances were related to me, firsthand, by royal counselor Sheikh Hafiz Wahba. The sheikh frequently accompanied Ibn Saud in the late 1940s on afternoon drives around Riyadh. On one of these drives, just outside Qasr al-Murrabba, they passed by a new concrete mansion under construction, its reinforcing rods showing through a cement foundation. Abruptly the king ordered the driver to stop and demanded to know who was responsible for this building. Hesitantly, until the monarch raised his voice, the chauffeur replied that Crown Prince Saud had ordered the building erected as his own palace. Furious, the king directed the driver to return to Murrabba, where he ordered Saud to report to him at once. Sheikh Hafiz begged to be excused but was ordered to remain. The prince arrived posthaste and crouched, Bedouin-style, before his ruler. The dialogue ran more or less as follows:

"Did you order that house built of concrete and steel?"

"Yes, *tawwil amrak.*"

"Destroy it! Know now, if you've not yet learned, that as king the example you set to your people is vital to the stability of your rule. All of us, you included, are of the lineage of the *black tent.* Don't you ever forget that! Live simply in a building of native materials [sun-dried mud mixed with straw], as do your people! Otherwise, you will foster the wrong leadership and be surrounded by sycophants and greedy flatterers who will bring catastrophe to your people!"

The crown prince received this rebuke manfully, but did no more than leave the mansion unfinished until after his father's death in 1953. He then proceeded to build as many palaces as he wished. In Riyadh, the grandest had a huge *majlis* with rows of chandeliers suspended over vast overlapping Persian carpets and upholstered gilded chairs arranged around the wall for perhaps two hundred people. Outside in a garden of many acres, which King Saud showed me personally in 1961, was a geyser-fountain illuminated by shifting colored lights. In Jeddah, in the center of the new city, was a palace built for pilgrimage receptions. Before the entrance was a high welcoming archway bearing the royal seal of crossed swords below a palm tree. Its interior was sumptuous. At a beach residence outside Jeddah on the northwest waterfront, where the great coral reef approaches closest to the shore, was a string of unused pavilions with an embarkation for pleasure boats. Outside al-Madinat al-Munawwarah was a huge unfinished and unattended palace. An unoccupied small palace at Abha, high in the mountains, overlooked the Red Sea and had a small airstrip. It was a recreational home at a cool altitude, visited only once by King Saud. At Dammam was a working palace, the sixth that I had seen.

The total cost of these structures in 1966 was estimated conservatively at $3 billion, drawn from the royal treasury. Until Faisal took over as managing head of state, it had been treated as the monarch's own fund, for which there was no public accounting and on which obligations often exceeded cash at hand.

The second instance concerning Saud that Sheikh Hafiz related to me occurred sometime in the last years of King Ibn Saud's life. The monarch was alone with his royal counselor in Qasr al-Murrabba, and he suddenly decided to summon his two eldest sons, Saud and Faisal. Again, Sheikh Hafiz begged to be excused but was ordered to remain as witness. When both princes were present, the king commanded that Faisal swear fealty to Saud effective at once, to be publicly repeated upon the death of the king. Faisal obeyed and the king demanded he repeat his pledge six more times, which he did. He then turned to Saud and demanded the same number of pledges that Saud be loyal to and listen to his younger brother—"He is smarter than you are!"—and take his advice. Saud complied and repeated his pledge seven times.

As the relationship between these elder princes unfolded before my own eyes over the years, I must credit both men, who were reputed never to have been on the best of terms, with a real measure of loyalty to that very exacting oath. In 1964, however, as recounted in chapter 9, Saud precipitated a head-on confrontation that ended badly for him. Even then, Faisal's position was simply put: I will do nothing against my brother; but I cannot govern if authority is removed from me.

At Jeddah airport, 1942, Sheikhs Yusuf Yassin and Ibrahim ibn Mu'amer greet Alexander C. Kirk, US minister to Egypt (1941–1944), accredited also to Saudi Arabia, with two legation aides and Second Secretary Raymond Hare. Courtesy of Clarence McIntosh.

Acting Secretary of State Adolf A. Berle, Jr., greets two Arabian princes arriving in Washington as guests of President Franklin D. Roosevelt, September 30, 1943. From left: Berle, His Royal Highness Prince Faisal, and Faisal's son Abdul Aziz. Courtesy of Clarence McIntosh.

First United States consulate in Saudi Arabia, housed in an ARAMCO-leased building, Dhahran, summer 1944. Except where otherwise indicated, photos are courtesy of P. T. Hart.

Consul Parker T. Hart in the consular residence, Dhahran, 1945.

His Majesty King Abdul Aziz al-Saud (Ibn Saud) visits the US experimental farm near al-Kharj, riding in front with his driver, late 1944.

Near al-Kharj experimental farm, 1945, His Majesty King Ibn Saud receives Dr. Glen F. Brown, US Geological Survey, and Dr. David Rogers of Arizona, head of the US government–sponsored al-Kharj Agricultural Mission.

King Ibn Saud meets President Franklin D. Roosevelt aboard the USS
Quincy *in Great Bitter Lake, Suez Canal, February 1945. US Minister
to Saudi Arabia Colonel William A. Eddy (kneeling at left) interprets.*

*James McPherson, ARAMCO chief administrative officer (second from
left, with glasses case in shirt pocket) welcomes His Highness Saud bin
Jilewi, Emir of the Eastern Province (center), and his interpreter, poet and
protocol officer Ibrahim Jindan (between them), Dhahran, 1946.*

*In a ceremonial tent in Dhahran, Crown Prince Saud (seated, in
dark glasses) and one of his sons are received by Emir bin Jilewi
(standing behind the king) and his retainers, 1950. Seated at left is
Consul General Parker T. Hart. Photo by T. F. Walters, ARAMCO.*

His Majesty King Saud ibn Abd al-Aziz, holding his son, Prince Mashhur, whom he has brought to the United States for medical treatment, leaving the airport with President Dwight D. Eisenhower, during the king's official visit at the president's invitation, January 1957. White House photo.

His Majesty King Saud ibn Abd al-Aziz (seated, left), Emir bin Jilewi (center), and Ambassador Parker T. Hart, August 23, 1961. Photo by B. H. Moody, ARAMCO.

Parker Hart presents his credentials as first US ambassador to Kuwait to Emir Abd Allah al-Salim al Sabah (far right), January 7, 1962.

*His Royal Highness Crown Prince Faisal meets President John
F. Kennedy at the White House, October 5, 1962. White House
photo, courtesy of the John Fitgerald Kennedy Library.*

Ambassador Hart converses in Arabic with the Emir of Jauf, Abd al-Rahman al-Sudairi, in garden of guest quarters at al-Sakaka, north of the great Nefud desert, 1964. Bowl of local dates is in foreground.

(Left to right) Richard W. Murphy, US embassy political counselor,
Ambassador Hart, and His Majesty King Faisal ibn Abd al-Aziz,
Presidency of Council Building, Jeddah, May 5, 1965.

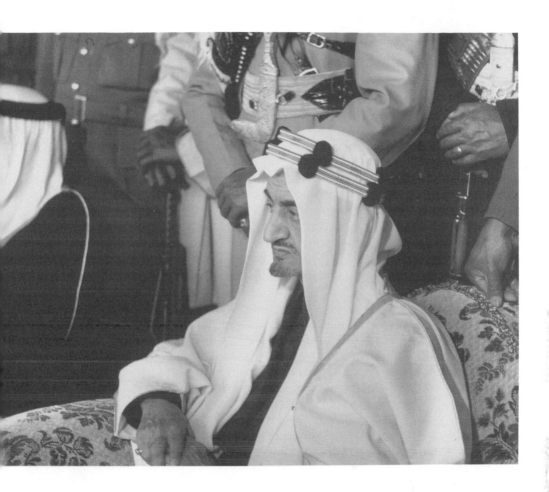

King Faisal in Jeddah, 1965.

King Faisal at UN Headquarters with Saudi Defense Minister Prince Sultan and UN Secretary-General U Thant, June 24, 1966. From Sun and Flare, *published by ARAMCO, July 13, 1966.*

Parker Hart with (then) Crown Prince (later King) Fahd bin Abd al-Aziz at the Saudi Embassy, Washington, 1977.

PART THREE

COLLAPSE OF AN
ANCIENT SYSTEM

5

BUILDUP TO CONFRONTATION:
EGYPT, YEMEN, AND SAUDI ARABIA

 In early September 1962, Prince Faisal summoned me to Ta'if for a private conversation, without any note takers in attendance. The king, he said, would soon be going abroad (to Europe in October) for health reasons. In assuming full responsibilities, Faisal felt that in view of forces at play in the Middle East, his own time had come to meet President Kennedy and determine whether the president fully subscribed to earlier United States pledges of support for Saudi Arabia's integrity and independence. Did I think that the president would be agreeable to his visit to Washington at this time? I personally felt sure that he would and said I would at once send a message recommending it. Washington's reply was immediate and affirmative.

By agreement with the White House and Faisal, I decided to send Isa Sabbagh with Faisal. Sabbagh was the best of any bilingual interpreters I knew, a man on friendly personal terms with the prince, and one who would report fully to me on his return. It was better that I remain on watch in Jeddah; the king was still in the kingdom and international Arab tensions were high, reflecting Syria's breakaway from the UAR on September 28, 1961, and Nasser's efforts to reverse or compensate for this major setback. From countless messages, I knew that President Kennedy was being kept closely informed on all these events and would find Faisal's intelligence and natural dignity a reassurance that US support of his leadership would not be misplaced. I also felt that Faisal and Kennedy would hit it off personally, and they did.

Faisal and Kennedy had but one encounter, on October 5, 1962. They never again met face-to-face. Nonetheless, the indelible impression each made upon the other was positive. There was a White House luncheon hosted by the president and attended by some of Kennedy's close civil and military advisors, followed by an unusual private audience (one on one), attended only by Sabbagh as interpreter. It was here that specific understandings were reached:

1. Kennedy reaffirmed the Truman pledge of 1950 that any threat to the independence and integrity of Saudi Arabia would be a matter of deep and immediate concern to the US government, which would take measures to counter such a threat.

2. The United States would demonstrate its interest in Saudi security through stepped-up naval visits to Saudi ports, notably in the Red Sea.

3. The United States would provide pilot training and counter-insurgency training to Saudi personnel.

4. In response to a query by Faisal, Kennedy said the United States would consider its pledge of general support to apply to threats against Saudi Arabia activated from without and from within. However, with due sensitivity to Faisal's pride and responsibilities, the president made it clear that US measures of assistance would be taken on the basis of Kennedy's understanding that Faisal intended to take early steps to abolish slavery and to institute fiscal and other reforms in the Saudi judiciary and its practices so as to bring about strong public support and greater participation of educated Saudi youth in the administration of the state. The US government would find it hard to justify to its own people a deep commitment to a system of government that was corrupt or bore the stamp of slavery and arbitrary denial of civil rights and personal freedoms.

Faisal had prepared for this and fully agreed. This understanding, therefore, was not exactly a "deal," but a meeting of minds. Its general terms quickly became known and approved in Saudi intellectual and business circles, which were quite fed up with the retrogressive and insulting image of their country reflected in world, and especially Arab, media.

REVOLUTION IN THE YEMEN

Earlier, on September 25, Faisal had gone to New York City's Waldorf-Astoria to update himself, as foreign minister, on the United Nations scene. He had not much more than arrived when the revolution in the Yemen broke out on September 26 and the report of massive Egyptian support for the insurgents reached him. He asked, by phone to the Department of State, that Isa Sabbagh come up from Washington to see him. When Sabbagh arrived, he found Faisal alone and worried. His concern centered on Nasser and Egypt's intentions toward Saudi Arabia. He was certain that Nasser intended the Yemen to be a stepping stone toward taking over Saudi Arabia, directly or by proxy forces within the country. He wondered whether the United States would really stand by the kingdom against imminent sabotage from within as well as attacks from abroad. He wanted a very specific answer.

Sabbagh had to refer such a matter to Washington and returned there at once. Assistant Secretary Phillips Talbot took Sabbagh with him back to New York to reassure the prince that the United States would, if necessary, take measures to help Saudi Arabia resist attacks from within or without and would expect Faisal to concentrate on domestic reforms as the best means of defense. This Faisal subsequently volunteered to President Kennedy that he would do, when they finally met on October 5. It was Talbot's view that Faisal should return to Saudi Arabia as soon as possible and take the helm. The United States had not yet decided whether to recognize the new regime in the Yemen but held the view that outsiders should not interfere in the Yemen's internal struggles.

Faisal was not at all reassured on Washington's attitude regarding the Yemen, even after his meeting with Kennedy. He had shown his extreme anxiety that Egypt be actively opposed, preferably by a US Navy show of force at Hodaidah, Yemen's primary port. He also wanted a US warning to Nasser to withdraw his troops from the Yemen or face the consequence that the United States would step in. Faisal made clear that Saudi Arabia would support the Yemeni royalist opposition. Here began the problem of implementing the Kennedy pledge of support, a problem that was to remain acute through the rest of 1962 and all of 1963. Nevertheless, Kennedy had made a warm personal impression on Faisal, and Kennedy's regard for Faisal had no parallel in the case of Nasser or any of the Yemen's leadership.

By long and careful preparations, Kennedy had earlier sought a personal dialogue on fundamentals with King Saud, as well as with Nasser and other Middle Eastern chiefs of state. However, as stated earlier, Saud's intemperate and ill-considered response to Kennedy's letter on the Arab-Israeli question had gotten Saudi Arabia's leadership off to a poor start with him. For that reason, and because Saudi Arabia as an entity was important to the United States, the personal impact of Faisal's dignity, intellectual strength, and concern for a better standard of living for his people gave him a key position in the president's continuing evaluation of forces in the Middle East. This accounts for the extraordinary sustained personal attention given by Kennedy to this crisis in an area then little known to most Americans. There were, after all, major preoccupations elsewhere, not the least of which was the deepening US involvement in Vietnam. However, both Egypt and Saudi Arabia tried to exploit the Kennedy touch, but neither really succeeded. All interested parties, except the royalists, benefited in the end by Kennedy's efforts to avert a wider conflict. After his assassination, both sides were able to tone down their adamant positions. The shock of his death to both Egyptian and Saudi public opinion bore postmortem fruit in reinforcing the desire of both sides to avoid further bloodshed.

The story began on September 30, four days after the coup in the Yemen, when King Saud received an urgent appeal from King Hussein of Jordan to help Yemeni prince Hasan, the deposed Imam Ahmad's eldest brother and pretender to the Hamid al-Din imamate. Without consulting Faisal, or even informing him, Saud responded with both arms and money. Hasan arrived at Riyadh the same day. There Chief of Staff al-Tassan was put in charge of assisting Hasan to reenter the Yemen. Planes with military cargo were sent to the border area of Jizan. Saudi military aid to the royalists was thus initiated.

Faisal returned to Saudi Arabia in late October 1962. Before Faisal left the Waldorf-Astoria on October 17, King Saud had made him prime minister (he was already foreign minister). On October 25, 1962, just prior to Faisal's return, I had a long and detailed session with Deputy Foreign Minister Sayyid Umar al-Saqqaf. Before proceeding to urge against Saudi intervention, I gave him the latest US estimate of the Yemen situation:

The royalists could harass their enemies but not recover control. The Egyptian military presence in the Yemen could be expected to remain in force until the outside threat to the republic disappeared, though Egypt was already wearing out its welcome. Abd Allah al-Sallal, the leader of the revolution, in contrast to his vice president, had adopted a conciliatory approach toward the United States. He had informed Robert Stookey, US chargé d'affaires (at our legation in Taiz), that he wanted good relations with Saudi Arabia, the United Kingdom, and the United States and would not be ordered about by Egypt.

Saqqaf agreed that Hasan was unlikely to be able to do more than harass the newly proclaimed Yemen Arab Republic (YAR), but he feared that Sallal's indirect appeal to Saudi Arabia had come too late. The Saudi government had already made an enemy of the Yemen republic. I contested this, pointing out that up to now it was King Saud, not Faisal, who had made hostile moves.

It was clear that Saqqaf was personally much opposed to Saudi involvement in the Yemen. We compared assessments, and he soon was able to report to Faisal that the United States stood fully with the Saudi government against any external attack; that the US government would probably recognize the YAR; and that Faisal should note that while Nasser, operating from the Yemen, was a danger to Saudi Arabia, a greater danger would be for the Saudis to back Crown Prince Muhammad al-Badr, the deposed imam's eldest son (who was erroneously reported killed in the coup), who would be unable to pacify the Yemen but could attract Egyptian attacks on Saudi Arabia. Saqqaf stated to me later that he had incorporated my assessment and recommendations into his own advice to his chief. Faisal was not easy to convince, however. To him, resistance to Egypt was imperative for Saudi security. The United States had no ground or air forces in the area on whom the Saudis could count.

The close relationship between Saqqaf and me was to continue unbroken throughout the long crisis. It certainly did not arise from an earlier friendship, for we had not known each other (as I had known Faisal) from my earlier assignments to the kingdom. Rather, it was the result of a shared concern for the future of a weak and undeveloped Saudi Arabia. We both felt strongly that Faisal's program of reforms must not be put in jeopardy by an unwinnable Saudi conflict with a dynamic Egypt. Neither of us saw the likelihood of any US military backing of Saudi participation in a Yemeni civil war. Faisal was a popular and determined leader; though irreplaceable, he was nonetheless alone in his great gamble, and his country was highly vulnerable.

As for US interests in the kingdom, centering on oil, they had been recognized by Washington policy-makers as highly important (even vital) to long-term US security. The United States had no comparable interest in the Yemen, but the Cold War had made the Red Sea and Egypt important in their own right. President Kennedy had sought to find points of common interest with Nasser rather than allow US policy to be steered entirely by points of US-Arab disagreement over Israel, as it had been during the Eisenhower period. The idea was for this policy to be implemented by periodic letter exchanges between Kennedy and Nasser. A tone of cordiality and a resumption of US economic aid (interrupted by Eisenhower) would reduce the probability of a rupture, but would also make clear to Nasser that the United States could not tolerate an attempted takeover of Saudi Arabia or a military operation against it. It was a tightrope walk, as Saqqaf fully understood. So did Faisal, who found it inadequate against immediate peril from Egypt and who therefore gambled that the royalists could be equipped to fight a successful guerrilla war.

In pursuance of Kennedy's policy, the Department of State and the

White House worked on a formula for disengagement from the Yemen, to be presented to Nasser, Faisal, King Hussein, and Sallal. Accompanied by a friendly letter from Kennedy, the essence of the formula was that, following the cessation of Saudi aid to the royalists, Egypt would initiate a withdrawal of its forces from the Yemen. US determination to protect the integrity and independence of Saudi Arabia as a vital interest would be strongly reaffirmed. The United States would call on all three parties—Egypt, Saudi Arabia, and (through Egypt) the YAR—to agree to this formula. The YAR would undertake to cease its propaganda attacks on Saudi Arabia and the United Kingdom, and Egypt would see to it that the YAR carried out its share of the agreement. In return for these pledges on all sides, the United States would recognize the YAR.

The evolution of this concept derived from what Washington believed Egypt would accept, not from what Faisal would accept; nor was my advance opinion asked. Speed, as far as Washington was concerned, was vital to prevent an all-out confrontation between Egypt and Saudi Arabia. It was therefore deemed essential to slow the pace of events, particularly on the part of the stronger party, Egypt. My concern was that the entire package favored Nasser's strategy and would thus be rejected by Faisal. It was. Nonetheless, the dialogue between the United States and all the parties continued because of Kennedy's insistence.

EGYPT'S POSTURE ON OUTSIDE INTERFERENCE IN THE YEMEN

In Cairo, editor and journalist Muhammad Hasanein Heikal had been a close friend and confidant of the Revolutionary Command Council since before July 23, 1952, when he accompanied the "free officers" in their overthrow of the monarchy. He had the inside track on national policy, was regarded as authoritative by Egyptian readers, and had presented himself to the US ambassador as a personal but unofficial messenger of President Nasser. In early October 1962 Heikal now called on Ambassador John Badeau at the ambassador's office for an exchange of assessments and views on the Yemen.[1] It was apparent that Nasser needed a dialogue and would much prefer to avoid a clash with the United States.

Heikal's assessments paralleled those we had just received from Chargé Stookey in Taiz, namely that the YAR controlled most or all of the Yemen, except the northern and northeastern frontiers, and enjoyed wide popular support, including that of the principal tribes. Nasser, Heikal maintained, wanted to avoid all foreign military involvement and clashes between Egypt and both Saudi Arabia and Jordan, two countries in which the United States had deep interests. Egypt, he insisted, had sent technicians and matériel, but no major troops, to the YAR. Egypt had no intention of resuscitating its bond with the Yemen as the "United Arab States" and had refused YAR pleas to do so. He urged the United States to quickly recognize the YAR to counterbalance incipient Soviet ties with the new republic.

This was the opening of an Egyptian gambit, pursued often over the next year and a quarter, to exploit US fears of Soviet influence in the Red Sea straits as a lever to obtain active US opposition to Saudi-Jordanian involvement in the Yemen. Heikal argued that such interference would invite the YAR to swing toward Soviet ties as a counterpoise. Nasser, he said, had no intention of embarrassing the United States. He saw Saudi Arabia as discontented and ripe for revolt, but he understood and accepted the US interest in protecting oil supplies. Egypt, furthermore, did not want to see Saudi Arabia in chaos or the YAR interfering with British interests in Aden. Only UK support of the royalists could change this.

In general, Heikal's slant on Nasser's motivations seems to have gone over well in the Department of State and the White House. It corresponded to their own assessments and to their worries. It cleverly reinforced US fears that Saudi-Arab aid to the royalists would cause the YAR to seek an increase in the small Soviet military presence. At the same time, a Saudi military defeat by Egypt—total Saudi forces numbered only about 15,000, with little combat training—could shake the Saud regime.

The next day, Ambassador Badeau called on Egyptian vice president Anwar Sadat at Sadat's request, and the two of them compared notes. Sadat made no accusations of current US involvement in the Yemen, but "advised" the United States to recognize the YAR. He assured Badeau that Egypt would commit troops there only as a last resort, after increasing the supply of Egyptian "technicians," and then only if foreign forces threatened the overthrow of the YAR. The same day, Heikal made the same assertion to the British ambassador to Egypt, Harold Beeley.

These coordinated Egyptian diplomatic steps strengthened US fears of a total Egyptian military commitment. They would likely propel, in response, a Saudi overcommitment, the collapse of which, in military confrontation with Egypt, would threaten a fragmentation of Saudi Arabia. The United States also feared that British aid to Hasan risked an Egyptian green light to the YAR to press irredentist claims to Aden and might lead Egypt to resurrect the military pact of the 1956 United Arab States. It might then assert in the UN Security Council—where Egypt had Soviet support—an Egyptian right of intervention in the Yemen's claims. Thus could a wider war begin.

US-SAUDI CONSULTATION

From Taiz, Chargé Stookey had been summoned to San'a by YAR Vice President and Deputy Prime Minister Abd al-Rahman al-Baydani on October 2, 1962. (San'a had been restored by the YAR as the traditional capital.) Baydani had weighed in heavily, declaring that the US diplomatic mission, like that of the British, would not be allowed to function, even in coded communications, until it had formally recognized the YAR. In the same breath he stressed the anticommunist nature of the revolutionary government and its desire for expanded US aid. It would live up to all existing agreements with the United States.

On his same-day return to Taiz aboard a YAR plane, Stookey and the small diplomatic corps accompanying him made an emergency landing in Aden. On that plane was the Italian minister to the Yemeni kingdom, Amadeo Guillet, who had been a trusted friend of the imam. To him, Stookey had entrusted a report to Washington to be sent by the American consulate in Aden. Because of security measures, Stookey could not alight without being barred from returning to the plane, whereas Guillet had received a special exit permit from YAR chief of state Sallal. In his briefcase, Guillet carried Stookey's classified telegram to Washington and one from British minister Christopher Gandy to London via the Aden governate. He was apparently the only passenger to leave the plane in Aden.

In his message, Stookey advised Washington that the pressure of Saudi troops on the Yemen's northern border could trigger a YAR call for more Egyptian reinforcements. Stookey had weighed and now supported official Yemeni assertions of its independence of control from Egypt or other outsiders and its desire to honor existing treaties and establish peaceful relations with both Saudi Arabia and the United States. Stookey therefore strongly urged recognition of the YAR. If ever a country needed reform, he declared, it was the Yemen. A return of the Hamid al-Din clan to the imamate would mean—despite some possible reforms—a restoration of the Sayyid aristocracy, which was ignorant, bigoted, venal, and avaricious.[2] The United States owed nothing to Prince Hasan, who had usually voted against it at the United Nations and sided with the Soviet bloc. As for Badr, he had always been cool toward the United States and had snubbed the US minister, this author, in June 1962.[3]

Stookey, like his British colleague, had been far from well treated by Vice President Baydani. Under the latter's direction, the government of the YAR destroyed US coded telegrams, incoming and outgoing. As the legation had no transmitter of its own, this amounted to a communications blackout except where Stookey managed a covert operation via friendly hands like those of Guillet. The Yemeni government even interfered, under Baydani's direction, with operations of the US Agency for International Development (AID) mission, intimidating Yemeni employees and sabotaging the vehicles sent before the revolution by the US Bureau of Public Roads to assist the Yemeni effort to build basic overland links. This tactic implicitly threatened to obliterate a US role in Yemeni development in favor of the Soviets and communist Chinese, who were apparently quite willing to duel for a monopoly of the YAR development program.

In retrospect, the effrontery and cynicism of the YAR leadership appear eminently challengeable, but in those days of the Cold War Washington believed that Soviet spheres of interest in as backward a land as the Yemen would quickly evolve into spheres of control. Stookey's rejection of Baydani's insistence that diplomatic recognition of the YAR precede permission for the United States to send or receive coded telegrams apparently reached, and did not please, chief of state Sallal, who reversed the order by Baydani (and later transferred him to Cairo). Sallal then endeavored personally to reassure Stookey, calling him to San'a and strongly affirming the YAR's independence from Egypt and its eagerness for friendly US ties (and US aid).

Stookey's recommendations to Washington to recognize the YAR impressed me as based on the long-term US interest. I saw no such interest in the return of the imamate. In November, after much deliberation from Jeddah, I decided to support Stookey. I recommended, however, that recognition be postponed until there was tangible evidence of Egyptian troop withdrawals. I did not recommend that it be done without prior discussion (sure to be difficult) with Faisal.

On November 10, 1962, I had a lengthy talk with Faisal, now acting for King Saud in his absence and in his presence. Faisal had become acting king (implicitly subject to Saud's revocation) and was not obliged to refer matters for decision to Saud, who at this time was still in Europe undergoing medical treatment, without any indication of his time of return. Up to that date I had felt I could assure Faisal that our recognition of the YAR was not imminent. I was not yet aware that Washington was now in great haste to recognize.

Faisal's and my assessments of the situation in the Yemen were as far apart as they could possibly be, especially regarding the relative strength of popular Yemeni support for Hamid al-Din rule vis-à-vis that of the YAR. He estimated strong, even decisive, support by the principal tribes for the royalist cause. I regarded this as wishful appraisal carried to an extreme. We agreed, despite wide general disagreements, to keep up exchanges of current information, and we did so.

Among the assessments I passed on to Faisal were those of Stookey, who, in his messages to Washington, repeated to me at Jeddah, challenged Faisal's evaluation of popular support for the YAR. Stookey had pointed out that to achieve tribal backing—crucial to so-called public opinion in such a tribally organized country—the northern and most heavily armed Baqqil and Hashid peoples had to be won over on a large scale. These tribes, which had traditionally supported the imamate of the Hamid al-Din dynasty, had been badly handled by Crown Prince Badr, however. He had tried to emulate his father Ahmad by taking a tough line, thereby antagonizing some seventy ruling sheikhs. As a result, when the revolutionists approached them on the eve of the coup, they responded positively and were in the streets, heavily armed, when action began against the palace in San'a. The next day, some of these sheikhs spoke over San'a radio in support of the new regime. To consolidate this strategic gain, the YAR formed a defense council composed of these leaders, gave them the salaries of ministers, and sent them home to maintain local security. To assure loyalty within the army, salaries were doubled and a month's bonus granted.

In return for information that I provided, Faisal sent me a huge package of messages from YAR field commanders to their headquarters, intercepted by the Saudis and apparently authentic. They reported that royalists throughout Yemen's northern area Maidi up to Najran, Saudi Arabia, were giving the YAR forces great trouble. Commanders were urging military relief to break sieges, asking for provisions, water, blankets, guns, and ammunition. They also reported Egyptian use of napalm from aircraft on population centers and attacks (probably in error) from Egyptian aircraft on YAR troops.

In Amman, US ambassador William B. Macomber sought to persuade King Hussein against military involvement on the side of the royalists. The king had already sent a few Hawker Hunter aircraft to Taiz. Macomber assessed Jordanian popular sentiment as favorable toward the YAR and anti-imamate. He tried to persuade the king that his shipment of planes and personnel to the front at Najran ran against his own best interests and gave his people the wrong image of him. However, the king, like Faisal, was emotionally involved, and both equated Nasser's search for hegemony with communist penetration of the Arabian Peninsula and Red Sea. This was intended to alarm the United States into direct confrontation with Nasser or, at a minimum, to dissuade it from recognizing the YAR. It is a bit ironic that Egyptian officials and Heikal also agreed, in private, on the need to reduce Soviet influence in the Yemen, but they advanced US recognition of the YAR as a way of doing so.[4]

The British position throughout the October postrevolution period was hesitant, affected by contrasting evaluations from the Colonial Office and the Foreign Office. The Colonial Office, taking its information largely from reports by Aden governor Sir Charles Johnston, was strongly opposed to British recognition of the YAR at this or any foreseeable time; the UK minister to the Yemen, however, strongly urged recognition to the Foreign Office in London. The minister noted that Prince Hasan, whom the governor favored assisting, was inactive and wasting his momentum. The republic's leadership had the better chance of guiding a new Yemen. In London the result was paralysis and no recognition. For the rulers of the Aden protectorates, there was a crisis of confidence with London.

The possibility existed that these chieftains could be subverted by the YAR, which might pressure them to agree to annexation by San'a. Annexation was a cry for unity that had deep resonance in Aden. This pressure could be greatly augmented by the anti-imamate, pro-republic sentiments of a majority of the very large Yemeni population of the colony and of the protectorates. The Foreign Office also feared that a weakening of the British position in Aden would adversely affect British control of sheikhdoms in the Persian Gulf.

EARLY US-YEMENI RELATIONS

That such a crisis as that of the Yemen might well occur had come home to me in 1961 during my first days in that country, where I was taking stock of the situation as newly appointed minister plenipotentiary. My most important contact in the Yemen was the deputy foreign minister, Sayyid Abd al-Rahman Abu Samad Abu Taleb, who for many years had been the Yemeni chargé d'affaires in Washington. He had later been posted to Cairo while I was there, so that by this time we were on very easy terms because of our innumerable discussions of the dynamic political scene in the Middle East. Abu Taleb was unique among my Arab diplomatic colleagues in his objectivity and emotional detachment. He pointed out that Nasser, whom he knew well, absolutely required a success after the resounding defeat he had suffered by Syria's 1961 defection from the United Arab Republic. It was a question not of annexing another Arab state to fill the hole left by Syria but of reasserting his primacy in the guidance of Arab revolution, unity, and change. The Yemen seemed to fit that objective.

As Yemen's ruler, Imam Ahmad had visited Cairo in 1958 to obtain membership, in some form, in the UAR. His purpose was to buy protection from Nasser's revolutionary drive for Arab unity under the banner of socialist republicanism. Nasser considered the imam and his kingdom the epitome of backwardness and a far better target for attack than for political partnership. However, he could not completely put aside an opportunity for enlargement of Cairo-dominated Arab unity. He therefore accepted a compromise worked out by Yemeni crown prince Badr, the fiction called the "United Arab States." The low regard Nasser held for the imam and his regime was highlighted at a dinner held in Cairo in early 1958, ostensibly to celebrate the creation of their union. Nasser, in his speech, ignored Imam Ahmad, the guest of honor, and addressed himself to Iraq, urging it to join the UAR and its march toward Arab unity, socialism, and anti-imperialism. Nasser's preoccupation with revolutionary Iraq was genuine and deep. He feared it as a rival and sought vainly to capture it in the UAR.

In our 1961 encounter, Abu Taleb told me that Nasser would take some action against the regime in the Yemen through the undercover organization of the Free Yemenis, an opposition movement that had begun in Aden and was active in Cairo. He noted that since the Syrian coup of 1961 all but two Egyptians who had been working in the Yemen had left the country. Meanwhile, he confided that, without any sign of success, he had long urged specific reforms and government reorganization measures upon the aging, infirm, and stubborn imam. Abu Taleb was discouraged. He knew the Free Yemenis and had been invited to join them, but he had made up his mind to do what he could for the country from within[5]. The time was at hand, however, when the Arab Socialist movement of Nasser, with its powerful symbolism of radical change, would bring external pressure to bear and win broad support through much of the Yemen.

It was not clear, at first, why the United States should give the Yemen much more attention than the Saudi government gave it, which was minimal. Nonetheless, on May 20, 1961, I had been appointed minister to the Mutawakkilite Kingdom of the Yemen to serve concurrently with my appointment as ambassador to Saudi Arabia. Our ties with the imam were far from close, and my larger responsibilities lay in Saudi Arabia. I did, however, make three trips to the imamate at six-month intervals, beginning soon after my presentation of credentials in October 1961. My first visit, accompanied by my wife, Jane, was to Taiz, where the imam had his residence and his office. Chargé Stookey met us in Hodaidah and took us to Taiz, where he also had his residence. Deputy Foreign Minister Abu Taleb welcomed us warmly and oversaw all arrangements from there on, starting with the formal presentation of credentials to the imam.

The presentation ceremony was so unique that it deserves mention. I had been aware that the imam was ill, unreasonable, and cantankerous toward all foreign delegations and that for reasons of Arab politics, as well as of bile, he liked to demonstrate his high station by keeping western ("imperialist") diplomats waiting, not minutes but often weeks. I therefore had made clear in an early message via Stookey to Abu Taleb that I had only ten days set aside for this first visit and could not extend it, much as I would like to, for even one day. Abu Taleb kept the imam to the time limit.

No advance details were available at first regarding the ceremony, but soon after my arrival I began to hear discordant trumpet sounds from the direction of the imam's dwelling, an ancient and picturesque castle outside the city walls. Only at the site of presentation did I later learn what they were: the sincere effort of the royal guards' band to cope with perhaps the most difficult of the world's national anthems, "The Star Spangled Banner." The result was at first unrecognizable. At the wide courtyard, Abu Taleb made it clear that I was to review this guard, and as I was about to begin, but before I had taken the first step, certain bars brought my hat over my heart, and I stood still until the rendition was finished. The royal Yemeni anthem followed. The tuba players were unforgettable, their cheeks and eyes bulging from air pressure at nearly one mile of altitude and from the chewing of qat. They looked at me appealingly. I wanted to express my appreciation to the band and so signaled to Abu Taleb. I would also have given much for photos, but that had not been arranged, and protocol demanded quick entry into the castle so as not to keep the imam waiting.

To my surprise, Abu Taleb led us up four flights of a stone tower to a bedroom so small that I realized at once why our official party had been limited to four men, myself included. The imam, in his rather dingy knee-length cotton tunic, was sitting cross-legged on a wide bed, without robe, headgear, or footgear. From the ceiling, over his bed, a woven cord hung with a ball attached some three feet above bed level. This had been used by him to hoist himself from a reclining to a sitting position. Abu Taleb joined him at bedside to introduce our little group. All of us received perfunctory handshakes until the fourth and last of my team, Isa Sabbagh, was introduced. As an unparalleled master of Arabic and English, Sabbagh had broadcast BBC news and commentary in both languages during World War II. His resonant voice and nuanced, sophisticated Arabic had captivated the imam, who now exclaimed in delight and grabbed his hand, pulling him to his bedside.

It was the only bright spot in a quaint but not very encouraging meeting. I had prepared, with Sabbagh's assistance, a presentation speech in Arabic similar to the one I had used in Ta'if with King Saud. Abu Taleb, conferring briefly with the imam, suggested I pass the written text to the imam for him to read. He scanned about half of it, put it down, and then delivered to me an extended indictment of US failure to tackle the British regarding their "repression" of Yemenis in Aden and the protectorates. Abu Taleb interpreted. The imam said, in effect, "South Yemen is our land and our people, separated from us by force. British planes have just bombed our villages, killing fifty sheep. It is enough to make one cry. You Americans are responsible. You control the British. They will do what you say!" I remonstrated at once that this was far from a statement of the case. He rejected my exceptions with scorn and would listen to no discussion or even to my request for details from him. After expending his venom, he turned to Abu Taleb and asked where was the "American gift." In the Yemen, gifts by a newly accredited emissary were customary, and we had brought with us a good portable reflector telescope. Abu Taleb informed the imam that it was already installed on the palace roof for his use. There was no word of thanks. He was not in a good mood.

The imam signaled that the audience was over, so we bade him goodbye. I was to see him only once more, nearly a year later, under very different circumstances. On that occasion he summoned me to apologize for a considerable discourtesy by his eldest son, Crown Prince Badr.

I had met Badr at the suggestion of Abu Taleb during my initial visit to the kingdom, but he had been absent thereafter. I was now to make a formal call on Badr, with the expectation of a substantive talk. Al-Badr had acceded to my request, made from Jeddah, and the call was set for a date in June 1962. He had designated San'a as the place and fixed the hour. I was there, but he was not, and the representatives he had left behind him were obviously embarrassed. They had no message to me from him. They mumbled that unspecified business had required a last-minute change, and the crown prince was in Umran, a city northwest of San'a. They urged me to go there but could give no official assurance that I would find him. I knew then that the snub was deliberate and politically motivated. I therefore declined at once, whereupon the retinue was startled and argued that, indeed, I must go and would find him. I replied that I had a lineup of engagements that would be discourteous of me to fail to meet.

I returned to Taiz. Some hours later I received a call from the palace that the imam wished to see me immediately. I replied that I would be ready in fifteen minutes. No, that was too long, the protocol officer said, you must be ready right now! I responded that this was unreasonable and I would be ready as stated and no earlier. The car arrived on time, and the imam on this occasion was fully dressed and seated alone in his study. He made a pretense of struggling to rise but did not succeed, and I urged him to remain seated while I took a chair near him. He made apologies for his son, giving unconvincing reasons for Badr's sudden business in Umran. I told him that such things happen to high officials, and he should not worry about it. The imam did not offer to arrange for another call nor did Badr.

In retrospect, I explain the imam's behavior as prompted by two things. First, the imam and, notably, Badr were attempting for Nasser's benefit to project an image of defiant "Arabism" toward the United States. They were anxious for Nasser's support and were very worried that they might not get it. It was (correctly) feared that Egypt would withdraw support of Badr in favor of a republican coup. I doubt that the imam quite shared Badr's concern. He had already lost the sharper edges of his judgment. His mood was that of resentment that he had not received the major economic aid from the United States that he had expected.

This latter factor was also the second reason for his behavior: In 1957, during the Eisenhower administration, Secretary of State Dulles had dispatched US congressman and special ambassador James P. Richards, accompanied by Deputy Assistant Secretary of State John J. Jernegan, on a rather poorly thought out and even more poorly financed mission to corral Arab alignment. This was to be accomplished in the form of signed declarations against international communism. It was part of the so-called Eisenhower Doctrine and compliance was to be rewarded by US aid more or less on the spot.[6] For convincing his targets, Dulles had a total of $200 million to distribute throughout the Arab world, and by the time Richards called on the imam the best that had been budgeted for the Yemen amounted to about $3 million. The imam terminated the meeting with Richards by ostentatiously walking out in anger, indicating that he was insulted by such a low rating of his country.

The United States had certainly not given a deliberately low rating to the Yemen, but the country had a limited capacity to absorb aid. Additionally, US funds for these essential programs were short. What was needed most were funds for education abroad and a program in the Yemen of preparing Yemenis for advanced study. This was clear from the beginning of the US-Yemeni relationship, which dated back to 1946, but the imams and their Zaidi followers were not eager to see a foreign-educated class of Yemenis arise to challenge their political supremacy. They were a ruling Shiite minority over a Shafi'i Sunni majority. It was a continuing dilemma for the last Zaidi imamates, nurtured in traditional isolation but knowing they must bring to the Yemen technological progress obtainable only from industrial powers.

It was in 1945 that a long-reigning imam, Yahya bin Muhammad Hamid al-Din, had decided to take decisive action. He sent Sayyid Hussein al-Kibsi to Cairo to contact the US minister plenipotentiary to Egypt, S. Pinkney Tuck, and through him to invite the United States to send a mission to the Yemen to establish relations. Referral to Washington resulted in instructions to the US consul in Aden, Harlan B. Clark, to proceed to San'a to make inquiries. Clark thus became the diplomatic pioneer in establishing official US-Yemeni contacts. He was most warmly invited to make a visit to San'a by no less than Prince Ahmad, eldest son and subsequent successor of Imam Yahya. Clark reported a fine reception in San'a, providing State with a wealth of fascinating detail and advising that the imamate would welcome a US mission to conclude an accord of friendship and commerce.[7] In response to President Truman's subsequent telegram of November 2, 1945, Imam Yahya, on December 2, 1945, formally accepted such a proposed mission. Truman then picked his minister to Saudi Arabia, William Eddy, to head it up.[8] The sons of Imam Yahya were split over the prospect of diplomatic ties with the United States, with the exception of Prince Ahmad, who clearly favored them at that period of his life.

The mission arrived in San'a in April 1946, after an arduous but fascinating auto trip from Hodaidah, to find itself surrounded by palace intrigue. Nonetheless, all began well. The titular foreign minister was a Turk, Muhammad Raguib Bey, who for thirty-one years (going back to 1915) had served Imam Yahya competently and loyally. He had married into the ruling family and considered the Yemen his adopted land.

However, a son of the imam, Prince Hussein, now maneuvered to take over the Yemeni negotiating responsibilities and to oust Raguib Bey. How Hussein managed this has never been explained to me.

What had been a friendly Yemeni approach to a basically routine draft agreement of friendship and commerce was now the subject of exception to every phrase. Hussein particularly objected to Article III, which stated, "Subjects of His Majesty the King of the Yemen in the United States of America and nationals of the United States of America in the Kingdom of the Yemen shall be received and treated in accordance with the requirements and practices of generally recognized international law." Emphatically, Hussein declared that for Yemenis there could be but one law, that of the Qur'an, and that this language was therefore unacceptable.

Coming after other time-consuming exceptions demanded by Hussein and a number of changes of text that had to be referred to Washington by the mission's shortwave radio, this uncompromising stance suggested that the prince had found the means to destroy the negotiation. Minister Eddy began to make preparations for departure, at first discreetly, then openly. Article III was a sticking point. Eventually, Eddy announced his regret that no further concessions were possible and that he had commitments elsewhere he had to meet. He would leave the radio as a gift to the kingdom, with sincere thanks to the imam for courtesies.

Before their departure, however, Imam Yahya received the delegation in his *majlis* and inquired from Eddy as to the cause of the deadlock. Not wishing to cast blame on the imam's son, Eddy passed to him a letter explaining the sticking points. He proceeded to explain, point by point, that the draft text held no traps for the Yemen but was standard language for agreements of this kind. The objective was expanded trade with reciprocal assurances of the fair treatment of nationals on a most-favored-nation basis. This draft held some special exceptions on the US side regarding Cuba and the Panama Canal Zone, which may well have struck the Yemenis as odd and irrelevant, but they hardly involved any Yemeni interests. Imam Yahya responded that he could see no special reason to consider that the text held difficulties, and he evinced puzzlement as to the cause of the deadlock. He ordered that Raguib Bey come forward and be again put in charge of negotiations.

Raguib Bey, seventy years of age, arose from the back of the *majlis,* came to a table directly in front of the imam, and burst into a torrent of eloquent Arabic. He stated that he had served the imam faithfully for thirty-one years. He repeated what he had often told the imam: every small nation, to survive in this century of great wars, needed the friendship of a strong power; the United States was the only strong power without imperialistic designs. This agreement, he said, would have been the crowning achievement of his career, but just as he was about to conclude it, he was kicked out of the imam's palace "like a dog." In his place was the unskilled Hussein, who dropped the diplomatic master-piece. All progress had stopped. Now, said Raguib Bey, he was being called back like a sweeper to pick up the pieces, but would not be pushed around like a slave. He resigned as foreign minister and asked permission to return to his native Turkey to die. Raguib Bey's emotion rose as he talked. He shook his finger in the face of his sovereign, whereupon the chief bodyguard of the imam, Qadi Kolala, advancing behind the foreign minister, drew his *jambiyya* from its scabbard, laid his left hand on the shoulder of the speaker, and peered at the imam for permission to use his weapon. Slowly, the imam shook his head, and the guard sheathed the blade and withdrew. The imam urged Raguib Bey to quiet down and take a rest so he would feel better. Raguib returned to his seat.[9]

The imam then turned to Eddy and asked when he and his party must depart. Eddy replied that firm arrangements had been made to depart within the hour and could not be postponed, owing to air connections. Could adjustments of text be made in that time, the imam queried. Eddy replied that he had made all the concessions possible, and he could make no more. The imam then told Raguib Bey to resume talks, but Raguib pointed out that he was no longer minister of foreign affairs. The imam then instructed Abd al-Karim Mutahhar, as acting minister of foreign affairs, to see if matters could be settled within the hour, and the two missions, minus al-Hussein, withdrew to reconsider the text. Mutahhar pressed for no further changes. Clean copies were made of what Eddy had already indicated was his final offer, and within the hour the ex-change of notes in Arabic and English was approved by the imam, signed for the Yemen by Mutahhar, and entered at once into full effect on May 4, 1946.

As Eddy and his party were leaving the government guest house at San'a, they encountered Raguib Bey, on foot, carrying a suitcase. He explained that he was leaving the Yemen at once and for good, returning to Turkey. Eddy gave him warm praise for his courage and forthrightness and expressed his great appreciation for his assist in the completion of the US special mission. They exchanged what turned out to be their last handshakes and best wishes.

THE YEMEN BETWEEN YAHYA AND THE REPUBLIC

Imam Yahya was assassinated in 1949, allegedly by Sheikh Murad, paramount sheikh of the Abida tribe (who was in turn executed later that year). In the years that followed Imam Yahya's assassination, the Yemen was disturbed by a new dynastic struggle for power between the great houses of Hamid al-Din and al-Wazir, the traditional Zaidi contenders, by wealth and by influence, for the imamate. For a time the al-Wazirs were on top, but tribal allegiance is not a constant thing in Yemeni history.

Prince Abd Allah bin Ahmad al-Wazir, head of the house, desperately sought recognition from Ibn Saud by sending him a delegation to explain and justify what had occurred. Ibn Saud, however, wanted no part of blessing regicide. It was one of the al-Wazirs' most serious setbacks and was soon followed by others. Imam Ahmad and the house of Hamid al-Din regained control, with the valuable blessing of Ibn Saud for his legitimacy. He also inherited from the late Imam Yahya the problem of deciding on a US request for a resident mission and for the right to fly the US flag.

Consent to these steps, normally given quickly and pro forma by one state to another, are rarely held up by security considerations. In the Yemen, however, there lingered a distrust of all foreign officialdom, deeper by far than in Saudi Arabia.[10] The establishment of a mission in the Yemen presented one frustration after another for the Department of State, which had to explain the elementary needs of a diplomatic mission to a medieval mindset—Imam Ahmad's. The consequent series of delays in obtaining a legation site and permission to fly the flag retarded the ability of the US government to fulfill its main purpose in the Yemen: to grapple with the developmental requirements of a kingdom in need of every kind of progress and reform. The State Department endured these frustrations as the specter of the Cold War powered US foreign policy in the Middle East. The communist seizure of Eastern Europe and a dynamic Kremlin foreign policy created an exaggerated fear of a "house of cards" collapse in the Third World. At length, by the late 1950s, the United States leased a building and flew the flag from it. A small American school served children of mission personnel (and of Yemenis on a space-available basis).

An impediment to a fully developed aid mission and to timely improvement in the Yemen's development program was the almost total lack of cooperation by the imam's government with US efforts at practical assistance. It gave virtually no help, for example, to the distribution of PL-480 wheat, much of which rotted in the hot, humid harbor of Hodaidah for lack of storage and of trucks for distribution. US aid personnel were told that the United States must pay the imam's officials—with a suspected percentage for the imam himself—to contract for distribution. The rates were exorbitant. The absence of a road network was basic, but trucks, while scarce, could get around, if the will and the money were there. I found in my visits an air of expectancy and—not then unusual in the Middle East—a clearly defined effort to shame the US government into providing instant gifts of expensive infrastructure.

I remember an interesting afternoon in 1962 with Prince Hasan bin Ali, minister of public works, who came by horseback to call on me at the residence of Chargé Stookey. A handsome young man of princely bearing and a fine horseman, he did his best to convince me that the United

States should bestow as gifts to the kingdom a variety of costly public improvements, all no doubt urgently needed. Knowing that our government had neither the necessary money nor the intent, I did my best to persuade him that a continuing reliance on grant aid from the United States or any other power was not the best course, or the most dignified, for a developing country of a proud and ancient culture. I recounted a recent experience I had had with Egyptian attitudes when, in the mid-1950s, I witnessed at Cairo a decline in relations between Egypt and the United States in proportion to the very extent of US aid.

I was convinced that the Yemen, like Pakistan and Turkey, would benefit most by taking its aid from a group of friendly powers, rather than just one. It should first establish a permanent relationship with the World Bank and International Monetary Fund, starting with membership in the fund; it would be easy then to arrange for a visiting bank mission to study, free of charge, the entire economy and development of the Yemen. That done, the bank and the kingdom would arrange for the establishment of an international consortium of lender powers. This body would permanently advise and oversee agreed development projects that, by stages, would augment the Yemen's ability to help itself. Thus, the Yemen would avoid both the feeling of overobligation to one patron and of going overboard beyond growing capabilities. Warming to the subject, I said that I knew well a fine officer of the World Bank resident in Jeddah. He was Anwar Ali, a Pakistani economist on loan to the Saudi government as head of the Saudi Monetary Agency and as advisor in Saudi developmental planning. Through him I could send to the Yemen full details on how to start this relationship with the bank. The Yemen faced a long road of development and should have the best of collective help over the many years ahead.

I could see the prince's unspoken disappointment. We were talking past each other. He wanted to be able to announce a huge American grant-in-aid program and a bilateral Yemeni-US relationship to counterbalance Soviet influence. Nonetheless, I did follow up with Anwar Ali, who cooperated fully, and I sent Stookey details for the prince. Nothing came of it, as the bloody revolution of September 1962 intervened. Hasan bin Ali, who hid out in a village near San'a, was discovered and killed at once, his head mounted on a pike atop the walls of San'a.

Reflecting on the Yemen in its last prerevolutionary days, I retain, along with a sense of pathos and regret at the slaughter of all the top officials of the imam's government, a strong impression that the house of Hamid al-Din, once keen on the need for development and technical education, had become tired and was stalled in time. Nothing could really advance matters as long as Imam Ahmad governed, for he had come to focus first and foremost on his personal benefit. He was an old tribal infighter, street smart and ruthless, with several bullets still in his body, giving him much pain in his declining years. He wanted to see dramatic progress and take credit for it, but he saw no reason not to grab what he could as foreign aid supplies and equipment passed his door.[11]

Within the Yemen, the imam had sought to generate foreign aid by spectacular projects, pitting the United States against the Soviet Union and mainland China and the latter two against each other, while the imam took sole credit for positive results. Yemenis were most eager to educate their youth. The Soviet Union responded with free scholarships to Moscow institutions, with living expenses and transportation, all on a scale alarming to the US aid mission. US budgetary limitations offered little more than a handful of scholarships. This was a strategic initiative in the Cold War that I much regretted the United States could not begin to match. Our scholarship programs were qualitatively good but few, compared to those of the Russians or the Chinese. Furthermore, there was absolutely no prospect of increase. It was clear that Washington was not captivated by the long-term importance of the Yemen.

The communist Chinese aid mission built a surfaced highway from Hodaidah to San'a, a major accomplishment, while the United States organized, trained, and equipped the Yemen's first highway department. Under its supervision until the revolution, US-trained Yemenis were building a gravel-surfaced highway from Taiz to the coast near Makha (Mocha), and another northward from Taiz to Ibb. Instead of thanks, and clearly on the imam's orders, we received complaints that the roads were not surfaced as the Chinese highway was. We also sought to help Yemeni farmers in the better grading and packaging of their excellent Makha coffee, but this did not become sufficiently organized to be remunerative.

There was never the slightest sign of official gratitude for US assistance, but at the village level the undeniable competence and brotherly approach of our technicians and teachers toward the people won immediate and touching response. In a stratified society we made common ground with the rural population. Indeed, it was a labor of love to assist the hospitable, kindly Yemeni villagers and countrymen. The women, unveiled, working the fields alongside the men, were the backbone of the country. They were dimly aware that beyond their mountainous borders conditions were better and progress possible. About 2 million Yemeni men worked in Saudi Arabia, Kuwait, and other gulf states, usually leaving their tough and resilient wives at home and sending back their remittances.

My mission to the Yemen lasted from September 1961 to September 1962. Detailed and prescient warning of the upheaval to come had been provided by Chargé Stookey in July 1962. On economic matters the legation was well served by Foreign Service officer W. R. Brown, whom I had known as a first-class analyst from our service together in 1955 in Cairo. Following is a summary of the views of Brown and Stookey.

Economically, the Mutawakkilite Kingdom of the Yemen was an adjunct of the British colony of Aden. It had no independent economic identity, including no currency except the Maria Theresa thaler, a large silver coin that bore the likeness of the buxom eighteenth-century queen of Austria. During the centuries it was variously minted in Italy, England, and Austria for circulation in the Arabian Peninsula. There, where paper currency was far less widely acceptable than coin, its high silver content made it generally popular. I recall the rate at about forty US cents as a collector's item, but its value rose and fell with fluctuations in the price of silver. There was no control by the Yemeni government over its circulation and exchange. These matters, by tradition, were regulated by banks and trading firms in Aden, but the system was awkward for Yemeni merchants, who kept offices in Aden for large payments. For much of their domestic and foreign trade they used East African shillings and instruments denominated in shillings, drawn on banks in Aden. There was no balance of payments problem, but there was also no integrated national economy.

During the kingdom's last twenty years, economic conditions steadily worsened. There was no industrial capacity, merely handicrafts such as milling, production of sesame oil, weaving, dyeing, and tanning. Since World War II, however, these crafts had not been able to meet the competition of imported products. The departure of virtually all Yemeni Jews for Israel after 1948 removed a famous class of skilled silversmiths.[12] The quarrying of building stone, limestone, gypsum, soapstone, and agate was small, crude, and disorganized. Salt from domes at Salif was exported to Japan, but delays in the handling were so crude and haphazard that demurrage eliminated most profits. Agriculture in the Yemen provided the principal livelihood but at a subsistence, barter level. Former substantial exports of grains, coffee, ghee, live animals, and hides had dropped off by 25 to 60 percent. One minister of agriculture had asserted that his ministry was on the back of his mule.

With a few exceptions, the kingdom was poorly served by the general caliber of its ministers. With the exception of Abu Taleb and a few others, most of them had no education in the modern sense, kept few records, and were totally ignorant of the field of activity they were supposed to direct. Over half of tax levies were collected from farmers in kind and amounted to 25 percent of an arbitrary estimate of crop value; yet this was inadequate for the needs of the state. The hoard of silver that had been accumulated by Imam Yahya was practically exhausted by the imamate under Ahmad, which was thus in no position to invest in development. The imam not only took his cuts on local vehicle traffic, he levied a personal tax on hides and coffee, payable in foreign currency to him personally. Imports were taxed 20 to 30 percent, exports 10 percent. Thus, the kingdom was broke, not because of any lavish spending but because of oppressive, ill-considered taxation and tax farming. This was not even profitable to the regime, as it was estimated that less than one-half of the taxes paid by citizens ever reached the government.

One can understand why the regime was against programs of reform but in favor of public works as gifts. The latter, like the Chinese-built road, could represent a visible accomplishment of the imam's shrewd diplomacy, while the former threatened the demise of his entire system.[13] In 1962, however, the prospect of foreign or domestic investment in the future of the Yemen was essentially zero. The Yemeni business community had no confidence in the regime or its future. No one really wanted what the Yemen could offer on the world's markets except the Soviet Union, which took 30 to 50 percent of the Yemen's coffee exports. Such little capital as was accumulated went to Aden banks and overseas.

A major political factor in prerevolutionary Yemen was its well-known religious split. The tribes of the Yemen were deeply influenced by divisions of power built on tradition. The Yemen had been ruled by Zaidis, a Shiite offshoot and a minority in the Yemen. The governed majority were Shafi'i Sunnis. Generally and with conspicuous exceptions, the Zaidis were of poor and exclusively religious education. They were determined to keep the Shafi'i merchant class in its inferior hierarchical place. To protect their earnings, Shafi'ites invested in Aden and overseas and took their revenge on the regime by so investing, charging exorbitant brokerage fees to the Zaidi government, and providing it with substandard or worthless merchandise.

In this sterile picture, US aid, employing 1,000 Yemenis on a $65,000 monthly payroll, plus $55,000 in local monthly purchases, fostered less fundamental change than additional discontent toward the imamate. To our legation it was clear that Crown Prince Badr was eager for quick and spectacular development and was attempting to beat the clock and appear an independent reformer in action. The Sayyid class was fully on the imam's side, fearing loss of their privilege and control if real reform occurred. Time was running out. Fearing a violent revolt at any time, Badr had, since March 1962, led a cabinet of his own in San'a. It was a parallel government in which the imam was not cooperating. Badr seems to have been serious in his efforts to at least improve his own image. Also in March 1962, he ordered the establishment of a committee to delimit the functions of all ministries and government departments and draft regulations for their operation. Most of them were in San'a, the traditional capital, which the imam shunned in favor of Taiz. (At least one of the bullets he harbored in his body had been delivered in San'a by an ambush some years before.) The membership of Badr's committee, headlined in *al-Nasr* on March 22, 1962, "Constructive New Organizational Measures," included some able people, in contrast to most of the cabinet residing and pretending to work at Taiz.

The resulting contest of wills between Badr and his father generated hesitation and instability. Indeed, vacillation at the highest levels presented a continuing impression of weakness. In January 1962, communists—Taiz had three cells—had circulated leaflets against the regime. In February shots had been fired at the San'a house of the crown prince. On March 16, tank corps officers had been briefly imprisoned in Taiz on suspicion of being disloyal to the imam and to the crown prince. In San'a the crown prince had sought, without much success, to rally tribes to suppress a revolt among the Khawlan, the Harith, and the Baqqil. Only the small Hamdan tribe responded favorably to Badr's appeal.

On July 24, a strike occurred, stirred up by communists and labor agitators from Aden. On July 30, 130 secondary students demonstrated in Taiz and marched on the radio station carrying pictures of Nasser. Police fired over their heads, and some participants were jailed. Abu Taleb informed me that the Egyptians had spent 35,000 Egyptian pounds on propaganda and subversion during that June and had attempted to ship in explosives, which were discovered and seized. A spirit of uncertainty and apprehension prevailed in the Yemen but especially in the palace. Abu Taleb, perhaps the only friend of the United States in the Yemen, was appointed minister of economy and then minister of public works, replacing Prince Hasan bin Ali.

Then, on September 26 came the revolution, with dramatic suddenness. Imam Ahmad had shortly before died of natural causes, and his son Badr was at once invested as imam, promising extensive reforms.[14] After eight days in office, however, Badr was overthrown in an army coup led by his chief bodyguard, Abd Allah al-Sallal. He escaped death by inches and seconds from a point-blank artillery assault on his stone palace and made his way to a cave in the north, where he established his political headquarters. From there he visited Saudi Arabia and received aid.

In the Cairo of 1958, reports of covert Egyptian plans to overturn the system in the Yemen had been numerous. The tree was ripe. When the fruit fell in September 1962, Egypt was ready for it, with at least one ship loaded with personnel and equipment to support the revolutionaries. In both Jeddah and Cairo, it was immediately apparent that if Nasser had not organized the uprising, he had blessed its preparation.

6

YEMEN: COLLAPSE OF AN ANCIENT SYSTEM

News of the Yemeni revolution came over Yemeni radio as I was packing in Jeddah for my fourth official visit to the kingdom. On September 26, 1962, the Yemeni army, headed by Brigadier Abd Allah al-Sallal, had seized power. As monitored by our Jeddah embassy staff, the high command made a series of public announcements on September 27. Accompanying these proclamations, reports came into the Jeddah embassy from various other sources that the entire Yemeni cabinet had been summarily executed. The US legation in Taiz had been silent on September 26 and 27. Since it depended basically on Yemeni government radio, I had to conclude that access was blocked by the revolutionary authorities or mobs, or perhaps both. The welfare of the small American community in Yemen, almost all of whom were legation or AID personnel, was in doubt and a matter of direct and immediate concern to me as minister.

I therefore wired the Department of State on September 27 that I proposed to use the US Military Training Mission's C-54 to proceed on September 28 to Aden, accompanied by air attaché Major Clark Scott and his secretary, to ask the cooperation of my friend, Sir Charles Johnston, the British colonial governor, and meanwhile to attempt to reach our legation in Taiz via such limited radio equipment as that on the C-54. I would avoid Yemeni territory, including the coast, in my flight, and would return as soon as possible. The department gave rather reluctant but quick consent—reluctant, because it thought I could perhaps learn as much in Jeddah. I had doubts on this point, however, and wanted to be closer to sources.

On my arrival in Aden, neither Sir Charles nor others had much information for me, nor any contact, at first, with his own chargé in Taiz. However, as visits by Yemenis to the Aden protectorate were frequent and uncontrolled, it was not long before our consul in Aden, Stephen P. Campbell, was able to tell me that a reliable Yemeni source who had just arrived assured him that all US hands in Taiz were safe and not under immediate threat. This was later reinforced September 29 by the British head of secretariat at Aden. Both the dean of the diplomatic corps in Taiz, Amadeo Guillet, and the British chargé, Christopher Gandy, asserted a revolutionary authority had assured them that the "interests of [the] foreign diplomatic community would be respected."

On September 28 a communication had finally arrived from Chargé Stookey in Taiz. It was the unclassified text of a circular note from the "Foreign Ministry of the Arab Republic of Yemen" informing the legation of the "blessed revolution," whereby the Yemen Arab Republic was now a proclaimed fact, and stating that the army command would continue to hold the reins of power until general elections were held. The YAR would be bound, meanwhile, by the provisions of the UN Charter, the Charter of the Arab League, and the resolutions of the Bandung Conference. It would fulfill its international obligations, and its policy would be "positive neutrality" and the maintenance of world peace. It would also raise Yemeni living standards. Stookey added that he would await instructions before acknowledging this note, the implication being that any acknowledgment would constitute US recognition if he used the only form of address acceptable to the YAR.

I reported from Aden that the news of the overthrow of the Mutawwakilite Kingdom had been greeted with palpable enthusiasm by the Aden Yemeni community. Our consul general in Dhahran, John E. Horner, reported the same reaction by the large Yemeni labor force in eastern Saudi Arabia, despite a negative Saudi official attitude, soon to be openly expressed. I reported October 1 on a private dinner with Governor Johnston. He expected that the United Kingdom and the Saudi government would lend help in resisting the revolution and would probably extend that help via Yemeni prince Hasan. In Washington, Mutawwakilite chargé Ahmad Zubara urged the US government to declare itself against all outside intervention in the Yemen and to recognize Hasan as the new ruler. Hasan was then in New York representing his government at the United Nations. All this was based on the early belief that Imam Badr had been killed by gunfire at the start of the revolution, since his home had been bombarded point blank and no communication from him had been received by any of his subjects or emissaries abroad. Prince Hasan was declared by the Mutawwakilite embassy in London to be the legal imam.

In calls on Adlai Stevenson, US ambassador to the United Nations in New York, and on Talcott Seelye, a Foreign Service Arabist at the State Department, Hasan requested money and aircraft to fly to the Yemen but received no response from these approaches. It soon developed that Badr was alive. He had made his escape by stages, at night, to Wahsha, in northern Yemen, beyond reach of the revolution, where, from a cave, he used a portable radio to communicate with royalist troops and officials. Mutawwakilite embassies soon made the public correction that Badr was "king" (or "imam") and Hasan prime minister.

I decided that I had done as much as I could in Aden and flew back to Jeddah on October 2. As my mission to the Yemen was finished, so was my privilege of entering the country. I regretted this, as I was much attracted by that country and its people. However, I had been accredited to a regime that was anathema number one to most of its public and to most expatriate Yemenis. If the US government decided to recognize the YAR, a new presidential appointee would be required.

As I flew to Jeddah, I pondered the grisly newscasts from YAR radio recorded by our Jeddah embassy monitors: After "deliberations" by a "people's court" in the Yemen, the top officials of the kingdom were sentenced and immediately executed by firing squad. The jails were reported full, and prisoners were being selected for execution as authorities might direct. The numbers and rank of those executed with or without summary trial signaled the ferocity of the army's action and its disregard of long-term tribal and family consequences. The Yemen, as its history shows, had almost always conducted its changes of supreme leadership by violence and regicide, but this was a special case. It was an indiscriminate purge, and, what is more, there was the Egyptian factor.

THE GREAT EGYPTIAN GAMBLE

On September 27, 1962, Egyptian vice president Anwar Sadat proffered a bit of "advice" to US ambassador John Badeau, delivered before Badeau had learned of the Yemeni army's seizure of power. The advice was that the US government would be unwise to support Prince Hasan or other counterrevolutionary forces in Yemen, and, in particular, to join King Saud in such support. Badeau quickly obtained instructions permitting him to tell Sadat that the US government—supporting Badeau's own recommendation—had no plans to interfere or give aid to Prince Hasan as long as US vital interests were not threatened, particularly in the Persian Gulf area. However, US security interests depended on continued peace and stability in the Arabian Peninsula, and that included the

United Kingdom's position in the Aden area. The United States could not accept a campaign against this position—such as was now emanating from Radio Yemen—by high-level YAR spokesmen, and the United States looked to Egypt to influence the new Yemeni regime in the direction of international stability and development, and not toward external adventures.

The responsibility of Egypt in the support, if not in the planning, of the Yemeni revolution was now clear. Sadat was believed to be a major coordinator in the opening phases. On the minds of all of us was Nasser's September 1961 setback—Syria's domestic coup d'état and its immediate withdrawal from the UAR. Egyptian backing of the Yemeni revolution offered clear opportunity to restore Nasser's prestige and military hegemony and a stepping stone to mastery over Saudi Arabia.

In its initial stages, the Yemen Arab Republic conducted its revolution with a heavy hand, shocking and antagonizing Washington, London, Riyadh, and Amman. The Arab League was thrown into disarray, split down the middle between those sympathetic with the YAR for its action in ending a corrupt, oppressive, and utterly backward regime and those who feared the revolution's direct impact on their own societies or their vital interests. In general, intellectuals in the Arab states, including those in Saudi Arabia and Jordan, were at least partly convinced that Egypt and its leader had done well in helping to topple a regime that brought shame and disgust upon the Arab world. In other circles, however, feelings were widely mixed, as leadership groups feared a gathering momentum of Egyptian imperialism. Active opposition to the YAR was initially led by King Saud, just as he was leaving the kingdom for medical treatment. As stated earlier, Saud ordered arms and money assembled and sent to the royalists in sufficient quantity to threaten the republican regime. This quickly led to confrontation between Egypt and Saudi Arabia.

Chargé Stookey managed to get to us a rough sketch of the situation on the ground, confirming that the Revolutionary Army was under orders to protect the safety of Americans and other foreigners. It did not sound, however, like a very friendly protection. On October 2 the official attitude was made clear to Stookey by Abd al-Rahman al-Baydani, deputy prime minister of the YAR. Baydani, a prerevolutionary paid agent of Nasser's government, treated Stookey to a menu of threats and demands and radio listeners to a diatribe against the Saudi regime. He vowed to meet Saudi or British troops if, as expected, they invaded Yemen and to pursue them clear to Riyadh or Aden. With Stookey he adopted a threatening and bullying posture at first, but this subsided when it yielded no results.

Commander-in-Chief Sallal, on September 29, asked the secretary-general of the United Nations and the president of the UN General Assembly to inform all delegations that his government was firmly in power. The Secretariat circulated this message, along with a cable of October 7 from Prince Hasan claiming recognition for the Mutawwakilite kingdom as the legitimate government of the Yemen. Both sides indicated they would send delegations to the United Nations. A protracted war of credentials had now begun. Bolstering the YAR claim to recognition was the situation in the Yemen itself, namely, its reasonably well-established capture and control by mid-October of San'a, Taiz, Hodaidah, Makha, Ibb, Qatabah, and Baydah. Bolstering the claim of the royalists was their alleged capture, by October 7 and 8, respectively, of Saada and Ma'rib. At the time, sources believed there were as yet no royalist forces loyal to Hasan in Yemen, but sporadic border fighting was reported in the Najran area of Saudi Arabia, an indication of border mobilizations and clashes yet to come. There were reports of troops invading the Yemen from the Aden protectorate. A survey of conflicting stories in early autumn 1962 indicates that the royalists were in the formative stages of mobilization planning and supply and not yet really engaged.

The YAR had provisional control over the main centers of the population, but for the long haul the republic certainly needed Egypt. It had no operational military aviation, as I had been able to verify personally on my last visit. Its only known air base, unusable by jets, was three miles south of San'a (elevation 3,900 feet), where some twenty Russian YAK trainers (piston-engine aircraft) had remained canvas-covered and unused in the open for more than a year. Also reported to be in inventory were two Ilyushin piston-engine IL-14 transports (modeled on the US Convair); two medium and two small Russian helicopters; two DC-3s; two "Aerocommander" six-seater, two-engine passenger aircraft; and two grounded Yemeni Airlines DC-3s. There was no maintenance, except for Russian light servicing at Taiz, where the 600-foot runway had a considerable hump and a "built-in crosswind," making it usable by small craft only in the morning before winds developed. Civilian airports north of San'a and at Hodaidah had short, gravel runways and were treacherous. Nonetheless, piston aircraft from Egypt were to use them.

By mid-October the US legation at Taiz was able to file most enlightening reports on the revolution and on the degree of acceptance by the Yemeni public. These showed that despite the leadership role of the army, Yemeni civilians had had a vital part to play in planning the overthrow; noncommunist youth had blocked procommunists from controlling the streets, through the use of placards and loudspeakers among other means. Civilians and military personnel even cooperated in preventing anti-US agitation and in turning demonstrations in front of the legation away from destructive mob action. There was no open xenophobia, and street orders had been given against harming foreigners. Citizens were ordered not to interfere with USAID programs, which the legation reported were scarcely interrupted.

Economic counselor W. R. Brown, who had served in Egypt during the revolutionary period of 1953–1956, was able to compare the 1962 YAR revolutionary experience with that of Egypt in 1952. The consolidation of the revolution in Yemen showed inspiration by, but no copying of, the Cairo experience. A YAR People's Congress was set up to assist the army high command in convoking rallies of support for the new regime.[1] The direct ties between the Congress and the high command also served to block communist inroads into public-relations programs.

The YAR organization (with fast-growing Egyptian authority replacing early Egyptian "advisors") was simple, and, as the Egyptians moved into place, quite ineffective. The core of the central high command at San'a was the National Revolutionary Council, ten officers and eight civilians, headed by Sallal, who executed decisions of the council as prime minister and chairman of the high command. Subordinate revolutionary councils were established in Taiz and other provincial capitals. A cabinet of twenty men was made up largely of the membership of the Revolutionary Council. As Mutawwakilite Yemen had had virtually no functioning ministries (excepting foreign affairs), and even the most minor questions had had to be referred to the imam personally, many ministers of the new regime had little to guide them. A five-man committee of army officers and civilians was set up to coordinate work between the high command and the cabinet.

In the towns and the cities, civilian governors were installed but given no authority. In tribal areas, leading sheikhs were selected as governors and given more authority than in the towns. One early product of the revolution for the Yemenis was a horde of cash; some 25 million Maria Theresa silver riyals were taken from Imam Ahmad's premises and other imamate sources. It appeared enough to carry the costs of YAR administration for a year. Meanwhile, October passed with swift consolidation of YAR rule in major Yemeni towns.

The aftermath of the revolution in San'a found the "royalists" with much of their potential civil and military leadership killed, believed dead, or active abroad. The Hamid al-Din had cards to play, however, and were encouraged by supplies and money (initially provided to Prince Hasan by King Saud) and matériel (from King Hussein of Jordan). A royalist guerrilla organization was able by November to mount attacks near Haradh and Sa'da in the north of Yemen. Severe fighting ensued, and Cairo entered the fray to avert a YAR setback.

As ground forces of the YAR counterattacked on November 2, Egyptian planes bombed five Saudi villages north of coastal Maidi, and planes and warships bombed and shelled the small Saudi coastal villages of

Mawassam and Samata. Ostensibly, these attacks were carried out by YAR forces, but, as already noted, YAR military airplanes were nonoperational and the Yemen had no navy. On the morning of November 2, I was summoned to the Saudi Foreign Ministry by Deputy Foreign Minister Umar al-Saqqaf and informed that Egypt was responsible for the attacks on Saudi territory and that diplomatic relations with Cairo were being severed. The public broadcast of severance the next day was accompanied by a circular note to all diplomatic missions in Jeddah proposing the immediate withdrawal of all Egyptian troops from the area under impartial and neutral supervision but without mention of any reciprocal withdrawal of Saudi forces from near the Yemeni frontier.

Damage to the Saudi villages was minimal but the attacks revealed the Saudis' inability to respond. The best (and only) Saudi defense of that coastal area at the time was the coral reef structure, which extends, with interruptions, along the thousand miles of Hejazi coast. The absence of reliable charts forced Egyptian vessels to give wide berth to these submerged dangers and made naval bombardment or amphibious landings very difficult. The Egyptian air force's actions were clearly designed to discourage the Saudi supply effort to royalist positions in the Maidi-Tihama plains region[2] and to intimidate the Saudis, as Egyptian ground forces were in no position to conduct amphibious landings or a long overland ground operation through arid territory.

By mid-November, US observers estimated the defensively committed Saudi forces at about 2,000 men, consisting of one brigade (700 to 800 men) of the "White Army" (the Bedouin national guard) in Jizan; 180 paratroops from the regular army, sent to Jizan to train forces; and the regular army's Third Battalion of the Tenth Infantry to hold the border area. Possibly 300 to 400 Saudi troops may have been in the Yemen, but not in combat, although the Saudis consistently denied having any troops there. Once Badr was installed in his cave as titular commander of royalist forces, however, the Saudi army supplied him with complete communications equipment, operated by Saudi technicians.

The general weakness of the regular Saudi army of about 15,000 men was a clear deterrent to its extensive involvement beyond Saudi borders. US observers believed only 5,000 to be combat-ready. In addition, the bedouin White Army, also numbering about 15,000, had minimum training, and its weapons were limited to rifles. A Royal Guard of 2,000 was well-trained, but its loyalty was questionable, and six of its officers were under arrest. The Royal Saudi Air Force suffered three defections to Cairo, with US-built planes, in the early phase of this confrontation with Egypt. Its flying officers were put on accelerated training out of the Dhahran Airport, but only about six were considered combat-trained at that time. In general, Saudi leadership evidenced distrust of its air force. While the air force was eventually restored to duty status, this meant training rather than operational activity throughout the critical period. Its best planes were a few F-86s. Six British Hawker Hunters arrived November 10 from Jordan, piloted at first by Jordanians, who provided combat assistance to royalist guerrillas in the Ma'rib-Jawf sector of the Yemen. The provision of weapons for royalist resistance even extended into the international arms market. Saudi purchases from Pakistan—which was sympathetic to the Saudi cause—amounted in early 1963 to 10,000 rifles of .303 caliber and 5 million rounds of ammunition.[3]

REACTIONS TO THE YEMEN CRISIS

Like most of its neighbors, Saudi Arabia was taken by surprise when the Yemen erupted into violent revolution. From visits to Taiz and San'a in 1961 and 1962, I had taken note of the low priority Riyadh had given to its relations with the imamate. Its mission in Taiz was manned at the top level by a very junior secretary of legation who appeared inactive and who counted the days until he could return to Saudi Arabia with his family. He evidenced little interest in the Yemen as such. The same could be said for most Arab diplomatic missions, Egypt's and Jordan's excluded.

Among non-Arab missions, interest was split. The Italian, British, American, Soviet, and communist Chinese missions were directed by trained Arabists or by leaders who recognized the strategic potential of the Yemen's geographic position. These sought to direct such potential toward realization of their own national interests. As in other Middle East countries, the Chinese interest in the Yemen appeared to be centered on countering Soviet influence. So pervasive were Russians among European faces that I was taken to be one by the Yemeni populace and greeted in Russian by street urchins.

The British handled security of the Red Sea straits, and in Aden they had the second largest bunkering port in the world, backed by a naval presence. They had no visible aid program for the Yemen and mutual distrust characterized Yemeni-British relations. London had been permanently on guard against the imam's hostile speeches and his machinations in boundary areas against British colonial rule. Across the straits of Bab al-Mandab, Ethiopia was in the friendly, pro-Western hands of Emperor Haile Selassie. His rebellious Eritreans presented no immediate problem to US control over Kagnew Air Station, a major relay center for military and State Department messages in the Indian Ocean region.

It was clear that the posture and behavior of Imam Ahmad and his son Badr had made a negative impression on US policy-makers. The White House saw little reason to get worked up over the Yemen and found it hard to justify a heavy investment in goodwill when the Yemeni leadership showed less than no appreciation. Even after the revolution and throughout the international crisis that followed, the interest of the

White House centered not on the Yemen per se, but on Saudi Arabia's integrity and stability and on the preservation of US access "on reasonable terms" to the vast Saudi oil resources. Relatively few Foreign Service officers and Arabic speakers had served in the Yemen, but these were touched by the clear needs of the Yemeni populace at large and empathized with its genuine struggle for knowledge and modernization.

Jordan's King Hussein regarded the revolution as a threat simply because it was backed by Nasser, whose henchmen had more than once sought the assassination of Hussein and his replacement by an Egyptian-oriented republic. The king informed the US embassy on September 29, 1962, of his conviction that the revolution was the work of a group of young Yemeni army officers who leaned toward Nasser and enjoyed little support within the Yemen. To the king, Nasser's influence was synonymous with communism, or so he chose to label it. He was certain that tribal sheikhs, in general, opposed the revolution, and he asserted that Prince Hasan would rally his people against it. Because he saw the hand of communist forces in the YAR, he would not extend recognition to it. He hoped the United States and others would also decline to recognize it. His prime minister, Wasfi al-Tel, urged the United States to support Prince Hasan as the best defense against communism in the Yemen and affirmed that Jordan would send him arms and technicians. Thus did King Hussein in 1962 bury forty years of Hashemite resentment toward the Saud clan that had snatched from his great grandfather his pretensions to kingship over the better part of the Arabian Peninsula and his heritage as custodian of the two holiest shrines of Islam.

During October 1962, the government of the Sudan split over the sudden recognition of the YAR by key members of its Supreme Council, despite the lack of formal council proceedings. The move was made without consulting Foreign Minister Kheir, who was greatly concerned over Egyptian influence in the new Yemeni regime and possible involvement of the Soviet Union. In part, this irregular act reflected Egyptian pressures on the Sudan to facilitate air traffic from Egypt to the YAR, which had become quite heavy as massive Egyptian military intervention in the Yemen got under way. By late October it was estimated that Egypt had 13,000 troops in the Yemen, and a divided Sudanese government opinion did not in any way appear to hinder Nasser's escalating deployments.

In Syria, President Nazim al-Qudsi, who was friendly to the United States, appealed on November 6 to those Arab states not directly involved in the Yemeni situation to consult one another and mediate the conflict. Though fearing a new effort by Cairo to spread its influence north through Saudi Arabia, his government had promptly recognized the YAR to avoid being bracketed with Arab "reactionaries."

Israel showed concern over any expansion of Nasser's influence, fearful it could upset the Arab-Israeli balance of power. Considerable wishful thinking lay behind Israel's early assessments that the Yemeni royalists were putting up a good fight in the north and causing Egypt to suffer heavy losses. Israel considered Saudi Arabia to be quite fragile and likely to crumble under the pressure of an Egyptian-dominated Arabian Peninsula, jeopardizing Israel's use of Eilat. The Israelis urged the United States not to recognize the YAR.

Gulf states, such as Bahrain and Qatar (whose foreign affairs were still under British control), and chieftains of the Aden colony and protectorates all looked to the United Kingdom to support Prince Hasan. They were worried about the stability of their own regimes in the face of the violent collapse of traditional Yemeni government. The Yemen, with a much larger population than any of these principalities, represented power. Furthermore, it had long claimed sovereignty over the British-controlled territories to its south.

For the most part, Arabs distant from the Yemen tended to favor the revolution and to back YAR membership in the United Nations. By November 20 a number of states had recognized the new republic: Egypt, Lebanon, Iraq, Tunisia, Syria, India, Somalia, Mali, all the Soviet bloc states, and the Federal Republic of (West) Germany. Those states closest to the scene were divided. Even the urban populations of Saudi Arabia and Jordan were divided, but in both those countries, as in Egypt, the ruler's emphatic decision was what counted. The vigor of opposing commitments thus brought the White House into one of the most time-consuming of presidential preoccupations, and one of the most arcane.

KENNEDY'S PROPOSAL

An intensification of the crisis between Egypt and Saudi Arabia in November 1962, spearheaded by their strong-minded leaders, brought President Kennedy into action. Faisal's aid to the royalists was intrinsically defensive, limited in scope and objective. Nasser's actions were nominally directed toward protection of the Yemeni revolution, and were certainly so intended, but there was the clear implication of wider Egyptian intentions. Nasser's moves bore the color of aggressiveness, and took place against the backdrop of Cairo's bitter radio attacks on the house of Saud and efforts to incite the Saudi people to overthrow its rule. Egypt's posture and its air and sea operations against Saudi targets could presage a much wider military campaign, which would bring US action into play to protect its interests.

Accordingly, the State Department and other agencies prepared for President Kennedy's approval a proposal to put a brake on Egypt's military activism in the Yemen. Its immediate purpose was to forestall any further buildup of Egyptian forces in the area, effect a drawdown of those forces, and discourage further attacks on Saudi territory. To deprive Nasser of the excuse for such attacks, the proposal sought the removal of Saudi and Jordanian joint concentrations just north of the Yemeni border. Washington was also motivated to test Nasser's intentions by seeking his advance concurrence on a disengagement package and placing him under the restraints of its program. After discussions in Washington with Egyptian ambassador Mustafa Kamil, a draft text was presented to Cairo. Full concurrence was quickly received.

As noted above, this move by Washington was taken without any advance discussion of strategy or tactics with me or my colleague in Jordan, William Macomber. Given the exceptional cordiality and mutual regard that had characterized the Kennedy-Faisal meeting of October 5, 1962, I had expected the first US approach to the parties to be simultaneous, secret, and tentative. If preferential treatment were accorded to Nasser, Faisal would reject the proposal out of hand. Therefore, I was chagrined to learn in the telegram that spelled out the proposal that it had already been cleared with Nasser, thereby putting Kennedy's overall relations with Faisal in question, not to mention my own.

The proposal already accepted by Egypt and being submitted to Saudi Arabia and the YAR called for the following:

1. Termination of all external support to the Yemeni royalists (meaning Saudi and Jordanian from the north, and British out of Aden in the south).

2. Phased withdrawal of Egyptian forces from the Yemen. (I at once recommended this be changed to "expeditious withdrawal." The final text added the word "expeditious," to read "expeditious and phased withdrawal," which did not help much.)

3. Withdrawal of Saudi and Jordanian forces from the vicinity of the Yemeni border (meaning concentrations near Jizan and Najran).

4. A public statement by the YAR reaffirming its intention to honor its international obligations, seek regularization of its relations with neighboring states, and concentrate on domestic matters.

If the above were accepted all around, the parties involved would act as follows:

1. The United States would announce its recognition of the YAR (contingent upon the acceptance of the rest of the package).

2. Egypt would issue a public statement of its willingness to undertake reciprocal disengagement and a phased withdrawal of troops from the Yemen when:

    a. The situation was therefore stabilized.

    b. Saudi and Jordanian forces were removed from the Yemeni frontier.

    c. Saudi and Jordanian support of the royalists ceased.

    d. The YAR, simultaneously, made the public announcement described in (4) above.

    e. The United States sent a separate presidential letter to Faisal affirming the US intention to support his efforts to carry out a program of internal reforms.

    f. The United States recognized the YAR (which would be conditioned on the complete cessation of further Egyptian military acts that could exacerbate the situation).

I was to carry the foregoing to Faisal with the option of his releasing the presidential letter for publication, if he so wished. I did so with foreboding, for the die had already been cast.

On November 17, I took the proposal, as slightly amended, to Deputy Foreign Minister Saqqaf with an advance copy of an explanatory letter by President Kennedy addressed to Faisal. While he read both, my colleague Isa Sabbagh brought to him an Arabic version he had edited. After reading both texts carefully, Saqqaf protested that Kennedy's recognition plan would be a victory for Nasser, as the proposal was very one-sided. It required the Saudis to stop all aid to the royalists in return for a declaration of intent by Nasser. It would therefore not be accepted. After Sabbagh left and we were alone, Saqqaf put on his "personal hat," as he described it, and told me that Faisal would be deeply shocked by the message but that it had one virtue: it would ultimately oblige Faisal to face facts. Saqqaf suggested that, in delivering the Kennedy letter to Faisal, I emphasize that

    • The US government firmly supports Saudi Arabia and Faisal's regime and finds YAR claims on southern Saudi territories, such as Najran and Jizan, inadmissible.

    • The Yemeni revolution is a fact and must be reckoned with.

    • Once the Egyptians were out of the Yemen, Saudi Arabia could have better ties with the YAR than would Egypt.

    • Deep involvement by the Saudi government in Yemeni affairs would seriously impede its own reforms and the fulfillment of Faisal's other promises to the Saudi people.

    • The imamate of the Yemen did not resemble the Saud family in any way.

    • The struggle to restore the imamate was not popular with Saudi citizens, nor with the people of Jordan, where an upset of King Hussein would be more dangerous to Saudi Arabia than the establishment of the YAR.

    • King Hussein had extended himself dangerously and was not a political asset to Faisal.

Saqqaf explained to me that Faisal had been opposed to a Saudi-Jordanian pact that had resulted from a proposal by Hussein to King Saud in Italy the previous summer. After Saud's return to Saudi Arabia, Hussein had sent a message that he would like to visit Saud, who had put on an act of disapproval before Faisal and asked Faisal, as the telegram was being read, what Hussein could have in mind. Before Faisal could reply, the king had answered his own question: "Maybe money." Finally, the king had said, "What can we do? Let him come." The result was a pact signed without real consultation with Faisal. Saud then set up direct radio contact with Hussein from the Riyadh palace and asked Hussein for technical aid, including a security team to check on the loyalty of Saudi officers and officials. This program involved some forty Jordanian "sleuths," which was disturbing to Saudis who were aware of it. The Jordanian detail of six Hawker Hunter aircraft to Ta'if, and later Najran, was also the direct result of a Saud call to Hussein.

A danger lay in Faisal's disappointing high popular expectations, Saqqaf continued. In October 1962, deeming the timing right for one reform that could have dramatic and favorable effect in the United States, the United Nations, and still-divided Arab circles outside his country, Faisal had proclaimed an end to slavery. It had been an embarrassment for many years to Saudis and to their now traditional role as defenders of the Islamic faith and its two holiest shrines, that Muslims, notably Africans, were held in bondage, even in these holy cities.[4] Faisal's move was astute, and it was prompt. President Kennedy received quiet credit among Saudi intellectuals, diplomats, and high officials. As for Faisal, it was one of his finest moments and greatly improved his international image, not only in Washington but also in the Arab East.

Now, the Egyptian Office of Information was spreading the story that Faisal would do nothing about reforms and development. As Saqqaf noted, most Saudis were indifferent about who ruled the Yemen; but thanks to the Saudi Monetary Agency's regular reports, they now knew where much of the country's money was going: hundreds of millions of riyals (each worth at that time about 40 US cents) that had been allocated to that year's unfulfilled development program were sitting in the agency, unspent.

Faisal had to set an example of progress and enlightenment, Saqqaf concluded, and therefore suggested that I urge him not to support outworn institutions. As I look back on this conversation, I feel considerable admiration and gratitude toward Saqqaf. One could not possibly have had a better advance briefing for a difficult session with an emotionally aroused ruler.[5]

President Kennedy had sent letters fairly identical in form to the involved heads of state, and each party—Saudi Arabia, Egypt, Jordan, and the Yemen Arab Republic—was informed that all the others were receiving the same proposal. A copy also went to the US embassy in London for the foreign secretary, Lord Home, with a note pointing out that the proposal included termination of any intervention in the Yemen by south Arabian tribal rulers. The US mission in New York was to inform the secretary-general of the United Nations, U Thant, or his under secretary, Ralph Bunche, of the general nature of the Kennedy proposal, to be held in confidence.[6]

On November 19 I met with Faisal and Saqqaf. The prince was very grave, having received a full briefing from Saqqaf. He read President Kennedy's letter and the proposal and, in an uncharacteristic display of anger and disappointment, slammed both down on the desk before him. He declared that the United States had been taken in by Nasser and had fallen for his program; Nasser would not fulfill his side of the bargain. The only way to get him to withdraw his forces from the Yemen was to insist that this be completed before termination of Saudi aid to the royalists, not after.

An argument then developed and went on vigorously for some time. I stressed that both Faisal and Nasser knew, from demonstrated US actions, our commitment to the integrity and stability of Saudi Arabia; it was a vital US interest. Also, Nasser knew that we had very recently sent six F-100s and a destroyer on a demonstration visit to Saudi Arabia. I used the material Saqqaf had provided (though toning down his references to King Hussein and to the monetary agency) and developed the thesis that the proposal was designed to help Faisal and definitely not to offer any help to the royalists, whose return to power would be of no advantage to anyone.[7] Gradually, Faisal calmed down, but he insisted that the package was unworkable unless Nasser saw that he must withdraw his forces before aid to the royalists would be stopped and before other forms of pressure on him by the United States had worked their effect.

The main difficulty Washington had with Faisal's formula was that Nasser clearly would not accept it. Nasser's pride and ego demanded a success. Preserving a Yemen Arab Republic closely linked with and guided by Egypt would help restore his predominance in the Arab world.

Nasser apparently saw Saudi Arabia as ripe for the picking (before Faisal's reforms could take hold). Likewise he saw Aden and south Arabia as possible entries into his orbit. However, some thought he could be dissuaded from precipitous action on these two Arab lands if British willingness to use armed resistance were made clear. The United States hoped to dissuade Nasser from attacking Saudi Arabia, for a start by offering to recognize the YAR and continue its economic assistance to the Yemen, while making it obvious by naval and air visits to Saudi Arabia (already promised by Kennedy to Faisal) that the independence and territorial integrity of the kingdom was a vital and long-established interest of the United States.

Faisal, for his part, felt that a resounding defeat of a power-driven Nasser in the Yemen was required for Saudi security and that only the royalists (whom he personally disliked) could have a chance of accomplishing this. He would take large security risks in opposing Nasser in this way, and he hoped the United States would protect his flank. He showed no intention of deploying his meager combat forces inside the Yemen, knowing the country as he did from personal military experience.

Protecting Saudi Arabia's intervention in the Yemen, as distinct from protecting Saudi Arabia's integrity and independence, was not seen by Washington as a US interest. That interest lay in Saudi stability and Faisal's reform measures, now barely begun, and in not seeing their success imperiled by expensive and dangerous foreign operations. One other factor apparently was weighed in Washington at this time. It was the degree of dynamism in Soviet Middle East policy. The Red Star seemed to be on the rise, and while it showed caution on the subject of Arab unity, it was politically allied with Nasser in preaching "scientific socialism." It was not a viable US policy to appear to embrace traditionalism in order to assure access to oil.

Just before I boarded the plane in Jeddah for Riyadh, on November 19, to deliver President Kennedy's proposal to Faisal, the former royalist minister of the Yemen to Saudi Arabia called on me in a last-ditch effort to affect US policy. Muhammad Ali al-Murfiq, a frank and likeable man who for more than a year had been a fountain of information for me on Yemeni tribal affairs, was obviously aware that official US opinion was not going his way. The royalist mission in exile was still active and, as yet, still officially recognized in Washington. Naturally, Murfiq urged the United States to lend assistance to the royalist forces, who he claimed were having success. They had cut the road from San'a to Hodaidah, and in the area between Taiz and San'a, royalists had control of the ancient fortress of Shihari. They had also seized al-Qaflah. In the south, they held al-Barq on the Taiz-Makha road.

The Yemen, Murfiq added with emphasis, had now learned its lesson and would never again seek a close relationship with the Eastern bloc. The United States would have the field to itself in providing economic assistance to the Yemen and could use Yemeni terrain for military bases, if it so desired. The implication that the United States had now earned the privilege of being the sole provider of economic aid to the Yemen showed that the royalists' mentality had not changed. Nonetheless, it was too late for a serious consideration of Murfiq's promises, hollow in any case. I passed on to Washington a full report for information.

FULL US INVOLVEMENT

Faisal's rejection of the first Kennedy package was not regarded as his last word. Kennedy's efforts were just getting started. Faisal, meanwhile, sought to gain a position of strength at home and abroad by publicly launching his own proposal for disengagement based on Egyptian troop withdrawal under international supervision. His wording was general, intended to put Saudi Arabia on the side of peace and nonintervention in Yemeni affairs while highlighting Egyptian intervention as a violation of international law. On November 19 at the United Nations, the US delegation held discussions with Under Secretary-General Ralph Bunche on the feasibility of a UN observer mission to supervise the withdrawal of all outside forces. Bunche took a positive view, but stated that the secretary-general would need specific authority, which could be explored in formal consultations with members of the Security Council. Financing would best be obtained from the countries directly involved. If much larger funds were needed than the parties could agree upon, however, the secretary-general would have to appeal the matter to the General Assembly. In the Yemen, Deputy Prime Minister Baydani, ostensibly speaking for Prime Minister Sallal, rejected the idea of UN observers to monitor Egyptian troop withdrawals.

By November 21 the White House had formalized, in consultation with the United Kingdom and Egypt, a public statement to be issued twelve to twenty-four hours after Egypt and the YAR had issued public communiqués reassuring to Saudi Arabia and to the United Kingdom. The draft text was intended as bait to Egypt and the YAR:

> The United States welcomes the declaration by the government of the Yemen Arab Republic that it will honor its international obligations, that it will seek normalization and the establishment of friendly relations with its neighbors and that it intends to concentrate on its domestic affairs. The United States Government also is gratified by the statesmanlike appeal of the Yemen Arab Republic to Yemenis in Aden and elsewhere in the Arabian Peninsula to be law-abiding citizens. Further, the United States Government welcomes the declaration by the United Arab Republic signifying its willingness to undertake a reciprocal disengagement and expeditiously phased removal of troops from the Yemen as external forces are removed from the frontier and as external support of the Yemen royalists is stopped. In believing that these declarations provide a basis for a solution to the conflict over the Yemen and in expressing the hope that all of the parties involved in the conflict will cooperate to that end and that the Yemeni peoples themselves be permitted to decide their own future, the United States has today decided to recognize the government of the Yemen Arab Republic and

to extend to that government its best wishes for success and prosperity. The United States has instructed its Chargé d'Affaires in the Yemen to confirm this decision in writing to the Ministry of Foreign Affairs of the Yemen Arab Republic.

In Cairo, the US embassy urged the Egyptian government to withdraw a battalion from the YAR at an early date, as a sign of goodwill toward the Kennedy proposal. On November 24 the United States sent a circular to its embassies in the Eastern Hemisphere instructing them what to inform their host governments: following on US approaches to Egypt, Saudi Arabia, Jordan, and the YAR, which were designed to obtain eventual disengagement in the Yemen, US recognition of the YAR in the near future was likely. On the same day, the Saudi ambassador to the United States was so notified. The royalist Yemeni chargé in Washington, Ahmad Zubara, was notified two days later. He took it quietly.

Shortly after these steps, the Egyptian government sought to make tendentious changes in its proposed declaration regarding the Yemen, to which Washington responded sharply, pronouncing the suggested text entirely unsatisfactory and reminding Cairo that the United States was in no hurry to recognize the YAR. Nasser quickly accepted a certain number of Washington's textual changes, but the Egyptian text was still not entirely acceptable to Washington. It was pointed out that satisfactory language was also being awaited from San'a and was a condition of US recognition of the YAR. The United States wanted San'a's declaration to include specific reference to Aden and to the southern federation of emirates in the proposed YAR public call on its Yemeni brothers to be good citizens. This US proviso was an assist desired by London's Foreign Office in its running contest of wills with the Colonial Office.

On December 18, 1962, Baydani issued the expected and approved communiqué to the press. His quick turnaround had been propelled by the ongoing YAR-royalist credentials fight in the UN Credentials Committee. A meeting of that body was scheduled for December 19, and a General Assembly plenary session was also about to convene that would decide who represented the Yemen. The agreed-upon Egyptian declaration immediately followed, whereupon that of the White House was issued the same day.

The beginning of 1963 saw no progress toward the goals set in President Kennedy's November proposals. Washington began to focus on a suitable intermediary and an associated observer team that could undertake what it now considered to be phase two of the developing crisis. Again it approached the United Nations for assistance and advice.

In Jeddah, I received for evaluation the following proposed steps:

1. Egypt was to be persuaded to quickly remove one military element

from the Yemen. This would imply a stop to reinforcements and to attacks on Saudi territory.

2. Faisal was to be persuaded to suspend, in return, all arms shipments to Najran.

3. An observer mission would be allowed to monitor compliance with (1) and (2); the mission would consist of ten Lebanese, Sudanese, and UN Emergency Force (UNEF) officers, the latter as senior members. The YAR government was to accept this team and permit it to travel freely, and the Saudi government was to be persuaded to admit the team to the Najran area.

I concurred in this program and recommended as intermediary and chief of observers Ambassador Pier P. Spinelli, whom I had met in Jeddah. An able and high-ranking Italian diplomat, Spinelli was an under secretary to UN secretary-general U Thant. US ambassador Macomber in Amman and Chargé Stookey in Taiz supported the choice of Spinelli. In mid-January the US diplomatic team at the UN approached U Thant regarding Spinelli as a possible intermediary and broached the concept of an observer team. An approach on the same lines was made by our diplomatic missions to Cairo, Jeddah, San'a, and Amman. The Saudi and Jordanian responses indicated readiness to discuss the problem with Spinelli, but Faisal was not in accord with the American program.

A continuation of Egyptian attacks on Saudi territory stirred Washington to reassure Faisal of US general support—making a show of US military strength and White House concern—and to seek at the same time a pledge of disengagement from Faisal. To demonstrate US concern and military strength, Washington would hold special exercises with Saudi military participation and deploy a US air squadron, which would be immediately withdrawn, however, if the Royal Saudi Air Force should attack the YAR. Such deployment would be conditional on the cessation of Saudi flights, with mercenary pilots, to transport arms to the royalists. Washington by now saw Faisal as trying to use its support as a protective shield behind which he could support the royalists against Nasser. Meanwhile, owing to difficulties in prying Spinelli loose from the secretary-general's office, another figure had volunteered his intermediation, James Terry Duce.

A retired vice president of ARAMCO, Duce had been something of a "secretary of state" for the company over a span of two decades. He had volunteered his services as a troubleshooter to Secretary of State Rusk through an old friend, George C. McGhee, then under secretary of state for political affairs. Rusk had telegraphed me instructions regarding Duce's mission, and he arrived in Jeddah with his wife, Ivy, around February 3, 1963. His cover story was that he had come to help members of the Saudi government, with some of whom, including Faisal, he enjoyed warm friendships. He would be proffering advice on economic development, notably in the field of geology and mineral exploitation. In reality he was there to attempt to deflect Faisal from his preoccupation with the Yemeni question toward practical developmental concerns.

Duce and I were old associates from my Dhahran years. I gave him a comprehensive briefing, plus the hospitality of the residence, and sent him on his way on February 4 to Riyadh for a private meeting we had set up for him with Faisal. I also asked our consul general in Dhahran, John E. Horner, and Colonel W. W. Wilson, chief of the USMTM, to cooperate in providing him coded communication facilities. Nothing came of Duce's mission, which in any case was limited to informal contacts with the ruling family and could not carry the same weight as the awaited shuttle services of a UN envoy. It was a good try, however, as his telegrams showed.

Washington now instructed me to reiterate to Faisal its offer of visits by combat aircraft to the kingdom in exchange for the suspension of Saudi support to the royalists. Washington reaffirmed to Cairo its strong opposition to Egyptian border violations of Saudi Arabia, but to Faisal called attention to the provocation created by Saudi aid to the royalists. We were getting nowhere, but at least we were no longer insisting on the one-sided formula of demanding from Faisal a *permanent* ending of aid to royalists in return for, at best, a token withdrawal of one Egyptian military unit of undetermined size. We talked of the "expeditiously phased," but not necessarily complete, withdrawal. We were edging toward more even-handedness, as Washington's alarm deepened.

In general, at the end of 1962 the royalist forces appeared thin on the ground but were receiving sizeable arms shipments from Saudi Arabia and were likely to make themselves felt in the weeks or months ahead. The YAR forces, as such, were of even less importance, dependent entirely on Egyptian forces now gathering strength from sizeable reinforcements. The risk of open warfare on the Yemen's northern border had been heightened by Egypt's bombing and shelling of Saudi coastal villages. Thus, the armed struggle over the Yemen's political future had begun to have a momentum of its own. Inflammatory speeches proliferated on Cairo and San'a radios. Egyptian air strikes on Najran began on January 7, 1963, the first of many more to come.

EGYPTIAN BOMBINGS

An escalation of violence by Egypt against Saudi Arabia occurred in February 1963, in one instance with dramatic personal consequences for me. William Roe Polk, a Harvard scholar in Arabic and Middle Eastern studies and a member of the State Department Policy Planning Staff, arrived in Jeddah on February 10 on an official visit of reconnaissance. I took him on February 11 to call upon Faisal, to whom he expressed a desire to make an overnight visit to Najran, site of a supply depot for Saudi aid to the Yemeni royalists that had been the target of the January 7 Egyptian bombing. Najran lay in a plain just north of Yemeni mountain ranges then largely under royalist control. I indicated that I would accompany Polk, and asked Faisal's permission to use a USMTM aircraft. Faisal agreed at once and offered to facilitate our further entry into the royalist-held area of the Yemen for interviews with Imam Badr and Prince Hasan. This we politely declined, because it would have put the US government in a potentially awkward posture; we had broken relations with the imamate when we recognized the YAR two months earlier. Faisal did not press his offer.

Noting that hostile aircraft had overflown Najran during recent days, Faisal expressed the hope that there would be no trouble. A landing area closed following the attack of January 7 had just reopened. He would notify Emir Sultan ibn Abd al-Aziz, minister of defense and civil aviation, of our plans.[8] Sultan sent a telegram to Najran, addressed presumably to Emir Khalid al-Sudairi, politico-security chief for the area throughout the Yemeni crisis.

Because this trip had been contemplated by Polk in advance of his arrival, the Pentagon's consent had been obtained for use of a C-47, and the State Department had voiced no objection to our going. The "old workhorse" of World War II could land almost anywhere. An American pilot, Robert E. Ahearn, was found who knew the landing area, in the Wadi Najran, eight miles north of the Yemeni border. It was quite unmarked and consisted of a soft-sand plain with a few palms, no dragged strip, and no windsock. The site was a depot for airborne supplies normally offloaded at Khamis Mushayt, a good American-built airfield about 100 miles farther to the northwest, from which trucks now moved south with supplies for the royalists.

I took the precaution of notifying Ambassador Badeau in Cairo of our exact plans, so that he could pass word to the Egyptian government that an American military plane would carry official passengers to an area that was part of undisputed Saudi territory. Since Nasser knew any attack on Saudi territory would be regarded seriously by the United States, I felt that the expedition was not likely to encounter warfare. I was quite mistaken.

Our plane carried prominent USMTM markings with an orange nose and wing tips. The party aboard consisted of Polk and myself, Consul General Horner, USMTM chief Colonel Wilson, and other USMTM officers.[9] We took off from Riyadh about noon on February 12 and landed without problems about three hours later. We were met by an impressive young graduate of an American university who spoke flawless English and was a son of Khalid al-Sudairi. Four of us—Polk, Horner, Wilson, and I—were driven to the small government guest house in Najran village, where we rested until sundown (it was Ramadan, thus fasting was obligatory from the predawn hour). The remainder of the party slept beside the plane, partially hidden under palms.

After the sunset gun had signaled prayers, to be followed by the *iftar*—the meal permitted at that time—we all had a sumptuous picnic supper at a hillside camp, hosted by Emir Khalid and attended by the emir of Najran and other Saudi dignitaries. Except for the fire itself, no lights betrayed our location to aircraft or dimmed the intense glory of the stars. The evening was most pleasant, and we learned something of local conditions from Khalid. Polk's Arabic was excellent and important to the establishment of rapport. He brought out some old poetry that evoked recitations from Khalid, and reinforced my long-held conviction that, in the Arab world, a foreigner's facility in vocabulary and appreciation of Arab literature are of inestimable importance in opening the doors of friendship and information. There was no disguising that this was a working supply center for the royalists.

The predawn cannon signaling first-light prayers and breakfast broke our sleep, and not long thereafter we received an Egyptian visit. At 7:15 A.M. on February 13, in perfectly clear weather, three or four TU-16 bombers, coming from the southeast, bombed the Najran area for approximately thirty minutes. The Saudis at once opened fire. The bombing was random but seemed to be directed at the small resupply and cantonment area in ravines and foothills northeast of Najran village. No one on the ground was hit, and no property damage was noted or reported at that time.

Wilson, the senior military officer in our party and chiefly responsible for the safety of aircraft and crew, believed that the Egyptian bombers would soon be back and could attack his plane and crew. We therefore made our thanks for hospitality to the emir of Najran and through him to Emir Khalid and took off, heading for Jeddah and writing up our report on the way. Wilson's appraisals were given special attention. An expert from World War II, he had participated in the bombing of Tokyo in 1945.

Polk and I made a courtesy call on Faisal on February 14. The prince had received a report of the incident and expressed gratification that no one was hurt, but asked what the United States was going to do about this situation. We knew that Faisal had "kept his arms folded"—an expression he was to use with irony many times in 1963. Saudi Arabia could have obtained planes and hired mercenaries to retaliate, he said, but refrained from so doing, instead deciding to consult the United States, "our friend." What would the Saudi people think if he continued to do nothing?

Faisal then launched into a condemnation of Nasser, whom he described as once a close friend whom Saudi Arabia had propped up when he was down, even giving him access to a Swiss bank account. During the 1956 crisis at Suez, the Saudis had lost $50 million because of the closure of the canal. Nasser had access to Saudi oil and money, and now what did he want? To crush Saudi Arabia. Faisal asked if we believed we could guide him into being reasonable; he thought sheer force was what was needed. According to Faisal, Nasser expected to discredit the Saudi government with the Saudi people. He lamented that we had not seen rallies of the population at Riyadh and Mina.

In a message to the US embassy in Cairo, State *suggested* it approach Cairo governor Salah Dessouqi, who was friendly to Americans and thought to be close to Nasser. The embassy was to note that the Egyptian government knew well the US attitude toward cross-border attacks on Saudi Arabia and, since Dessouqi had personally known of Polk's visit to Saudi Arabia and his plans to visit Najran, that the US government wondered whether the coincidence in timing of the bombing meant that the Egyptian government was trying to prove some point. The US government would appreciate hearing from Dessouqi about this, especially since Polk's presence in the area was partly the result of Dessouqi's assiduous initiatives to establish contact with Americans who were influential in improving relations. Meanwhile, a corrective report from Najran came in to Faisal who passed it on to Polk. On February 13, after our departure from Najran, two Arabs were killed and two wounded, one seriously, in an afternoon followup raid. The target had been a palm grove assumed to harbor Saudi military personnel.

Dessouqi reacted without a sign of contrition, telling the US embassy officer that the air raid had good and bad aspects: bad if Polk and Hart had been hurt, good when it was considered that their visit to Najran showed what the Saudi government was up to, and how Egypt had to react, since Egyptians were dying as the result of Faisal's arms supply to the royalists. Nothing further was said by Washington to Cairo on the matter of Polk's and my presence in Najran, nor was there any word of congratulations on our survival.

NASSER'S AIR DROP

Of far greater importance on the politico-military scene and a catalyst to more vigorous diplomacy by Washington was the Egyptian air drop on the Hejazi coast three days after Polk's and my trip to Najran. Alone in my Jeddah office early February 16, I was sought out on an urgent basis by a junior US Air Force officer. He had just landed from an F-86 training flight with a Saudi student pilot. On the coastal plain some distance northwest of Jeddah, they had sighted a large yellow object on the sand and swooped low to identify it. It was a parachute attached to a large packing case. Alongside of it were two trucks onto which the drivers were attempting to load one of the parachuted bundles. Seeing the aircraft circling overhead, they abandoned their efforts abruptly, mounted their vehicles, and drove quickly away.

With their interest much aroused, the American officer and his student began to look further. There was no place to land on the neighboring terrain. A bit farther up the coast more yellow bundles were sighted, and the pilot then tracked down and counted several more before reporting by radio to headquarters. Joined by other aircraft, they found similar chutes and bundles scattered 100 miles up the coast from Rabigh to Yanbu al-Bahr. They signaled headquarters and returned to land at Jeddah, where the Saudi student made his report to superiors and my informant reported to me. He and his companions had counted a total of 108 parachutes and bundles. There were later found to be 11 more.

Quickly, the authorities sent out teams to find and collect the bundles. They encountered no individuals attempting to remove them. On the contrary, wandering Bedouins were reporting their presence to local police stations, a practice they had carefully observed for decades since the Saud clan came to power in 1925. Under the "peace of King Abd al-Aziz," theft carried Islamic punishments of the heavyhanded Hanbalite school. Picking up and appropriating something you might find in the great desert was construed as theft, and punishment was drastic and brutal. The standing injunction against such appropriation had translated into a universal habit.

The 119 bundles, once assembled in Jeddah at the *gishla* (a quadrangle barracks adjacent to what used to be the northern gate, known as the Bab al-Khamis), were found to weigh twenty tons. They consisted of Belgian heavy automatic rifles, British hand grenades, .30-caliber American ammunition, and mortars with ammunition. They were ready to be used at once. The parachutes and packing were of Egyptian style. Though their provenance was mixed, the style of Arabic writing on tags convinced Saudi inspectors that they were from Egyptian stocks at Suez. The lot had come from abundant canal stores left behind by British forces when they evacuated the canal area and its huge complex of warehouses in June 1956. Our military attaché and USMTM personnel estimated the drop would supply a 1,000-man force.

Three aspects were especially significant: (1) The drop appeared to be intended for trained military personnel on the ground who were friendly to the conspirators who had prepared it. (2) The drop was amateurish in the extreme.[10] (3) The drop preceded by only a day or two an assembly of the top Saudi leadership in Jeddah. I do not recall the purpose of their assembly, but it was probably to consider, along with the Yemen, some major organizational questions under study by Faisal. In any case, the presumption was that Nasser had received intelligence of the impending assembly of Faisal and his top command and had decided that now was the time, with his Saudi followers well armed, to accomplish a clean sweep.

The press and radio of Cairo, so far as I could determine, ignored the event completely. The diplomatic corps of Jeddah, then numbering in the fifties, was invited on February 20 to the *gishla* to inspect the opened bundles; the Saudi press was there to photograph and solicit comments. Particularly sought were remarks incriminating Egypt and denouncing Nasser's evil intentions. While avoiding this kind of comment, I sought to elicit the clearest of reasons for confirming Egyptian as against other origin. The next day *al-Bilad*, the principal Saudi daily, carried front-page pictures and much commentary, but the event seems to have attracted almost no press or radio attention in the rest of the Arab world or beyond. The Saudi military leadership, fearing further defection and an air attack by its own pilots, temporarily forbade instruction in shooting from air-craft. The fears were no doubt exaggerated, but the leadership felt isolated and alone in an indifferent world.

When Nasser learned how botched the air drop had been, he was reportedly furious and swore that his men would do better "next time." The episode demonstrated that Nasser, for all his charisma, had little notion of Saudi society and how it worked. There was little real support in the Saudi public for Egyptian revolutionary aspirations or for an integrated Arab state under Nasser's or any other foreign direction. Arab unity programs, in the estimation of Saudi Arabs, meant foreign control over a magnificent Saudi energy resource. This deposit of oil, as the Saudis saw it, had been awarded by Allah to a destitute Bedouin popula-tion. It was not to be handed over to or seized by others, but Saudi leadership could be generous in sharing its revenues, on its own terms, in the revered name of Arabism.[11]

The Egyptian paradrop and its obviously hostile intent solidified loy-alty to Faisal and his regime. Nasser's action was an expression of su-preme contempt, bringing a halt to what had been widespread, favorable public commentary, heard in business and some army circles in Saudi Arabia, contrasting Egypt's revolutionary discipline with King Saud's disorganization, corruption, and wasteful extravagance. Suddenly there was a pride of nationhood, of genuine Arab identity, and of recognition that Faisal was their hard-working leader who deserved their support.

Later indications that came to me suggested, but did not assert, that a small group of Saudi officers would have conspired to overthrow the Saud clan, if conditions had been right and if the United States had been willing to back or condone their cover. However, US support was clearly and openly for Faisal and for his reforms and development plans. Even in the worst period of King Saud's misgovernment, we did not condone and, in my opinion, would never have condoned any foreign takeover, especially a pro-Soviet Egyptian one, directly or indirectly. This position had been made clear to the Saudi leadership by every president from 1943 on.

The paradrop and further bombings in the area north of the Yemen border—Jizan on February 27 and Khamis Mushayt on March 1—resulted in my seeking a review with Washington of US policies and actions. I made the recommendation that, if we were not writing off Faisal in favor of avoiding confrontation with Nasser, we should reaffirm our support for Faisal and openly recognize the affirmative values of his regime. We should also recognize that a Nasser-provoked revolution in Saudi Arabia, if it occurred, would shatter the body politic of that country without any reason for confidence over the outcome.

I suggested, therefore, that, as earlier proposed by Washington, we consider sending a squadron of US fighter aircraft to Saudi Arabia as soon as possible, but with more of a mission than a brief demonstration of concern. It would be authorized to shoot down any intruding military aircraft clearly identified as behaving in a hostile manner in Saudi airspace. Nasser would not be officially informed by us in advance of this mission, but he would be left to learn about it from his own men. If having learned of it he nonetheless followed up with bombers against Saudi targets, his aircraft would be attacked by us while in Saudi airspace. Citing the 1958 US Marine Corps landings in Lebanon—I had been consul general with the personal rank of minister in Damascus at the time, monitoring Nasser's promotion of a civil war to overthrow Lebanese president Camille Chamoun—I pointed out the calming effect the landings had had on Syria and on the area as a whole, even dampening Nasser's headlong outreach for hegemony. I believed that Nasser would not break with the United States, because US ties with Egypt were critical to the equilibrium of his policy of "positive neutralism." Unless we were demonstrably willing to risk the possibility of a break with Nasser, however, I felt we would not be able to stop him from trying to use the Yemen as a stepping stone to the control of Saudi Arabia. At the same time, I proposed that we make clear that if Faisal failed to end his arms aid to the royalists, we would have to review our security relationship with him. At the time, neither Nasser nor Faisal had a firm basis for believing that the United States would make good on President Kennedy's 1962 pledge to Faisal. It had not been fully put to the test.

In reply to my suggestions, Washington indicated a firm intent not to provide air cover for Faisal should he continue and even augment his supply of arms and ammunition to the royalists. To provide such air cover would negate any leverage for disengagement. The Joint Chiefs of Staff asked for a special meeting with Assistant Secretary Phillips Talbot to discuss the military aspects of US policy toward Saudi Arabia, Egypt, and the YAR in light of my message and the possible use of deterrent force. From our embassy in Cairo, Ambassador Badeau entered the Washington discussions with carefully thought out arguments, partly at variance, partly consistent with my own. We were never far apart.

Meanwhile, President Kennedy became more and more personally involved in the problem as his interest in details and strategy grew. From my two personal calls on Kennedy regarding Saudi Arabia and our policy toward Faisal, I can testify to the strength of that interest, at the expense of many other weighty claims on his time. As 1963 wore on, this fascination did not lessen, despite scant attention given to it in the US media. I had the unique experience throughout the last year of Kennedy's life of receiving in Jeddah, time and again, direct instructions from the president, Secretary of State Rusk being "copied for information," aimed at maintaining his unfiltered personal relationship with Faisal.

In view of the sensitivity of all such messages, especially as they were to be put into Arabic, I kept Isa Sabbagh very busy at many hours of day and night applying his bilingual skills and elegant command of Arabic presentation. Each message had to hit the right tone not only for Faisal, with his special sensitivity and pride, but also for his royal advisors and aides, not all of whom, excepting Saqqaf, could be expected to read the president's messages with full understanding of the English-language nuances. These, therefore, had to be matched with nuances in Arabic, like English a language of extraordinary richness and breadth. Above all, to get favorable reactions, the message had to start on a very friendly personal tone. Where there was agreement, the level of relationship had to evoke gratification. Where there was disagreement, the tone had to be reasonable, respectful, egalitarian (above all no "talking down"), and clear.

We had these principles on our desks and in our minds, and they were tested again and again. Messages that often needed something of a small style change would arrive from Washington at two or three o'clock in the morning—the time difference between Washington and Jeddah was eight hours—and I would at once go over them for substance, then for manner of address. Always the incoming message bore the president's imprimatur and always it said, "Please pass, unless you see objection, the following to Faisal." Generally my recommendations for modification were not of substance and called for no radical changes. Though I know they irritated some of Kennedy's close advisors, my suggestions were usually accepted without material change. As a result, I was able to proceed in the knowledge that the president and I were in touch and that I had his apparent confidence and backing.[12]

Kennedy had gauged Faisal well when he met him and knew him for an intelligent, proud, and hard-working leader who was the best hope of Saudi Arabia in those days of tension and violence. Kennedy's continuing personal interest and receptivity also helped speed up our action in an accelerating political environment.

PART FOUR

VIOLENCE AND MEDIATION

7

THE 1963 BUNKER MISSION AND BEYOND

 The events in Najran and on the Hejazi coast described in the previous chapter were a turning point in US policy in the growing Egyptian-Saudi confrontation. The need for strong action was now clear, and President Kennedy grasped the helm firmly, with close attention to detail and to his relations with U Thant, Faisal, and Nasser. Kennedy's policy was to buy time for Faisal and his reforms, first by extricating him from the quicksand of the Yemen, making clear that he would support him and his government, if necessary, by a US military presence. If need be, the United States would repel aggression. However, this kind of guarantee was not to be exploited as a cover for further Saudi aid to the royalists: if it was protection of the integrity of Saudi Arabia and its regime against aggression that Faisal desired, he would have it; but reinstating the Yemeni royalists was not a US objective. As noted earlier, the proffered military presence, if so exploited, would be withdrawn, even if air attacks by Egypt continued thereafter. Had an attempt been made to take over the country and overthrow its government, I personally believe Kennedy would have intervened by force; but this was not the kind of policy to be spelled out in advance or for wide consumption. It was strongly implied.

Nasser was therefore to be made keenly aware that while the United States desired good relations with Egypt, a firm US objective in the area was to support the independence and integrity of Saudi Arabia, and especially (but not exclusively) the leadership of Faisal. Should that be threatened, the United States would react. As time went by, it was to be put to Nasser more bluntly that if he pursued a collision course with the United States, he could not win.

In applying these principles to fast-moving events, troublesome loopholes were at once apparent. Both Nasser and Faisal had already proclaimed separately and in principle their willingness to disengage, if it was a mutual course and carried out in good faith. Bad faith, however, was openly expected by both sides. There was a clash of strong wills and of fundamental objectives.

PREPARATIONS FOR MEDIATION

On January 8, 1963, the White House had released the text of a November 8, 1962, letter from President Kennedy to Prince Faisal giving assurances of US support for the integrity of Saudi Arabia in the context of Faisal's reform program. A day earlier, on January 7, Faisal on his own volition had reinforced the US assurance by proclaiming, over Radio Mecca, Saudi willingness to see the dispute over Yemen resolved in the following way:

1. All foreign armed military forces of any kind were to be withdrawn from the Yemen. (Faisal asserted there were no Saudi forces in the Yemen fighting alongside of Muhammad al-Badr's armies.)

2. After such withdrawals were completed, there would be a cessation of all direct or indirect intervention from the two disputants (Egypt and Saudi Arabia).

3. The Yemenis would be left to decide their own fate and to choose whatever form of government they wished, provided that a neutral international committee was appointed to execute and supervise steps of implementation to avoid a general killing by Arab weapons of mass destruction. (This could have been intended to worry Nasser regarding Faisal's access to such weaponry. So far as I knew, Faisal had none.)

Also in January 1963, the UN Secretariat had become the scene of preparations for mediation. Several able candidates were under active consideration by Secretary-General U Thant for a role under his direct auspices: Ralph Bunche, an under secretary of the United Nations, whose work on Palestine armistice talks in 1948–1949 and in the Congo, all of high quality, had nonetheless somewhat antagonized the Egyptian leadership; Andrew Cordier, the late secretary-general Dag Hammarskjöld's flexible and discreet American executive assistant; Eugene Black, who was favored in Egypt, where he was credited with helping to reopen the Suez Canal after the 1956 war; and UN Under Secretary Pier Spinelli, mentioned earlier.

U Thant preferred Bunche for this type of mission but only with a limited mandate to listen and record, subject to U Thant's review, and perhaps later to mediate. The United States also favored Bunche. The secretary-general was particularly worried about the attitude of Soviet deputy permanent representative to the United Nations Nikolai Trofi-movich Fedorenko, who was determined that no steps be taken by the secretary in the field of conciliation and solution of threats to the peace without reference to the UN Security Council, where he had a veto. U Thant had many arguments with Fedorenko, trying to protect his stand-ing mandate to further the peacemaking role of the United Nations, and he tended to be circumspect regarding this clash of prerogatives over the division of peacekeeping duties as set forth in the UN Charter.

Faisal also had problems with the UN machinery, mainly in communi-cation. He had managed in 1962 to send on "vacation" the headstrong Saudi UN permanent representative, Ahmad Shukairi. Under King Saud, Shukairi had been accustomed to largely having his own way in represent-ing Saudi positions before the United Nations. These were consistently anti-British (Saud had broken relations with Britain over the 1956 Suez War) and highly critical of US policy on matters relating to Palestine and Israel. Representations by Shukairi on these matters were part of his standing duties, but the language he used was fiery and often extreme. Faisal replaced him on an acting basis with a venerable family retainer, Jamil Baroody, a man totally devoted to Faisal. Baroody, however, was not as close to a full understanding of Faisal's policy problems as was needed if he was to advise him adequately. He and Deputy Foreign Minister Saqqaf by no means saw eye-to-eye, and Saqqaf complained to me about Baroody's interference, his literal-mindedness, and his preconceived notions of what Faisal required.

An invitation by Faisal to U Thant to send Bunche to Saudi Arabia for consultation on the Yemen crisis was required to start the process. To resolve problems of protocol, Saqqaf managed to get Faisal's approval to dispatch as special emissary to New York the royal counselor and "father" of the Arab League, Egyptian-born Abd al-Rahman Azzam. Of vast experience and seniority, Azzam was sympathetic to Saqqaf's gener-al pragmatism and approach to ending Saudi involvement in the Yemen. He was careful not to appear to replace Baroody, and his presence in New York was only temporary.

The core of the problem lay in Baroody's advice, accepted by Faisal, that since Bunche was to visit not only Saudi Arabia but also the YAR, he should visit the royalist leadership. This could be arranged by way of the Saudi northern frontier. U Thant could not accept this, as such a move would place the United Nations in an untenable position. The world organization had endorsed and accepted the new Yemen Arab Republic after a long credentials fight in the General Assembly. Saqqaf was able to persuade Faisal to convert the requirement of a visit to the royalists into a recommendation, but U Thant demanded a simple and unconditional invitation. A third invitation was therefore to be drafted. This might have resulted in Bunche being clearly and unconditionally invited to visit Faisal in Saudi Arabia except that Faisal felt he had already said enough to enable Bunche to come. U Thant, in any case, found Faisal's amended language still ambiguous.

U Thant became persuaded that the three disputant heads of state, Faisal, Nasser, and Sallal, should be invited together to a "summit" in a European or other disinterested setting. He favored Rome and pushed for acceptance. This was a nonstarter. Faisal, having been vilified by Nasser's radio, and his kingdom repeatedly attacked by bombers, was in no frame of mind to sit with Nasser, and in any case would not recognize Sallal. Nor would Nasser's ambassador to the United Nations, Mahmoud Riad, sit with an Arab "feudalist." Valuable time was wasted convincing U Thant that his summit project was ill-timed. President Kennedy now concluded that it was up to him to speed up disengagement under neutral observers, as the procedural snarls in the UN Secretariat were not quickly resolvable. He felt he must send a representative to prepare the way for, but not replace, a UN mediator.

ENTER ELLSWORTH BUNKER

Ellsworth Bunker was a business leader turned diplomat. He served as US ambassador to Argentina, Italy, India, and Nepal, and had been a successful mediator in the West New Guinea/West Irian dispute between Indonesia and The Netherlands.[1] He had demonstrably outgrown party influences during fifteen years of extraordinary dedication to public service in a succession of political appointments. U Thant liked and respected him, as did Republican and Democratic party leaders.

In approaching the Yemen situation, Bunker would be responsible to President Kennedy alone and thus not hampered by the UN Secretariat's internal politics. However, he would attempt to facilitate U Thant's efforts in the Yemen-Saudi-Egyptian crisis and, specifically, to promote a visit by Bunche, who was to follow him shortly as mediator, once Bunker had obtained unconditional acceptance for his visit in Riyadh and Cairo. Bunker would therefore "write the script," going as far as he could. If he could make progress on a set of terms acceptable enough to help Bunche, then he was free to do so. He was not bound to refer such questions to U Thant, but he would make reports to him at the end of each trip and would attempt to elicit pledges of disengagement under UN auspices by each of the contesting parties.

Kennedy had decided by February 5 to send Bunker first to Saudi Arabia and then to Egypt, but to avoid offending U Thant he had to wait until early March for the secretary-general to discard his "summit" proposal. Kennedy received Bunker on the eve of his departure for Jeddah and Riyadh and gave him final instructions. A special channel of communication was set up ensuring unimpeded, direct access to the president. Secretary of State Dean Rusk was to be kept informed but was not to issue major instructions; these were the prerogative of the president. The White House approved Middle East expert Talcott Seelye as an aide to accompany Bunker. Faisal promptly agreed to receive the Bunker mission, without conditions.

THE FIRST ROUND, MARCH 6–8, 1963

The opening session of the Bunker mission was held on March 6 in Dammam and was attended by Faisal, Saqqaf, Bunker, Isa Sabbagh (as interpreter), and myself. Bunker, with his courtly dignity and innate kindness, obviously pleased Faisal. The atmosphere was relaxed, unhurried, businesslike. Bunker presented a cordial personal letter from President Kennedy, translated into Arabic, which Faisal accepted with obvious gratification. It emphasized US support for Faisal and his reforms and US willingness to be of assistance in resolving the current problem, Kennedy's confidence in Bunker, and his positive view of US-Saudi relations. The president had instructed Bunker to present to Faisal a summary of his views.

Bunker began his remarks by emphasizing US readiness to help the Saudi government. He then stressed that aid to the royalists created a problem since it would make the United States an accomplice against a government (the YAR) that the United States had now recognized. The United States felt that it was possible to negotiate a start of Egyptian troop withdrawals simultaneous with a suspension of Saudi aid to the royalists. This would offer an honorable method of disengagement, the modalities of which could be worked out with UN representative Bunche, if the Saudi government agreed to extend an invitation to him, as Bunker strongly recommended. Neutral observers on the Yemeni border could verify when supplies were suspended, and troop withdrawals would at once begin. Bunker presented Faisal with a summary of his presentation in the form of eight points,[2] as follows, and it was agreed that talks on them would be resumed the next evening, March 7:

1. Agreement by the Saudi government to suspend aid to the royalists.

2. Agreement by Egypt to begin withdrawals simultaneously with suspension of aid to the royalists.

3. Agreement to station neutral observers in the Najran-Jizan area and at Hodaidah and YAR airports to certify the outward movement of Egyptian forces and equipment and the suspension of aid to the royalists.

4. Cooperation of the Saudi government with representatives of the secretary-general of the United Nations to reach agreement on the modalities of the foregoing steps and, through the secretary-general, with Egypt and the YAR. (Faisal interjected that he wanted nothing to do with the YAR, only with Egypt.)

5. Prevention by the Saudi government of efforts by the adherents of the Yemeni imam (Badr) to continue support from Saudi territory.

6. Implementation of the Egyptian pledge to remove troops and a public restatement of its determination to withdraw.

7. US military support to the Saudi government to deter attacks on Saudi Arabia and, if necessary, to shoot down intruding hostile aircraft. The United States would expedite the training of Saudi air force and air defense personnel.

8. Encouragement of moderation by the YAR (in its public pronouncements) and concentration by it on domestic affairs.

There was but one note of discord in an otherwise calm, reflective, and very friendly evening. In the course of reaffirming US support for Faisal's program of reforms and development, Bunker was attempting to put that support in the context of Kennedy's expectation that these reforms would be carried out. Unfortunately, he used the words "on the condition" that they be carried out. Faisal froze as Sabbagh used the Arabic *shart*. It was an entirely correct translation, but it carried the potentially explosive Arabic overtones of an ultimatum. Faisal declared this language was entirely unacceptable, and it looked as though the meeting was about to end. Saqqaf and I looked at each other, then Saqqaf said "ishtibak al-kalimah" (confusion of words). I waded in and said "on the condition that" in English carried less objectionable connotations than in Arabic, and really could be better construed as meaning "on the basis" or "on the understanding that." Bunker kept his silence as the semantic discussion proceeded. Sabbagh at first saw the implication developing that he had mistranslated. It was an offense against his outstanding command of both languages. He started to rise to defend his terminology. I put a hand on his arm. Faisal seemed to relax when Bunker then rephrased his remarks to use the more benign words "on the basis of," which evoked the Arabic *ala assass*.[3] The meeting was adjourned until the next evening, and Bunker left Sabbagh's summary in Arabic of his eight points with Faisal.

Day two of Bunker's mission was spent in reporting to Washington on day one and preparing for the evening session. Saqqaf summoned me in the afternoon to a private meeting in the home of one of his friends in al-Khobar, a port city of Dhahran. Saqqaf urged that in the coming session Bunker focus on his eight points and start his presentation with a statement that US support of Saudi Arabia was beyond question; that what the United States wanted was to advise the Saudi government, as a friend, on how to get the Yemeni problem off dead center; that we drop discussion of "conditions" and go down the eight points one by one, emphasizing that the dispute was between Cairo and Riyadh, not San'a and Riyadh. Saqqaf told me that he had warned Faisal that the Saudi government was totally isolated internationally in its position regarding the Yemen. It could, possibly, turn to the French for planes, pilots, and arms—the French would help in order to get revenge on Nasser for the 1956 debacle[4]—but France would not be a reliable friend and would pursue its own interests.

Faisal opened the evening session by saying that he accepted, in principle, the suspension of aid to the royalists, provided that he was assured that Egypt would indeed leave the Yemen. He therefore asked consideration of six points:

1. Egypt should stop all of its raids and other forms of aggression on Saudi territory, by air and sea.

2. Once a simultaneous disengagement was agreed upon, Egyptian forces should cease all military activities in the Yemen.

3. Egyptian forces were to return from field activities to bases in the Yemen, pending withdrawal under supervision of neutral observers.

4. Egyptian forces should then withdraw officers and men with all equipment they had introduced into the Yemen, such as tanks, planes, etc.

5. On agreement over these points, the Saudi government would order the cessation of all aid to the royalists.

6. There had to be a time limit for the withdrawal of all foreign forces from the Yemen.

Bunker responded that the foregoing points by Faisal should be addressed to the mediator (Bunche) for his action. Faisal then referred to President Kennedy's seventh point regarding US military support to deter attacks on Saudi Arabia and to expedite training of Saudi air force and air defense personnel. He asked for elucidation of the term "military support," particularly if Nasser's planes attacked before a disengagement was realized. Bunker replied that the president had already made strong representations to Nasser. This pleased Faisal, who then pleased his American guests by saying that he agreed "one thousand percent" with President Kennedy's message.

With the conclusion of this session, Bunker was ready to return to Washington and then to New York, to report to Kennedy and U Thant. Before closing the session, however, Faisal suddenly asked for US assistance in establishing television in Saudi Arabia. He wanted a television station for Riyadh and for the Western Province,[5] and he wanted to avoid importunities and arguments from Saudi business rivals by being able to say, "The American government is building this facility." I undertook to submit the request at once to Washington.

Bunker reported to President Kennedy and learned that to maintain the momentum of his first two meetings with Faisal he should be ready to return to Saudi Arabia if Ralph Bunche was not mandated to be mediator. Bunche had been in Cairo on March 7 on a fact-finding mission, following a visit to San'a. U Thant on March 4 had asked Adlai Stevenson, US ambassador to the United Nations, to suggest that Bunker urge upon Faisal a clear invitation that Bunche come to Riyadh. Although Bunche was ready and waiting in Cairo, nothing came of this, again largely due to fastidious attention to protocol by both U Thant and Saudi ambassador Baroody. U Thant received Bunker's report of his trip without apparent objection, including the various points put forth by Kennedy and by Faisal. Without prospect of an invitation to Bunche, U Thant took no exception to a return of Bunker to the area, this time to meet also with Nasser.

ROUND ONE IN ITS INTERNATIONAL SETTING

Before Bunker's first trip to see Faisal, Nasser's air forces had conducted several attacks on Saudi Arabian targets. On February 28, a bombing took place of Khamis Mushayt city and airport, which had become the major assembly point, recently moved from Jizan, for ground shipments to the royalists via Najran. On March 1, a forty-minute air raid was carried out against the Jizan area and city by four Ilyushins and a MiG. Saudi antiaircraft was reported to have scored one hit, setting a plane on fire. It flew toward San'a. Destruction on the ground by this raid was not detailed.

Faisal, in reporting these attacks to me, expressed regret over the failure of the United States—under long-standing pledges of support—to take action. In Cairo, vigorous objections to these attacks were voiced by Ambassador Badeau to Nasser on instruction from the State Department. The United States gave word to Faisal of its readiness to assist Saudi air force and ground-to-air defense through training. US manning of weaponry was offered until Saudi military personnel could take over.

The White House and State instructed me to tell Faisal that it had protested strongly to Egypt, but to add that Saudi supplying of the royalists provoked such attacks and that the earlier US offer to send combat aircraft to Saudi Arabia still stood, but was to be in return for cessation of support to the royalists. The United States was convinced that the only way to assure the integrity of Saudi borders was to terminate such aid and withdraw supply depots from the border area. This would enable the United States to put effective pressure on Egypt to honor its declared intent to withdraw troops.

When Bunche and Bunker were on peace missions to the area in early March 1963—albeit in separate countries—Nasser agreed to cease air attacks on Saudi Arabia for the duration of their visits. Nasser told Bunche that US land mines had been laid by royalists in northern Yemen and that discovery of this had been decisive in his decision to step up air raids inside Saudi Arabia. His most serious bombing before suspending the raids for the Bunker mission had been on March 5, when a hospital in Abha was hit, causing twenty-two deaths.

Under these circumstances it had been increasingly clear to me that State's use of the words "cessation" or "terminate" in regard to aid to the royalists was a flaw in our argument with Faisal. Aid was his only chip to play, and once it terminated, his leverage was lost. He had no air force as yet, and his ground forces were small and lightly armed. They were no match for Egyptian military power in the Yemen. Faisal was looking impotent to his people, as Egyptian air raids continued. The threat to the Saudi regime could only be abated by an agreement that came closer to equalizing political forces. Therefore, I had proposed dropping those terms and substituting "suspension" of arms shipments. This was accepted in February 1963, and Bunker used the term in point one of his March 6 presentation with good preliminary results.

Faisal had insisted that the Egyptian troop withdrawal from Yemen be full and complete before he stopped military aid to the royalists. He distrusted Nasser totally. Substituting "suspend" for "terminate" helped, and simultaneity of action—*start* of troop withdrawal in return for *suspension* of aid to royalists—moved Faisal in the right direction; but how was he to be sure that genuine troop withdrawals would actually occur or would continue? Who was to monitor compliance, and who was to ensure that Egyptian aircraft would not continue to bomb Saudi targets? These problems occupied the Bunker mission in its preparation for the second round.

Meanwhile, policy discussions by Saudi top circles produced a real division of opinion and advice to Faisal. In addition to Deputy Foreign

Minister Saqqaf, Prince Musa'id ibn Abd al-Rahman Al Saud was one of those opposed to Saudi involvement in the Yemen from the beginning of the crisis.[6] A younger uncle of Faisal, he was eventually named finance minister, then deputy prime minister.

Bunker and Bunche got together at the United Nations, and Bunche spoke of his just concluded visits to San'a and Cairo: Nasser wanted speedy assurance from Saudi Arabia that it would end its aid to the royalists; the YAR wanted assurances from Saudi Arabia and the United Kingdom that (1) they would cease infiltrations of opposition forces into the Yemen (from north and south), (2) the Yemeni royal family would be expelled from Saudi Arabia, and (3) Saudi Arabia and the United Kingdom would recognize the YAR. In return, the YAR would refrain from intervention in Saudi Arabia and Aden.

Bunker, in his report to Secretary-General U Thant, urged him to dispatch Bunche to Saudi Arabia at once, as Faisal was now in a receptive frame of mind. Air attacks by Egypt could be resumed at any time and cause the atmosphere to deteriorate. U Thant responded that he was ready to send Bunche to Saudi Arabia provided (1) that the Saudi government instructed permanent representative Baroody to make clear that Faisal would receive Bunche without requiring that he also visit the royalists, and (2) that encouraging reactions came in from Cairo and San'a on the substance of US proposals set forth by Bunker, with the exception of US military support (point 7) and the simultaneous start of Egyptian troop withdrawals with suspension of aid to royalists (point 2). These two points, U Thant indicated, were not prerequisites to sending Bunche to Saudi Arabia, but the others were. In other words, U Thant wanted most problems to be already well on their way to a solution before he would delegate a mediating role to Bunche.

At a March 11 strategy session with Bunker, President Kennedy agreed to the following objectives:

1. A first preference, *not* to be further pressed on U Thant, would be for Bunche to proceed to Riyadh by the middle of the coming week with authority to mediate.

2. If the secretary-general was not yet prepared to send Bunche, Bunker would return to the area by midweek as a US emissary, thus meeting the secretary-general's requirement that the eight points Bunker had put to Faisal on March 6 be put to Egypt and the YAR (via Cairo). Bunker would consult with U Thant before departure. He would visit Saudi Arabia first.

3. Bunker would be authorized to seek Faisal's agreement to drop his six points (of March 7), whose early acceptance was clearly impossible.

4. Bunker would seek Faisal's formal acceptance of a simultaneous

beginning of the process of disengagement by Saudi Arabia and Egypt, verified by impartial observers.

5. If the dispatch of a US Air Force squadron to Saudi Arabia should be necessary, Bunker had the authority to promise it to Faisal.

6. Bunker was to inform Faisal that he would stop in Cairo for negotiations.

7. Bunker would do his best to get Faisal to send to the UN secretary-general an *unconditional* invitation to Bunche showing Faisal's willingness to cooperate in disengagement.

ROUND TWO, MARCH 17, 1963, IN RIYADH

The second round of the Bunker mission was preceded, on its eve, by a Saudi rehearsal of the coming meeting. Those in attendance were Faisal, Deputy Saqqaf, Rashad Fira'awn (Pharaon), a Syrian-born royal counselor since the days of King Ibn Saud, and Tahir Radwan, the Saudi representative to the Arab League. Details were given to Isa Sabbagh by Saqqaf at breakfast on March 17, then passed on to me. The main subjects were the Bunker proposals and, secondarily, the question of the admission of the YAR to membership in the Arab League. Saqqaf called it a "screaming session." Saqqaf and Fira'awn, on the same track, urged Faisal to accept the Bunker proposals. They also urged him to accept (or, if necessary, abstain on, but under no circumstances to veto) YAR admission to the Arab League at a coming session in Cairo that Saqqaf was to attend.

Faisal was very emotional. Fira'awn stood up to him fearlessly and evoked the memory of King Ibn Saud and his statesmanship, urging Faisal to exercise the same standards of judgment. Radwan, anxious to please Faisal, opposed YAR entry into the Arab League and termed abstention cowardly. Faisal accepted Radwan's advice, whereupon Saqqaf refused to go to the Cairo session of the league.

The first meeting of the second round of the Bunker mission was held at Faisal's home in Riyadh the evening of March 17. It was attended by the same group as in the first round: Faisal, Bunker, Saqqaf, Sabbagh, and myself; it lasted two hours and forty minutes. Like the first, it began with a cordial message of greeting by President Kennedy to Faisal and an expression of thanks for receiving Bunker, all of this obviously pleasing to Faisal. Bunker related to Faisal that Kennedy had shown great interest in Faisal's desire for US assistance in establishing a television system to cover the Riyadh area and the Western Province. Kennedy had taken personal steps to prepare the way for American experts to come for a close study of the subject. Faisal expressed his deep thanks and instructed Saqqaf to send a telegram to the Saudi embassy in Rome to stop further arrangements with Italian experts who were to have executed this project.[7]

Bunker then proceeded to the business at hand. He recounted his first meeting with President Kennedy and then his session with Secretary-General U Thant and Under Secretary Bunche. Bunche's visit, he pointed out, would have been a fact-finding one, and Kennedy felt time was of the essence. Therefore, he had asked Bunker to return, especially in view of the pledge received by Kennedy from Nasser that he would commit no acts of aggression against Saudi Arabia that would interrupt these talks. Bunker was there with an acute awareness of time and, if Faisal agreed, would go on to Cairo to meet Nasser and seek his agreement on troop withdrawals. Bunker also told Faisal that US reports indicated that a revolutionary spirit existed and was increasing in Saudi Arabia. Faisal at once refuted this, saying that he knew his country better than outsiders, and that this brand of rumor was always traceable to American sources.

Bunker then said that the president was ready, upon agreement of Faisal to the suspension of Saudi aid to the royalists, to send a US air squadron, as discussed in their earlier March meetings, and would do his utmost to hold Nasser to his pledge to withdraw from the Yemen. Once agreement was reached, the United States would be able to stand by Saudi Arabia in the face of any threats to Saudi interests. The United States had already sent destroyers and planes to visit the kingdom, but a continuation of aid to the royalists would prevent Kennedy from keeping up the deterrent. Kennedy's message closed with best wishes and anticipation of Faisal's reply through Bunker.

Bunker then referred to the eight points he had transmitted March 6 and to Faisal's six points of March 7, but Faisal interrupted to comment on the Kennedy message. He pointed out that he had already agreed to all of the eight points that concerned Saudi Arabia, and that it had been Bunker who said that the six points should go to a mediator. Therefore, Faisal had said he was fully in agreement with Kennedy's letter handed to him at Dammam. The new element was Kennedy's observation that the Saudi government faced revolutionary elements within Saudi Arabia. He again refuted this.

There then ensued exchanges in which Bunker tried to reassure Faisal of US confidence in him, and Faisal asserted emphatically that the Saudi government was being led by him only as a public service and that if someone else qualified to lead the country could be found, he, Faisal, would be glad to yield. He then returned to practical realities, namely, that the kingdom was being attacked by Egyptian forces. Words were no deterrent in the present situation. Faisal needed to know how far the United States was willing to go to defend the kingdom, so that his government could see the road ahead. Saudi Arabia, he said, had the ability to defend itself by "various means."

At this point I intervened to say that both sides may have been talking at cross- purposes. President Kennedy's feelings had not changed, but he saw urgency in ending the Yemeni problem before it got out of hand. The first Bunker visit was on a fact-finding basis, but in view of difficulties over a Bunche trip to Saudi Arabia Bunker found himself in the role of international mediator. Because of this, Bunker wished to discuss additional points raised by Faisal.

Faisal then spoke of a recent incursion by Egyptian tanks in the south and the restraint he had ordered on Saudi forces and the limits of these restraints. Bunker rejoined that the US government had made the strongest protest to the Egyptian government regarding this raid and, as far as Bunker was aware, the raids had stopped. Bunker urged Faisal to issue a promise to stop aid to the royalists, so that he could go to Nasser and inform him of the Saudi attitude. Then it would be incumbent on Nasser to begin withdrawals and simultaneous disengagement; the United States would then be in a position to pressure Nasser to stop aggression. The United States, as the world's strongest nation, could defend Saudi Arabia with all its weight, including force, if need be, against Nasser or anyone else. Bunker stated that an air force squadron could be sent to Saudi Arabia on very short notice.

Bunker then went down Faisal's six points:

1. On stopping Egyptian raids on Saudi Arabia, the United States agreed and would incorporate this into its proposals.

2. On agreement for simultaneous disengagement and the cessation of military action by Egyptian forces in the Yemen, the United States agreed to its desirability. However, as put, the proposal failed to take into account possible royalist military action in the Yemen, including attacks on Egyptian forces as they withdrew. Faisal agreed, saying that he could deal with the royalists on this matter.

3. Regarding the return of Egyptian forces to bases and assembly areas in the Yemen, the United States agreed in substance but believed this would require time-consuming negotiations over what was a "base." Withdrawal itself would automatically cover this point.

4. Regarding the withdrawal of all Egyptian officers, men, and equipment brought into the Yemen, Bunker remarked that it was likely that the YAR would ask Egypt for a military training mission, since the YAR had virtually no military organization of its own. If no Egyptian mission were left behind, the YAR could, almost certainty, call on the Soviet Union for a training mission, a most undesirable thing for the Saudi and US governments.

5. Regarding Saudi suspension of aid to the royalists, when agreement was reached, this would be a point of conclusion with which the United States would not quarrel.

6. Regarding the need to set a time limit for completion of Egyptian withdrawals, Bunker said he believed this could be worked out with Nasser, since Nasser had told the US government that he had a plan for phased withdrawal.

Bunker stressed that it was important not to get into a time-consuming process of negotiating details, especially on points two and three. The process of disengagement would automatically take care of details. What was urgent was to get the process started, so that the United States could assist Saudi Arabia in repelling attacks by Egypt on royalist supply lines in the kingdom, which would in turn remove the motive for royalists to attack the YAR, whose regime the United States had recognized. What the United States was suggesting was that the Saudi government do no more than *suspend* aid and reinforcements, whereas the United States was asking Egypt to *withdraw* its forces from the Yemen.

Faisal then tossed into the discussion (perhaps as an offset to Bunker's unwelcome remarks on a "revolutionary situation" brewing in Saudi Arabia) reports that had come to him that the United States was engaged in a conspiracy against the kingdom. He did not believe them. Saqqaf interjected that many such insinuations had also come to him. Continuing, Faisal said he depended on the word of honor of the US government. Bunker expressed his appreciation of these sentiments toward President Kennedy and the US government and suggested that Faisal put the United States to the test by allowing it to proceed with the execution of its proposals submitted to Faisal. Faisal agreed. Bunker was now free to go to Cairo on March 18.

But Cairo was not free to receive Bunker. Nasser was deeply involved in a matter close to his heart—the reinvigoration of the United Arab Republic. He was now apparently in the process of its restoration through negotiations with Ba'thist Syria and Iraq. Both governments were basically anticommunist, fearing a trend toward intimacy with the Soviets, and desiring closer relations with Nasser in an Arab socialist context. They saw internal communist movements as a threat to their nationalistic aspirations and to the integrity of their independence from Great Power control. Iraq, in particular, had, under Abd al-Karim Qasim, suffered a close brush with internal communist efforts at street takeover by "popular militias." Both countries now had delegations in Cairo discussing Arab union with Nasser at the very time that Bunker finished his second round with Faisal. They were engaged in tense strategy talks on the need for a political organization that in all countries could curtail communist influence and advance the cause of pan-Arabism.

Nasser feared that a Bunker visit at this juncture would lay Cairo open to hostile accusations by the communist press, in Beirut and elsewhere, that it was being influenced by the US government. "Positive neutralism," Nasser's policy slogan of many years, called for pro-Sovietism in international politics and something more than tolerance of the United States in economic aid matters. Nasser needed both powers as rivals between which to box his independent compass. Neither should be allowed complacency about the role of the other.

Nasser's involvement in the Yemen was expensive and tiresome. It was politically unpopular at home and controversial among his Arab neighbors. He needed a face-saving disengagement but not a defeat, nor did he want the Soviet Union to step into his shoes as patron of YAR development and political "progress." He needed Bunker, but the timing was wrong, so he asked Ali Sabri, his lieutenant and fellow member of the Revolutionary Command Council, to call off the Bunker visit. Sabri made clear to Ambassador Badeau that Egypt had expected a UN mediator in any case, which would have been politically tolerable. Sabri maintained to Badeau that the image of Egypt being pressured by the United States was already current in Beirut and in communist newspapers. A Bunker visit appearing to confirm this would make it difficult for Egypt to lead Arab states toward an anticommunist program in the coming months.

Badeau wired this, with regret, to Bunker. Badeau was doing his best to change Nasser's mind and to rebut what we viewed to be a disingenuous Nasser exposition of his motivations. He asked Ali Sabri whether Nasser's decision was final, and Sabri confirmed that it was. Badeau then noted that Bunker was now in Beirut awaiting contact and suggested that he, Badeau, meet with Bunker in Beirut and then report Bunker's findings to Nasser. Sabri at once confirmed that this was acceptable and useful.

Arrangements were made for Badeau and Bunker to meet in Beirut on March 19. Washington was notified, but both Bunker and I were worried that this would convince Faisal that the United States was unwilling to put any real pressure on Nasser, even in the face of a remarkable Egyptian rebuff to Bunker, but that the United States was prepared to put plenty of pressure on Faisal. Furthermore, the explanation given by Sabri would be totally unconvincing to Faisal. I therefore urged that President Kennedy personally request Nasser to reconsider his decision and receive Bunker. The Department of State, however, rejected my recommendation. It then instructed Badeau to tell Nasser personally that an awkward situation had been created by his refusal to see Bunker and ask him to reconsider.

Badeau's appeal to Nasser was held up by a prolonged Egyptian wrangle with the Syrian delegation to the ongoing unity talks,[8] but Badeau saw him on the evening of March 23 and obtained his consent to receive Bunker on April 1. Bunker endured these complications and delays with characteristic calm and objectivity, notwithstanding that his wife was fatally ill with cancer in São Paulo, Brazil, and he desperately needed to be at her side. He nevertheless agreed to the April 1 meeting. Nasser also told Badeau that the Saudis and Egyptians had been in private contact since a meeting on February 27, and would soon meet again in the Red Sea area or in Baghdad or Yugoslavia, where the press could be controlled.[9]

On March 17, Kennedy had expressed to Faisal his thanks for accepting his eight points in principle, but stated that he was disturbed about one problem: Faisal's proposal for Egyptian disengagement could not, in US judgment, be successfully negotiated soon enough to avoid a broadening of the conflict. The 1963 coup d'état in Syria and recent trends in Iraq had created a new atmosphere, giving confidence to Faisal's opponents, and a new Egyptian military offensive in the Yemen appeared to the United States likely to succeed. Therefore, Kennedy saw it as in Faisal's interest to accept without conditions Kennedy's eight points and agree to let Bunche or Bunker work out with Nasser, with Faisal's concurrence, a date on which Faisal would suspend aid to the royalists and Nasser simultaneously begin withdrawals by moving out the first Egyptian military unit from the Yemen. Both suspension of aid and withdrawal of this first unit would be verified by impartial observers. These undertakings would be made by both sides directly to the UN secretary-general. Once such messages were sent, the United States was prepared to send an air squadron to Saudi Arabia. Nasser had already assured Kennedy through Ambassador Badeau, and Kennedy intended to press Nasser hard, on an expeditious phased withdrawal. The United States, Kennedy pointed out to Faisal, had already taken certain naval and other actions to make concrete US warnings to Nasser, but continued Saudi aid to the royalists made it extremely difficult for the United States to continue these demonstrations. Faisal's help was needed. So ended Kennedy's message, delivered orally by me, and Bunker was now ready to enter his first talks with Nasser.

ROUND TWO, APRIL 1–3: CONVERSATIONS WITH NASSER

Nasser received Bunker for the first time in the early evening of April 1 at his Cairo residence in Manshiet al-Bakri for an hour.[10] Accompanied by Ambassador Badeau, Bunker presented an oral message from Kennedy that outlined the purpose of his mission to the Middle East and asked for Nasser's cooperation in ending the Yemeni conflict. A written copy of the oral message was handed to Nasser, who apologized for the shortness of time at his disposal and proposed a follow-up session for April 2.

Bunker was able to summarize his conversations with Faisal and stressed that real progress had been made in changing Faisal's initial position on disengagement. Faisal was now ready to undertake disengagement on terms the United States felt were realistic and had shown some cautious interest in communication with Nasser (by permitting the private contracts noted above). The United States recognized the necessity of protecting the honor, dignity, and interests of all parties concerned. Bunker then asked for Nasser's reactions to the disengagement proposals he had transmitted through Ambassador Badeau.

Nasser recalled his November 1962 offer of reciprocal disengagement that had elicited no real response. On the contrary, Saudi aid to the royalists had increased, inciting Yemeni tribal action and necessitating a vigorous Egyptian military operation in support of the YAR. At first, Egyptian troops had not been very effective, being untrained in mountain campaigns; consequently, focus was placed on control of royalist supply routes and on isolating the tribes. This had been successful, and currently only one pocket of resistance existed along the borders. Given the unrelenting pace of Saudi support, however, he could not make a public reaffirmation of Egyptian willingness to withdraw, as requested in Bunker's proposal. Such a statement would incite the remaining royalist tribes, who would believe that as Egypt withdrew, Saudi support would continue.

Egypt, in any case, could not withdraw at once, Nasser observed, because the Yemenis had no significant army or security force of their own; a vacuum would invite tribal action with Saudi support. There would have to be a replacement of outgoing Egyptian forces by trained YAR forces. This did not imply an Egyptian unwillingness to disengage, as the Yemeni burden was costly in lives and money. Egypt, he said, currently had 30,000 troops in the Yemen. Not all would be needed if Faisal stopped aid, and some could be rapidly removed.

Bunker noted that the United States had made clear that it, too, was concerned for the reasonable protection of the new Yemeni government. As Kennedy's proposal to Nasser called for withdrawal in a specified period, Bunker asked whether Nasser had a timetable of disengagement. Nasser replied that two months after the beginning of Yemeni hostilities Egypt had begun to plan a disengagement schedule. Revisions were now necessary and were under study.

Badeau intervened to point out the difference between internal and external threats to the YAR. Nasser said he recognized the difference as it concerned Egypt's responsibilities to protect the YAR. Internal tribal difficulties were endemic in the Yemen. Taking hostages—which Nasser said had been the imam's policy, initially abandoned by the YAR—had recently resumed "out of necessity." Developing a good YAR security force suggested a way out of these difficulties. What concerned Nasser was Faisal's stirring up the tribes. If Saudi Arabia would recognize the YAR, there would be no problem.

Bunker restated his conviction that Faisal realized the dangers to himself and his government implicit in involvement in the Yemen, and that he was equally convinced that Faisal would honor an agreement on disengagement; the United States would strongly support such an agreement. He believed that Faisal was eager for a rapprochement with Nasser.

That would be difficult at present, Nasser replied, mentioning the 1958 episode when, he said, King Saud had paid 2 million pounds in an attempt to have him assassinated. He knew Faisal had disapproved of this and had been friendly toward the UAR. Faisal had also been in touch unofficially with Nasser through Prince Sultan and Ambassador Wahba. Nasser had indicated willingness to have these contacts carried on, but now he had heard that Faisal wanted to suspend them until the Bunker mission was well under way. Badeau expressed the hope that disengagement would not wait upon a Nasser-Faisal rapprochement; Nasser agreed.

Ali Sabri attended Nasser's second meeting with Badeau and Bunker. Discussion concentrated on certain specific points, the toughest being the character and timing of a token Egyptian withdrawal, which Bunker urged as absolutely essential to a Faisal commitment. Nasser resisted, arguing that no withdrawal could occur until he had actual evidence of the cessation of Saudi aid and until Egyptian forces could clean up pockets of tribal resistance. After very strong insistence by Bunker, Nasser finally agreed to withdraw at least one battalion of troops within fifteen days of Saudi disengagement, to be followed over an undetermined period by phased Egyptian troop withdrawals.

Nasser proposed an immediate demilitarized zone on both sides of the Saudi-Yemeni border. All Saudi and Egyptian troops would be withdrawn from this zone, and observers would be stationed in it for verification of the departure of Egyptian troops from Hodaidah and other YAR ports. Nasser strongly preferred UN observers to direct observation by Americans. Bunker then proposed a third meeting; Nasser agreed and set it for the evening of April 3.

Bunker sharpened his disengagement proposals to a high degree and presented them to Nasser at the April 3 meeting:

1. The Saudi Arabian government would suspend its support to the royalists on a date to be determined. (Nasser agreed.)
2. The Saudi Arabian government would prevent efforts of the imam's adherents to continue support from Saudi territory. (To this, Nasser said that to insure the discontinuation of the imam's efforts it would be necessary to withdraw Badr and Prince Hasan from the border territory to, at least, Jeddah and Riyadh. He added that all the Yemeni royal family should be so withdrawn. Responding to Bunker's query as to how many people this involved, Nasser said he thought about fifteen.)

3. Egyptian attacks on Saudi territory would cease. (Agreed to by Nasser.)

4. A demilitarized zone would be established, extending for a distance of 35 kilometers on either side of the demarcated Saudi-Yemeni border, from which military forces and military equipment would be excluded. (To this, Nasser objected that 35 kilometers would include Sa'da, which was the chief control point for the supply routes running from Saudi Arabia into the Yemen. Bunker responded that inclusion of Sa'da was not intended and that, according to maps he produced, it was 42 kilometers inside the Yemen. Nasser responded that the border was not well demarcated and that he preferred 20 kilometers. Bunker said that as long as Sa'da was not in the demilitarized zone, the actual depth could be easily and mutually determined. Twenty kilometers was ultimately agreed upon and included Najran on the Saudi side, but not Jizan or Khamis Mushayt.)

5. Within fifteen days of the suspension of Saudi aid, Egypt would begin withdrawals. (At first this was agreed to, but before the end of the day's talks Bunker apparently realized this was not even minimum simultaneity and would not sit well with Faisal. He urged Nasser to give an immediate token withdrawal of at least one company upon the activation of the Saudi withdrawal of aid. Nasser hesitated but then agreed, after discussion of what constituted a company: Nasser indicated it would be one hundred men and refrained from agreeing to Bunker's suggestion to make it two companies.)[11]

6. Impartial observers were needed. (Nasser agreed.)

7. Cooperation would be given by all parties to the UN secretary-general's representatives. (Nasser agreed.)

8. Egypt's good offices would be used in curtailing the inflammatory speeches of Yemeni leader Sallal. (Nasser agreed.)

Nasser raised a question regarding publication of the text of a disengagement accord, stating that he would have to make changes of wording if publication were to occur. Bunker responded that each government could give its assurances to the US government or to the United Nations. Badeau argued that there be as little publicity as possible, as otherwise both would feel the pressure to make statements that could injure the accord.

Bunker told Nasser that he did not intend to visit the Yemen, meaning that it was up to Nasser to obtain YAR concurrence to the proposals for disengagement. The YAR government had posed a precondition, namely, that the United Kingdom recognize the YAR. This was impossible, but once disengagement took place British recognition would come. Nasser responded that he had not yet informed Sallal of the disengagement talks but would do so.

Bunker made a strong pitch to Nasser that Egyptian radio cease its propaganda against the Saudi government, to go along with disengagement. Nasser replied that all parties were employing propaganda, but that a gradual cessation could accompany implementation of a disengagement agreement. However, he was unwilling to drop Egyptian propaganda suddenly, as that would imply that the United States had pressured him or that he was afraid of Faisal. To set the stage for reduction of radio warfare, Radio Mecca should stop its attacks on Egypt, and Faisal must surely stop his support for the royalists. Bunker told Nasser he intended to fly to Saudi Arabia the next day and would like a date to return to Cairo, if necessary. Nasser gave Bunker an open invitation to any day after April 6, which would be taken up with a Syrian delegation on Arab unity.

In my view, the meetings of Bunker with Nasser revealed several important features in the landscape of Egyptian involvement in the Yemen. The most salient was Nasser's recognition that his involvement had become unexpectedly costly in men and money, impossible to simply abandon, and very difficult to manage. Tribal politics in the Yemen presented Egypt altogether baffling problems with which it had little or no familiarity. A quick fix was out of the question, and Nasser feared Faisal's capability, financial and political, to drag out the royalist resistance. Money and arms were available to the prince in any amount he desired, while Nasser faced the prospect of a domestically unpopular struggle, as Egyptian casualties and material losses continued to mount. Nasser therefore had begun early to work on a disengagement schedule by which Egyptian troops would be replaced by YAR units trained on the spot.

In these circumstances, Nasser was unable to forecast how long Egyptian troops would have to remain in the Yemen to ensure the survival of its republican regime. To stay indefinitely could mean trouble at home, while to leave and see the republic overturned by the royalists was a prescription for political disaster. It would mean the end of Cairo's hegemony in an Arab world already split on the hows and wheres of unity under Nasser's chairmanship. Sensitive talks with Syria and Iraq taxed Nasser's diplomacy in any case. A defeat for Egypt in the Yemen would certainly wreck those negotiations.

On the broader international scene, Egypt's posture in the Yemen, supporting a new deal for the Yemeni people, was not a bad one. Cooperation with the United Nations was helping Egypt's image. Cooperating with the United States would also be useful, provided it was not well known and was subsidiary to cooperation with the United Nations. US efforts to pressure Faisal could be helpful to Nasser, for there was no alternative leverage available other than Egyptian radio propaganda and bombers. The use of these already worried the United States, but Nasser was enough of a brinksman to feel that he had not yet tested the limits of US patience and thus continued with both forms of pressure. Nonetheless, he left indications with Bunker that propaganda attacks could be curtailed if aid to the royalists stopped. Bunker used this with Faisal, but it was to be a half-hearted and hollow promise for some time to come.

ROUND THREE, APRIL 5–6: CROWN PRINCE FAISAL

The third round of conversations began in Jeddah and was attended by Faisal, Saqqaf, Bunker, Seelye, Sabbagh, and myself. Bunker, as usual, extended greetings from President Kennedy to the crown prince and his congratulations on the landmark reforms and programs of development Faisal had initiated, particularly the abolition of slavery and the earmarking of new revenues to meet needed economic and educational development in the kingdom. Bunker then reviewed in detail his conversations with Nasser, providing Faisal with negative as well as positive elements, including Nasser's expression of desire to improve relations with Saudi Arabia and his support of an extraofficial dialogue of representatives.

Faisal commented that Nasser's attacks had included an often reiterated indication that the Yemen was merely a stepping stone to reach Saudi Arabia; therefore, Nasser should hardly blame Faisal for opposing Egyptian occupation of the Yemen in the name of "Arab unity." He denied that he had ever authorized any unofficial talks between a Saudi and Egyptian official or that they had even taken place. He said that Egyptian-born Saudi ambassador Wahba had gone to Egypt on family business and had been approached there by officials for a dialogue on Egyptian-Saudi problems. Wahba, he said, dispensed with these approaches on the ground that Bunker was visiting both countries.[12]

Bunker then turned to the specifics discussed with Nasser. These constituted a reordering of the eight points, reducing them to six. Bunker omitted point five—that a fifteen-day period would follow the suspension of aid to the royalists before Egyptian commencement of withdrawals; and point eight—that Sallal be calmed down. Extended discussion followed on the need to incorporate a clause in point one, desired by Nasser, ensuring that members of the Hamid al-Din family in Saudi Arabia not use Saudi soil to carry out operations in the Yemen, as well as on Faisal's desire for a provision against Egyptian "mop-up" operations during the drawback of troops to bases in the Yemen prior to full withdrawal.

Faisal accepted points three and four—cessation of Egyptian attacks on Saudi Arabia and establishment of a demilitarized zone. On point five—impartial observers—he strongly desired their stationing at Hodaidah and San'a, as well as in the demilitarized zone. Bunker replied that the observers would be fully mobile, but promised a change of wording to emphasize this.

Faisal accepted point six—cooperation by Egypt and Saudi Arabia with the UN secretary-general's representative or other acceptable mediator—but then wanted a timetable for Egyptian troop withdrawal. Bunker explained Nasser's reluctance and commented that if a timetable were insisted upon, its length would have to be long enough for Nasser's compliance. He said that President Kennedy had expressed his intention to hold Egypt to expeditious withdrawal. Faisal reiterated that a timetable must be fixed. Bunker inquired whether the crown prince wished to accept the US offer of a fighter squadron to be stationed in Saudi Arabia, once Faisal agreed to a disengagement accord; Faisal gave an ambiguous answer. Bunker proposed a meeting for the next day, which was agreed upon.

The session on April 6 was attended by the same persons present on April 5: Faisal, Saqqaf, Bunker, Seelye, Sabbagh, and myself. Bunker began by once again emphasizing President Kennedy's deep interest in the issues at hand and his special concern to preserve the honor and dignity of Faisal, his admiration for Faisal's accomplishments in internal development, and his vital interest in the security and stability of the kingdom. The US government, Bunker again stressed, had a special relationship with Saudi Arabia that was different from its relations with other countries of the area. The United States shared Faisal's humanitarian desire to avoid further bloodshed, and it intended that any disengagement agreement have the full moral sanction of the United Nations in addition to US backing.

These comments, redundant perhaps to a reader of this account, were by no means excessive to the ear of Faisal. He needed the reiteration. Bunker then molded his comments into what was practicable, reasonable, and fair to both parties. The role of mediator is never easy, and it is always impossible to fully satisfy both sides. Politics may be the art of the possible, but a mediator must be selectively insistent on his top priorities. Bunker had given especially close attention to Faisal's views and had made some changes to satisfy Faisal's concerns. Above all, he sought to buy time and, through a network of procedures and commitments by the parties to the United Nations, to obviate any precipitous action.

Faisal expressed thanks for Bunker's welcome comments and called attention to concessions he had already placed on the table out of a desire to be reasonable and to show the kingdom's staunch friendship with the United States. Saudi Arabia sought clarifications, but it had no wish to quibble. It wanted to go along with US wishes. Faisal never gave his word unless he meant to keep it; therefore, he had to know all the details of an undertaking into which he was to enter.

Bunker then showed Faisal the changes he had made since the previous meeting:

1. Termination[13] by the Saudi Arabian government of its support and aid to the royalists and prohibition of the use of its territory by royalist leaders to carry on the struggle.

2. Beginning of Egyptian troop withdrawal simultaneous with suspension of Saudi aid to the royalists. Egypt would continue a phased withdrawal of its forces, in the course of which its forces would be withdrawn from field activities to their bases pending their departure from the Yemen. Egypt would refrain from taking punitive action against the Yemeni royalists on the basis of resistance mounted by the royalists prior to commencement of disengagement.

3. Cessation of Egyptian attacks on Saudi territory.

4. Establishment of a demilitarized zone extending for a distance of 20 kilometers on either side of the demarcated Saudi Arabia–Yemen border from which military forces and military equipment would be excluded.

5. Stationing on both sides of the border in the demilitarized zone of impartial United Nations observers, who would be free to travel outside the zone to certify the suspension of Saudi support activities and the outward movement of Egyptian forces and equipment from Yemeni airports and seaports.

6. Cooperation of Egypt and Saudi Arabia with the United Nations secretary-general's representative or other mutually acceptable mediator in reaching agreement on the process and verification of disengagement.

Although he could not guarantee that these changes would be accepted by Egypt, Bunker said he would do his utmost to gain Cairo's acceptance. He pointed out that, in accord with Faisal's wish, there was no specific mention of the imam or of the Hamid al-Din. When Faisal asked what activities of that family were to be proscribed, Bunker gave as an example subversive operations of all kinds, arms smuggling over the border, clandestine communications, sub rosa movement into the Yemen, and radio propaganda. I indicated to Faisal that proscription of such activities accorded with generally accepted international law. Faisal raised aspects he thought needed strengthening in point two—punitive action—and point five—freedom of observers to travel, but Bunker answered them, and there was no change.

The big point of discussion was Faisal's insistence on a time limit for total withdrawal. Bunker said that he felt it best to leave it open-ended, as Nasser was unlikely to agree to a timetable that Saudi Arabia could accept. In any case, President Kennedy had undertaken to hold Nasser to an *expeditious* withdrawal, and this was the more effective of levers. Faisal asked what Bunker felt was a reasonable timetable. Bunker replied this was extremely hard to judge, but a rule of thumb might be for Egypt to remove its forces at the same rate at which they had been introduced, that is, four and a half to five months. Faisal felt this was too long a period and pointed out that when he had led forces with his brother Saud against Imam Yahya (in the 1934 dispute over the Asir territory neighboring the Yemen) and a truce was reached, he had withdrawn his own contingent in fifteen days. There was no further discussion of this point.

Faisal then asked me directly if I was satisfied that Egypt would live up to its promises to withdraw expeditiously. Knowing Nasser a bit from two and a half years as deputy chief of mission in Cairo (1955–1958), I had my inner reservations. I replied that my trust lay not with the other party—the Egyptians—but with President Kennedy's determination to hold Egypt to its undertaking. Bunker remarked that only US government military experts could offer an authoritative estimate of a reasonable period of withdrawal, and he reiterated that adequate assurances lay in the commitment of President Kennedy's prestige.

At this point Faisal made a dramatic, pivotal, and rather emotional move. As a gesture, he said, of confidence in the president, the US government, and "your joint excellencies and assembled brethren," he was prepared to accept fully the proposals presented and amended. Bunker assured him that his sentiments were not misplaced, and asked whether Faisal still wished to have a squadron of US aircraft as soon as disengagement was launched. Faisal responded in the affirmative "in principle," but preferred that details be taken up with the respective military experts. Bunker then said he would leave the matter in my hands for consultation with military advisors. He reminded Faisal of the additional US undertaking to expedite the training of the Saudi air force and expand air defense training.

Bunker then requested, in view of UN involvement, that Faisal send a message to the UN secretary-general indicating his complete willingness to receive the secretary-general's representative, presumably Bunche. Faisal said he thought such a message had already been sent through his special delegate to the United Nations. Bunker, however, said that the secretary-general still had the impression that his representative would not be entirely welcome in Saudi Arabia, so he suggested a second message. Saqqaf said a clarifying message would go to Ambassador Baroody, and Faisal nodded approval.

Faisal, as a last item, expressed his great interest in building the television station and in developing a road construction program. He desired prompt guidance from the US government. I responded that consultants on the television installation project were being assembled to send to Saudi Arabia to determine the best type of equipment for the kingdom. He asked for a team of road experts to make a survey of the road requirements and hoped that this team could be sent at US government expense so that he could avoid aggravating the bureaucratic complications in which he already found himself. Once the team made its report, Faisal was to invite bids on the basis of specific recommendations.

After this meeting a new set of proposals incorporated a suggested change by Faisal in point five and added "in Yemen" at the end of point one—all to please him and not likely to be controversial with Nasser. Much later, as Bunker was about to fly to Cairo, Saqqaf urged that the word "expeditious" or "as soon as possible" had escaped his notice and must be inserted in point two of Bunker's draft in the phrase concerning phased withdrawal. Saqqaf insisted that Faisal demanded this and would not accept the draft without it. The demand was needless and covered by President Kennedy's frequent use of "expeditious withdrawal" in his oral messages to Nasser. Nevertheless, I wired Bunker in Cairo a full report and recommended the insertion, which Bunker made, using the expression "as soon as possible."

ROUND THREE, APRIL 9: CAIRO

Nasser accepted the amended text in all respects, except for an editorial phrasing in point five concerning travel by observers in Yemen "so as to avoid upsetting Sallal." The change was in form rather than substance. He also agreed to Bunker's urging that Nasser withdraw two companies simultaneously with the cessation of Saudi aid to the royalists, plus one battalion, possibly two, within fifteen days thereafter. Nasser declared himself ready to effect disengagement any time after April 12, three days hence.

Bunker now urged that Washington seek prompt action by the UN Secretariat to get Bunche out to the area as soon as possible after a briefing by Bunker. Bunker did not inform Nasser of the US intention to send an air squadron to Saudi Arabia, preferring that this notification be done just before the squadron's departure and that it be explained as a training measure in reward for Saudi agreement to disengage. Faisal had been promised a quick dispatch of the squadron and particularly wanted to have it in place before the beginning of the *hajj* on May 2. This consideration may have strongly influenced Faisal's acceptance of Bunker's disengagement proposals. The Department of State reacted by raising the classification of this part of Bunker's message with the Pentagon so that measures could be taken to avert a leak that could risk deployment of the aircraft.

Faisal approved the Nasser amendments and the full text on April 10. He was pleased to hear that Nasser offered to begin disengagement any time after April 12. Bunker, waiting in Cairo, received the news from me by phone and scheduled his flight to New York for April 11. If not otherwise directed, he would at once see the UN secretary-general and give a push to an immediate trip by Bunche to the area. There, Bunche would be able to negotiate detailed and final disengagement terms, including an observer force to monitor troop withdrawals and cessation of aid to the royalists. Bunker was optimistic of a very early start on this process.

This was not to be, though not for lack of trying by the US government.

DISENGAGEMENT: A CLIFF-HANGER

At the conclusion of the Bunker mission, Saqqaf, who had labored so hard for disengagement against heavy odds, was euphoric. Faisal too was pleased, expressing his joy to the elderly royal counselor, Rashad Fira'awn, who, in turn, relayed his reactions to our embassy. Bunker had made a superb impression and had shown special sensitivity to Faisal's and Saudi Arabia's integrity and dignity. Back of this was solid support by President Kennedy, proving that personal involvement by a US president could make the difference in handling sensitive problems in the Middle East.

Meanwhile, Nasser jumped the public relations gun—ignoring his own appeal to Bunker for secrecy—in a sure-footed move to put his case for disengagement in terms of an Egyptian victory. On April 13, *al-Ahram* and *al-Akhbar*, the two principal and well-controlled dailies of Egypt, with international Arab circulation, trumpeted in a series of articles that fighting in the Yemen was now over and a "crushing victory" achieved by Yemeni republic forces supported by those of Egypt. It was a unilateral Egyptian decision to withdraw troops. Saudi Arabia had no alternative but to recognize facts. Contacts with President Kennedy's advisor, Ellsworth Bunker, had revealed that the Saudi government wanted to find a way out from the defeat that it had suffered. Egyptian withdrawal would begin only *after* it was sure that the aggressors were living up to their part of the agreement.

The contents of the agreement were truncated and distorted by the Egyptian media: The Saudis had agreed to stop all aid to "aggressive forces" trying to infiltrate into the Yemen and had agreed not to allow such forces to use Saudi territory as a base. Verification of the agreement would be under UN supervision. *Al-Akhbar* added that Egypt would keep part of its forces in Yemen to "participate in building the Yemeni army and training it." Ambassador Badeau in Cairo protested to Nasser, who replied unconvincingly that all this was a leak from New York and could do no damage. So much for complete withdrawal, and so much for Nasser's avoidance of propaganda. Perhaps more important, official

Egyptian sources authorized United Press International to say that the first Egyptian ship left the Yemen April 12.

Adverse Saudi reaction over Egypt's going public was partially neutralized by a brief, surprise article in *al-Bilad*, the leading Saudi daily, on April 11. It dealt briefly with the Bunker mission and was obviously unauthorized. Saqqaf and I concluded that the Saudi case for protest to Cairo was weak, since the *al-Bilad* story antedated those of *al-Ahram* and *al-Akhbar*.

Annoyed, Faisal shrewdly seized the initiative in a broadcast on Mecca Radio on April 16, followed by an April 21 press conference in which he declared the Egyptian-Saudi dispute the problem of the day, not the Yemen itself, where he said he had no problems. He portrayed the United Nations as having the keys to a solution and bearing the responsibility of using them. This was followed on April 22 by a Saudi public rally attended by an estimated 100,000 people, at which Faisal emphasized two themes: (1) nonintervention in the internal affairs of the Yemen, and (2) the right of self-determination of the Yemeni people. The context in which these themes were placed was Egypt's violation of both, while Saudi Arabia sought no more than their observance. The rally was well organized and orderly, and the crowd was clearly attentive and friendly toward the crown prince. Faisal followed up this measure with published photos of the effects of the March 5 Egyptian bombing of Abha, capital of Saudi Arabia's Asir province: a British engineer officially reported an estimated 100 killed at the time.

Although the war of words had picked up, as had Egyptian air attacks and, presumably, Saudi aid to the Royalists, on April 19 the Cairo daily *al-Gumhuriyya* announced that two ships, the *Misr* and the *Sudan*, loaded with returning Egyptian troops, would arrive at Suez on April 26. Bunker, meanwhile, had made his report to Secretary-General U Thant and was warmly congratulated on his achievement. As an expeditious follow-up, he urged sending a UN emissary to prepare the ground for the observer team. He then reported to Kennedy and accepted the president's warmest thanks.

Ellsworth Bunker's mission had been essential to an agreement on disengagement, and this unified but separately pledged agreement, conveyed individually to U Thant by telegrams, was indispensable to the next steps the secretary-general was to undertake. In the course of his rounds of talks Bunker displayed unfailing concentration on the essentials, dismissed peripheral matters, and kept the terms of an agreement clear and simple. Like all international agreements that have a chance of acceptance, the words had somewhat different meanings to each side. Their implication was unmistakable, however, to wit, that a settlement could be achieved only by abandoning violence and by stages of disengagement to be honestly observed and verified by impartial observers.

Central to the success of Ellsworth Bunker in obtaining Faisal's agreement to the disengagement formula was further demonstration of President Kennedy's commitment to Saudi security against both external and internal threats. To this end, Kennedy directed that US naval visits be stepped up from a normal once-a-year call at Jeddah (and later Yanbu, 200 miles up the Red Sea coast) to one a month. On the Persian Gulf side, US Commander, Middle East Force, had already observed a schedule of visits sufficiently frequent that no step-up was needed. The east coast, in any case, was quite distant from the conflict over the Yemen. In the Dhahran area, Green Beret units were deployed to instruct Saudi officers in counterinsurgency.

There was no delay in launching these military programs. The big operation was to be the US air squadron deployment (dependent on the prior establishment of the UN observer mission, which was to testify to the cessation of Saudi arms aid to the royalists and to the start of Egyptian troop withdrawals). This deployment was known as Operation Hardsurface and quickly became public, although it attracted little outside notice at the time.

Washington had instructed Ambassador Badeau, on April 11, to inform Nasser personally as soon as possible that, since Bunker had obtained the agreement of both the Egyptian and Saudi governments to a formula for disengagement, the US government planned to undertake certain training exercises in Saudi Arabia that had been previously discussed with Faisal. Within the next few weeks, a survey mission would be sent to the kingdom to examine facilities and prepare for the arrival of an air squadron. The purpose was to carry out a US Air Force training program in long-distance flight under difficult conditions and to conduct exercises of the Saudi Air Force in cooperation with the USMTM. This activity, the message pointed out, related to the continuing US interest in the internal stability and security of Saudi Arabia and in the improvement of its defense capabilities.

The US government told Nasser it would make low-key public and private explanations from time to time. Since full Egyptian cooperation with Ellsworth Bunker had furthered the prospect of an end to the war in the Yemen, these Saudi-US military exercises could now be undertaken without implication that they related to the conflict there; it was to avoid such implication that the US government had delayed their initiation. The timing of this notification was a change from Washington's earlier intention to notify Nasser on the eve of the expected departure of the air unit. This was just as well, since the delay was to prove a long one.

Operation Hardsurface was to consist of eight F-100Ds, accompanied at first by one command-support aircraft and six KB-50s. Its true mission, to be accomplished at Saudi expense, was to demonstrate to the Saudi and Egyptian governments and peoples continued US interest in and support for Saudi Arabia and to provide a deterrent to Egyptian operations in Saudi airspace. If these intrusions nonetheless continued, proposals regarding an appropriate response had been put forth for Department of State, Pentagon, and White House discussion. Washington was not yet ready, however, to issue rules of engagement, despite the rather strong promises of US air interception given to Faisal by Bunker. It was expected that the air unit would have a very limited tenure, perhaps two months, and serve as a token air defense—labeled a training mission for easier acceptance by both Saudi Arabia and Egypt; but it would nevertheless constitute a US show of force.

The commander of Middle East Force at this time was Rear Admiral B. J. Semmes, who proceeded on May 21–23 to examine the full implications of his position and his contingency orders by making an exceptional formal visit to Hufuf, capital of the Eastern Province, featuring a call on the Emir Saud bin Jilewi, governor of the province. This, to my knowledge, had never been done by any of Semmes's predecessors and was a move of considerable potential utility to regional diplomatic and military relations. For about sixteen years, the Middle East Force commanders had visited Dammam routinely in the single small vessel they had used as a flagship, one of three commissioned seaplane tenders still afloat—the USS *Duxbury Bay*, the USS *Valcour*, and the USS *Greenwich Bay*—that rotated on duty.

In Arabian Peninsula protocol, Emir bin Jilewi held the highest rank of any Arab ruler fronting on the gulf, with the exception of the king (later president) of Iraq and the sultan of Oman. (In the British as well as the US lexicon of salutes, the emir rated fifteen guns, well above those of the emirs and sheikhs of statelets still under British treaty protection.) Bin Jilewi was hereditary viceroy of the immense province that included all of Saudi Arabia's then-producing oil fields. The province was therefore the beating heart of the Saudi economy, industrial and commercial. Furthermore, bin Jilewi personally was a repository of Bedouin history covering the entire peninsula fronting on the gulf. Calling on him for nothing more than payment of respects had yielded inestimable dividends to me as a consular officer in Dhahran over many years. Semmes's visit added another and needed dimension to our preparation to install Hardsurface and its backup services, with hundreds of uniformed personnel, into the area of Dhahran-Dammam. Semmes, a gracious southerner, was a superb naval diplomat.

The advance survey team mentioned by Badeau to Nasser arrived in Jeddah via Iran on April 18. Led by Colonel Robert H. Langdale, USAF, it included Lt. Colonel Marion Staudermayer, USAF. One diplomatic problem of a purely military nature bothered them among others—visas for up to 850 tactical and support personnel. USMTM, as a resident mission, had been required to obtain individual visas for its approximately 200 personnel. Another problem was where to base such a unit. Faisal wanted it based at Jeddah, but the timing was bad. It was almost the eve of the annual Muslim pilgrimage to Mecca, and the Jeddah airport was quite inadequate for the vast numbers about to descend and rush to the Plain of Arafat. Saudi army chief of staff General Abd Allah Mutlaq, who had succeeded General Tassan, worked closely with Colonel Langdale. They drew up a memo of understanding regarding these and other matters of deployment on April 23 that based Hardsurface at Dhahran. This was approved by Emir Sultan ibn Abd al-Aziz, minister of defense and civil aviation, but subsequently opposed by Faisal, who pointed to Bunker's memo of assurances that the United States would station fighter interceptor planes in *western* Saudi Arabia.

I argued with Faisal for a month in favor of Dhahran on the practical ground of availability of space, water, and general services; I convinced Saqqaf of this position. Finally, on May 22, Faisal agreed to a secondary basing of the air unit at Jeddah, leaving the main base at Dhahran. It was clear that Faisal wanted the deterrent capability to be located near Egyptian air activity, and I thus had to have his agreement to language that ensured the unit would be under US command at all times, along with a countervailing provision that no US air operations would be conducted without prior coordination with Saudi authorities. This was accomplished.

Another item on the agenda was how to bring the unit to Dhahran from the United States. From south to north, the airspace options were quickly weighed:

1. Routing through the Sudan would be politically embarrassing for the Sudanese.

2. The Egyptian route was undesirable, to say the least, although the United States was only exercising its international right of naval passage. It was not certain that Egypt would turn us down, but we did not want to ask.[14]

3. Transit of USAF aircraft via Israel and then Jordan would be politically embarrassing to King Hussein and would be refused.

4. Transit via Syria and Iraq would be refused.

5. Transit via our allies Turkey and Iran was selected, and the Turks, somewhat reluctantly, agreed, as did the shah of Iran. Logistical preparations were now worked out, laying in 150 tons of material and supplies and transferring three aircraft from bases in France.

CONTRETEMPS OVER SAUDI VISA POLICY FOR JEWISH US OFFICIALS

Saqqaf raised with me the need for an update of the US-Saudi status of forces agreement. We therefore scheduled a full-scale review and renegotiation. The talks were to include provisions regarding the USMTM, particularly paragraph nine, so as to establish the concept that all of Saudi Arabia, not just specific areas, was to be construed as a training area. Thus, if US servicemen were arrested anywhere in the kingdom for infractions of Saudi law, they would be immediately turned over to the chief of USMTM for appropriate trial and punishment under US military jurisdiction. Saqqaf, however, found, as did I, that time was now too short to negotiate all these matters on the eve of arrival of a new and much larger US service contingent. Informally, Saqqaf said, this amended provision was already in effect, and the time was not right to put it before Faisal. He suggested we table it, and Hardsurface could come with confidence. The chief of USMTM had excellent contacts in the Eastern Province, where most Hardsurface personnel would be located. I recommended to Washington that Saqqaf's suggestion be accepted, and it was.

A revised draft agreement that I had previously submitted to Saqqaf thus remained tabled. It included a US proposal that Saudi authorities issue blanket instead of individual entry visas to avoid routine but troublesome questions. Among such questions was the standing provision on all Saudi immigration forms that required the applicant to state his religion. This became a touchy issue.

On June 10, Radio Cairo and Voice of the Arabs broadcast a statement by Representative Emmanuel Celler (D-NY) to an American Jewish group that the Defense Department had assured him in writing that American Jews were among US officers training the Saudi armed forces. Celler added that the assistant secretary of defense had further stated that President Kennedy had insisted no American Jewish officers or servicemen be barred from duty in Saudi Arabia. Considering the political sensitivity and the prospective conflict of laws, I asked Washington for background facts. I told State that if, in the meantime, I was asked by the press, I would propose to reply that there were no Jewish officers in USMTM. As for Hardsurface, I would reply to queries that any screening of personnel would have a disruptive effect on the operation. It would be best, I would add, that all Arabs recognize that the US government was trying to assist, not embarrass, the Saudi Arabian government and that the best procedure would be to ignore the Egyptian story. In a message crossing my desk, State informed me that a *New York Times* report of Celler's remarks had grossly distorted the facts. It instructed me to handle the case, meanwhile, exactly as I had proposed.

My recommendations were based on several considerations: Saudi visa policy in those days was sharply discriminatory not only against people of the Jewish faith, but against people "not of the book," such as Hindus, who were regarded as idolaters and image worshipers and were excoriated by the Quran. The ambassador of India in Jeddah was therefore always a Muslim. All American officials dealing with this policy knew that in the case of Jewish visa applicants the objection was not religious; Jews were criticized, like Christians, for certain practices and beliefs considered contrary to the Quran, but were nonetheless "peoples of the book," to be respected and, if governed by Muslims, protected. The objection to their entry was on political grounds—the Palestine problem. Innumerable approaches by American officials pointing out the undesirable features of this policy had been ignored. It was Saudi law, and ARAMCO foreign personnel and those of USMTM all had to sign visa application forms that included a requirement that religion be stated. If the applicant was Jewish, the visa was automatically denied.

On duty as deputy assistant secretary in Washington during an earlier period, I had been visited more than once by spokesmen of the Jewish community demanding the implementation of a US policy that would have liquidated US ties with Saudi Arabia unless Jews, like other Americans, were readily admissible. This position would have led to a direct confrontation of laws. It had been at least tacitly recognized by several administrations that it was in the US security interest to preserve good ties with Saudi Arabia; it was decided that we would try to persuade from within rather than ostracize from without. Some, however, insisted that if we were "firm" and were ready to break all ties "on principle," the Saudis would have to give in. These advocates did not know the Saudi Arabs and, in most cases, could not have cared less about US-Saudi relations. A hard, immediate insistence by the US government that Saudi laws be changed so as to accommodate US laws and policies could not but be rejected out of hand by the Saudis. They were as sensitive as Americans to questions of sovereignty.

By this time, Saudi Arabia had no lack of European suitors to take over the US political and economic relationship, train Saudi forces, sell it modern weaponry, and extract and sell its oil. Europeans could do all this on at least as good terms as the Americans had so far offered. In the highest councils of the Saud clan, there was no lack of "hawks" who would tell the United States where to go. Exacerbating the situation, the press from Cairo carried special overtones. It was immediately apparent that Nasser would use a Jewish presence in Hardsurface to trumpet to all Arab societies that the Saudi leadership had to call not only on America but on its Jews to defend a corrupt regime from a long-needed cleansing, Egyptian-style, by revolution.

I watched for the theme to appear, and, sure enough, it was not long in arriving in the written press. On June 15, *al-Gumhuriyya* and *Akhbar al-Yom* ran front-page stories headlined "America gives the lie to the Faisal government and confirms the presence of Jewish soldiers in Saudi Arabia." *Al-Gumhuriyya*'s editorial castigated Faisal for "betraying Arabism and Palestine." The background facts I had requested from Washington now came in. The assistant secretary of defense had written a supposedly confidential letter to an interested organization answering its query, confirming that Jews would be in Hardsurface. When the confidentiality was inevitably breached, Celler learned of it and made a public statement. Then the other shoe dropped.

I was summoned by Saqqaf to his office in the Foreign Ministry—a quite formal touch in our long informal relationship. He had a statement for me from Faisal. It began with assurance to me that there was nothing personal in what he now would say. He liked and respected me and was aware of my efforts and my interest in Saudi-US relations. However, Celler's statement, if not clearly denounced by the US government, would make it impossible for Faisal (with all respect and appreciation) to agree to the USMTM's remaining in the kingdom or to the passage of any US forces through it. Faisal added that Saudi Arabia had nothing against the Jewish faith, but that Saudis believed that many American Jews were Zionist supporters; Israel was an enemy and would remain so. Therefore, Celler's statement and the nondenial of it, and even the inadequate explanation given to the Saudi ambassador in Washington by the assistant secretary of state, all added up to an unfriendly US position. It directly conflicted with Saudi beliefs and policies. Faisal would therefore ask Emir Sultan to tell USMTM chief Colonel Wilson not to allow further American military personnel to move into the kingdom until a reply was received from the US government.

Saqqaf was very depressed, and referred to the hard work he and I had exerted to strengthen relations. I had brought Isa Sabbagh with me at Saqqaf's request. The conversation now opened up three ways. I told Saqqaf that I could not offer the slightest hope that the US government would "denounce" the Celler statement or would give assurances it would not send Jews to Saudi Arabia or even declare there were none in USMTM. I took my leave. Sabbagh remained behind, where his colorful command of native Arabic might be a vehicle of persuasion that it was time for a new Saudi look at one of its favorite nostrums. He urged that Saqqaf marshall the support of certain princes, particularly Jamil Hujailan, minister of communications, a forward-looking moderate.

At home, I received a phone call from Saqqaf saying that Faisal wanted simply to have Celler's statement denounced. When I asked what that meant, Saqqaf responded that the statement should be publicly labeled "not true." I then asked for a meeting with Faisal. I had known him for almost twenty years, and it was time for a review of this matter between us. Saqqaf at once concurred and said he would set it up for the next day. My closing remark was that all this played right into Nasser's hands.

I reported everything to Washington with the highest priority and with the caution that we had not yet, in my view, received Faisal's last word. We should leave the door ajar so that he could back out quietly. We would then let the problem settle and wither. We would not cancel Hardsurface, but delay it; nor should we withdraw any members of the USMTM, except by normal rotations. We must let time and Faisal's advisors work *in camera*.

But the deployment of the air unit had to be stopped, and it was, on June 15, thirty minutes before its scheduled takeoff from McGill Air Force Base in Tampa, Florida—Faisal had hinted that it would be best not to proceed. The cancelation orders came from the Joint Chiefs of Staff. The detailed plans, so abruptly put on hold, had provided for the unit to proceed to Zaragoza, Spain, and Incirlik, Turkey; combat elements were to remain in Incirlik until UN observers were positioned in the Yemeni-Saudi demilitarized zone. I had been instructed to tell Saqqaf of this and remind him that final movement of the unit into duty in Saudi Arabia was predicated on *complete cessation* of all forms of Saudi assistance to the Yemeni royalists and on Saudi prevention of the smuggling of arms. The United States was convinced that supplies were still flowing from the kingdom into the Yemen. Hardsurface was therefore put on twenty-four-hour alert awaiting JCS orders.

State had agreed to tell Saudi ambassador Abdullah al-Khayyal, if he inquired, that the matter was now under direct discussion between Faisal and me and that no details were available as yet. This tack had the support of Saqqaf. It made clear that the position of the US government on discrimination was that it was of such overriding importance that it could not be compromised, even if the USMTM were expelled and US-Saudi relations deteriorated. Thus adamancy and deadlock loomed on both sides. The Department of State's press guidance ran as follows: "As you know, in conjunction with our training mission in Saudi Arabia, we have held a number of training exercises with the Saudi defense forces. We have had under consideration a further training exercise designed to enhance the air defense capability of Saudi Arabia. The timing of such an exercise, however, is not now determined." We would refuse to comment on reports that the exercise was called off, or that difficulties had arisen over the question of the inclusion of Jewish servicemen in the units.

By 3:00 A.M. June 16 I had a report to make to Washington:

> On June 15, I opened my talk with Faisal by saying that I did not want his final answer tonight. I preferred a further talk tomorrow. I urged he forget publicity, which he could afford to ignore. I read him our press

statement. Faisal objected that it was lukewarm, but showed his desire to reach a compromise by urging several formulae for a simple US government disavowal, even to just saying the *New York Times* report was "distorted." I told him that any volunteering of comment was sure to open up inquiries, whereas new press treatment on the topic was not now developing. What we did not need was a dialogue with the media.

Faisal, in turn, argued strenuously that he had never raised the question of the religion of members of our air unit and would not have raised it. Others had done so, and now the US government seemed to be helping to "cram it down his throat." The least he could expect, he said, was that the US government not be silent while this bomb exploded under him or imply that Celler was citing US policy.

Faisal said that President Kennedy (in September 1962) had asked him to do something about Jews in transit through the kingdom and he had done so. He had arranged that no queries be put to transients regarding their religion. He asked that I declare to the press that the Celler statement was distorted or have US ambassador Armin Meyer do so in Beirut. I made the obvious objections, whereupon Faisal said that if the US government could not do even this little thing to help him dispel intense criticism, it might be best to remove the cause of the irritation. Our friendship would remain, and there were other fields for US-Saudi cooperation.

I asked Faisal to weigh this carefully. The United States would withdraw, if he so requested, both the air unit and USMTM. What then would Faisal have achieved from this fateful and irreversible course? The great satisfaction would be Nasser's and that of the Soviet Union. Faisal responded that this was not his wish or choice, but what other choice did he have when the closest of friends on whom he had depended most to strengthen his position with his people, and in the Arab world, could not respond with the minimum he had asked. Celler was unimportant; Faisal was concerned only because his statement was ascribed to an American official. He would be satisfied with one word from an equal American source, "distorted," or anything else that would produce a way out.

Saqqaf intervened to suggest that he and I get together on "phraseology." I handed him the department's proposed press guidance and offered to go over it with him without promise of any voluntary statement or change in the text. Faisal appeared somewhat softened by Saqqaf, but very insecure with regard to the regional press and radio coverage coming in on him from all sides. He could not cave in, but he did not object to Saqqaf's proposal, so I took it as Faisal's silent consent to a gambit by Saqqaf that could produce a further cooling off. In fact, a cooling off was exactly what Saqqaf had in mind.

A "working" trialogue now began with a flurry of messages to Washington on June 16. I made various suggestions for additional press guidance, such as a statement that the US government did not know and did not ask about the religion of its employees, whether military or civilian. Saqqaf proposed to me language for a US press release that the United States did not practice discrimination on the basis of race, color, or creed, and that, at the same time, it respected Saudi laws regarding movements on its territory by "undesirable persons." I objected to the last two words. Washington favored stating in the press guidance that the Saudi government reserved the right, as a sovereign state, to screen all applicants for visas on the basis of its own policies, but no visa question had arisen in the case of American military units participating, from time to time, in joint training exercises in Saudi Arabia on a transient basis. The US government, for its part, retained its own policy of nondiscrimination, and US efforts abroad had been directed at obtaining recognition and acceptance of this principle. These efforts would continue. Secretary of State Rusk, at one point, suggested by message through me to Saqqaf that any political activity by any member of the air unit while in Saudi Arabia was most unlikely but would be dealt with at once by the US Air Force as a matter of swift military discipline.

Throughout this consultation, efforts were made by Washington and by me to find language that would reduce the size of the Saudi target against onslaughts by the Cairo-Beirut media without in any way compromising stated US principles of nondiscrimination. The fact that these discussions met with increasing flexibility by Faisal could not disguise the width of the gap still remaining. Nevertheless it led to a very useful airing of Saudi official opinion on the need to reevaluate current visa policies. What proved to be the most effective element of all was time itself, while within the Saudi leadership the arguments went on over such phrases as "undesirable persons" and the preference for "Zionists" in its stead. These were purely Saudi discussions in which we had no part, but on which Saqqaf kept me posted. They showed growing strength among liberal thinkers.

OPENING THE DOOR TO OPERATION HARDSURFACE

The Cairo and Beirut media continued their attacks, but the reverberations among the Saudi public were virtually nil. On June 17, I reported to Washington that the "temperature" was dropping, and I recommended that Hardsurface units be held in a state of readiness. A unit of UN observers arrived in Jeddah (including a liaison unit that in due course became an excellent informal source of information on disengagement). With Saqqaf, I continued to trade proposals of language without either of us ever saying a flat "no," and I was able to get away briefly to visit my other post, Kuwait, which was about to conclude a frontier agreement with the new Ba'thist government of Iraq. Shortly I had word that the Saudi leadership was seriously discussing the abandonment of questions regarding a visa applicant's religion and that not only did this apply to transients, but was likely to be made applicable to all visitors.

An important inducement to Saudi Arabia's more rapid decision to let the air unit come in came from a resumption of Egyptian bombings. On June 23 and again on June 24, Abha was hit. Accelerated discussion over press guidance took place, with concentration on a voluntary statement about the air unit's mission, to be issued as the unit became airborne, and on questions to be answered. In effect, the guidance would indicate that no visa problem over entry of the air unit had obstructed its movement. Almost imperceptibly, Faisal was brought into agreement.

Washington now ordered the embassy in Cairo to inform Ali Sabri that the departure of our air unit was imminent and to inquire how Egypt proposed to ensure that there be no US-Egyptian military clash. The Joint Chiefs of Staff directed the support elements of the unit to proceed at once to Dhahran. The fighters would be held at Zaragoza until the UN Yemen Observation Mission's (UNYOM) advance party of Yugoslav observers, escorted by US Major Lawrence David, was in place in Najran, Jizan, and Sa'da, a date estimated to be between June 30 and July 2.

In Washington a press briefing agreed to in advance with Faisal took place on June 29, and I informed Saqqaf of the statement and of the departure of the air unit. I also told Saqqaf that I had a letter to Faisal from President Kennedy, which Saqqaf read through twice, with obvious satisfaction. The *Washington Post* carried the briefing on its front page on June 30, including answers to queries, all of which I was able to give to Saqqaf to use with Faisal.

It had been a long delay since the May 4 date originally scheduled for the departure of Hardsurface. It had been even longer for the expectations and urgings that had flowed from the Bunker mission.

OPERATION HARDSURFACE AND THE UN
OBSERVER MISSION IN YEMEN

UN secretary-general U Thant always recognized the importance of observer missions, but he worried, with good reason, over the size and sources of their manpower and how to pay for them. Where possible he sought to avoid a time-consuming Security Council session on the handling of peacekeeping projects as a whole, and he tried to limit expenditures by borrowing salaried personnel from other UN units, such as the UN Congo Mission and the assemblage of bilateral armistice commissions between Israel and the Arab states, under the UN Truce Supervision Organization (UNTSO). He opposed a large observer mission to Yemen.

In early to mid-1963, while Bunker was engaged in his mediating mission, a major problem on U Thant's horizon was Nikolai Fedorenko, Soviet deputy permanent representative to the United Nations. Fedorenko was chargé of the Soviet delegation and apparently sought to make his mark with Moscow by taking a purist Charter position and by repeated efforts to bring all peacekeeping issues to the Security Council, where, he asserted, they belonged (and where he had a veto). There, the Soviet Union could talk to death measures it did not like. Fedorenko demanded from U Thant that the entire dispute over Yemen be docketed for full review by the Security Council so as to preempt a possible channeling into the General Assembly, where the Uniting for Peace Resolution of the Korean War days could strongly advise, if not empower, UN action. U Thant sought to avoid delay without antagonizing Fedorenko; his heightened sensitivity to Fedorenko's dogged insistence made him over-attentive to minutiae and economy at the expense of precious time.

Trying to help, US permanent representative Adlai Stevenson canvassed Security Council members and found that none, not even Egypt, desired a Security Council meeting. Fortunately, the influence of Egyptian permanent representative Mahmoud Riad carried weight with Fedorenko. Responsive to Nasser's desire for a good image, Riad sought to persuade Fedorenko against a Security Council meeting. In its effort to build influence in the Arab world as a whole, the Soviet Union generally followed Egyptian policy lines when the matter at hand concerned the Middle East.

Saqqaf and his sympathizers in the Saudi leadership had reason to be most anxious that momentum be sustained. Egyptian bombings in border areas were intensifying. Saqqaf, who was worried that confusion over a Bunche visit to Saudi Arabia would delay disengagement, suggested to Washington that the secretary-general be urged to send Bunche to the kingdom before May 1, when Faisal would be leading pilgrims to the Plain of Arafat for the most important of the pilgrimage rituals. Thereafter he would be taken up with still other *hajj*-related formalities. However, Washington decided that the direct transmission via Saudi ambassador Baroody to U Thant of Saudi acceptance of the Bunker disengagement agreement obviated the need for a Bunche trip to Saudi Arabia. This was a break in Washington's policy of deference to U Thant's agenda. Washington also wanted the observer team organized and in place on the effective date of disengagement. That timing was crucial for the deployment of the USAF squadron.

In Cairo, Ambassador Badeau was also anxious to maintain the momentum of the Bunker agreements, since the Egyptian government claimed that large Saudi troop and matériel convoys were moving toward the Yemen. An Egyptian spokesman complained to Badeau that Egyptian hands were tied by a one-sided disengagement agreement; Egypt must start withdrawals, while the Saudi government was free to send supplies. Badeau sensed from this an Egyptian threat of new violence, and he strongly advised Nasser's spokesman against a breach of the Yemeni-Saudi border. It would have unforeseen and serious consequences for US-Egyptian relations.

At the United Nations, U Thant called on Swedish Major General Carl Von Horn, chief of UNTSO in Jerusalem, to take over the command of the observer mission and to tackle at once the problem of finding, organizing, housing, and deploying an observer team. U Thant sent Von

Horn on April 26 to the Yemeni-Saudi border zone to examine the ways and means of disengagement verification and the size of the manpower requirements. Consideration was given, with strong US government support, to having Von Horn "drop off" a few of his accompanying advance staff of nine and constitute them as the advance party of the observer force to trigger the disengagement process at once. But U Thant rejected the idea, fearing a clash with Fedorenko. He did not want to be caught out on a limb, with no funds, and then be called to account by an unfriendly Soviet ambassador, invoking the prerogatives of the Security Council and angered by the secretary-general's initiatives, taken in the face of his repeated demands. This kind of paralysis slowed up and restricted the realistic and expeditious planning of UNYOM.

The US military representative at the United Nations, seeking to expedite matters, took up the logistic needs of UNYOM with Indian Major General Indar Jit Rikhye, chief military advisor to the secretary-general. Rikhye indicated that the observer mission need not be large, but required four helicopters, each accommodating eight passengers (the size of one observer group). The helicopters would be based at Sa'da, the main city of northernmost Yemen, but would require forward bases for refueling at Haradh (fifty miles southwest of Sa'da) and Naqa (thirty-five miles northeast of Sa'da). Maximum altitude of these aircraft was to be that of a pass north of Sa'da at 2,630 meters. This meant an H-34 or similar type craft was required. Three were to be supplied by Canada, while the United States would supply all other aircraft. The main supply base would be Hodaidah, where a C-47 from the United States would be stationed. Rikhye estimated a short duration of duty for UNYOM, so he felt that planes and helicopters with crews should be rented and maintenance personnel furnished by the US government.

Bunker had estimated that fifty observers would be needed, plus logistic personnel. This figure was provisionally adopted by the secretary-general. Rikhye estimated that the UNYOM budget for four months would be $5 million. This would include $250,000 per month for aircraft. UNYOM personnel would come from UNTSO and be already salaried by the United Nations; they would receive only an additional per diem of $10.

The delay in assembling and deploying the observer force resulted primarily from the secretary-general's problems in financing it. Dues for peacekeeping were controversial and not willingly provided by member states. U Thant had working capital of only $2 million, which would be quickly exhausted if used. If Saudi Arabia and Egypt would each accept one-half of UNYOM's costs, a debate at the United Nations could be avoided or made brief. Nasser was traveling, and no one else in Egypt could make the decision or even offer a temporary reply. The secretary-general made clear his willingness to accept payment in kind if convertible Egyptian cash was a problem. Saudi Arabia had the cash, but Faisal delayed a reply.

Rikhye recognized (as had Bunker) that fifty observers could not cover all infiltration routes from Saudi Arabia, and that their principal use would be that of a deterrent. Washington urged U Thant to notify Von Horn, who was planning to proceed to the border area on May 1, that royalist resistance on the Yemeni side of the demilitarized zone was likely to continue during his visit and even after disengagement had begun. Dangers to personnel should not be minimized and precautions should be taken.

In Jeddah, Saqqaf and I set up a meeting with Von Horn, whom I knew from an earlier encounter in Beirut. U Thant's choice of Von Horn seemed ideal. An impressive man of wide UN peacekeeping experience, Von Horn was ready to proceed at once into an area of irregular warfare conducted by Bedouin snipers unlikely to distinguish UN soldiers from Egyptians. That did not bother him. What worried Von Horn was what he felt were U Thant's ambivalence and lack of realism, the vagueness of the UNYOM mandate, and the practical needs of that force. After one good look at the wild, precipitous, and almost trackless terrain of northern Yemen, Von Horn had begun to feel that UNYOM could not execute its mandate. He was also forthright in expressing his concern that his mission would not be well supported in New York.

RESUMPTION OF VIOLENCE

Two months and quite a trail of violence followed the Bunker mission and its April expectations that disengagement would occur within a matter of days. As the United Nations wrestled over putting an observer mission in place, the frontier began heating up in May. Alleging that Saudi Arabia had sent weapons to the royalists, Egyptian forces first attacked targets in the Saudi border area, though without much result. While Badeau sought to make his points against bombardments to Nasser, I was instructed to express concern that such supply movements had previously provoked Egyptian bombings. Saqqaf, on April 29, had assured me that all aid to the royalists had ceased two days earlier, on April 27. Faisal reacted angrily to the Egyptian attacks and told Saqqaf that he would now resume full aid to the royalists until the observer team was in place.

The Egyptian air force then increased its activities, occasionally overflying Jeddah and the whole Hejazi coast to demonstrate Saudi military impotence; actual bombings, however, were confined to the Saudi border region. Al-Kuba, a few kilometers from the Yemeni border, was hit May 21 as was Dhahran al-Janub,[1] ten kilometers from the border. An area seventy-five kilometers east of Najran was hit on June 3; an area thirty kilometers east of Dhahran al-Janub was hit on June 4; and in the Najran area, the Wadi Jizan village of Shuwayha was struck on June 6. Jizan city was hit severely, resulting in casualties, and reports of damage to a hospital, homes, and the airport. Jizan and Khamis Mushayt were bombed again on June 8, the day after the US formally declared the disengagement agreement fully operative.

The vigor of Egyptian activity against Saudi targets may well have had several causes: (1) a real increase in Saudi aid to the royalists, permitting them to lay in large stocks before disengagement cut off supplies; (2) a genuine Egyptian alarm over the progress made by royalist forces against nondescript YAR forces and mobile Egyptian targets; (3) a considerable decline in Egyptian troop morale and the need for troop rotation; (4) a desire to compensate through shows of strength for the uncertain loyalty of allied Bedouin tribesmen; and (5) a rise in Egyptian ground casualties at outposts where royalists had the advantage of cover and surprise.

An Egyptian brigadier, Hamdi Wasaf, revealed a drop in morale to our chargé in San'a, indicating that it had begun in early spring 1963. It underlay Nasser's willingness to take out the two shiploads of troops just as Bunker concluded his mission; it was useful to Nasser as a misleading signal to Washington and to the world that in withdrawing his troops he was truly cooperative. Such apparent readiness to start a major withdrawal would help offset the adverse impact in the United States and at the United Nations of bombing Saudi targets, an action that could be explained away as necessary to protect Egyptian troops during regroupment preparatory to withdrawal.

Meanwhile U Thant continued struggling with his funding problems, resolved provisionally, after further delay, by agreements with each party: Egypt and Saudi Arabia would each pay $200,000, or the equivalent, to the UN Secretariat every two months. Saudi Arabia would pay in hard cash, Egypt in Egyptian pounds. The Secretariat's accounting department feared this was insufficient to cover costs, but it was anticipated that no more than four months would be needed to verify complete Egyptian troop withdrawals. As for Saudi cessation of aid to the royalists, that had to be done at once and would remain final if withdrawals were completed. These expectations were to prove optimistic, even naive.

On June 11, Fedorenko finally got his Security Council meeting; but, swayed by Riad, he did not use it to attack the Bunker agreements or impede the establishment of the UN Yemen Observer Mission. He abstained on the enabling resolution, 179 (1963), creating UNYOM. It was over in one day. The Security Council put the seal of its approval on the Bunker agreements and the initiatives taken outside the council by U Thant.

Von Horn and his advance party arrived in San'a on June 13, two months after Bunker had urged on the secretary-general that an advance party of observers be sent immediately. Out of fear of displeasing the Soviets, U Thant had withdrawn the few Americans in the group from participating in UNYOM, except for Major Lawrence David, Von Horn's Arabist aide and deputy commander of UNYOM. As noted, the United States had jumped ahead of Von Horn's arrival date in declaring the Bunker disengagement agreement to be operative as of June 7, the day that UNYOM's advance group was ordered to proceed to the Yemen and Saudi Arabia.

Although the United States and the United Nations combined forces to ensure the transport of experienced men for the establishment of Von Horn's observer team, that team was pathetically small. More a symbol than a reality, it comprised:

1. *A reconnaissance military group*: 114 Yugoslavs from the UN Emergency Force monitoring the Egyptian-Israeli border, arriving by ship July 4. It was deployed in Jizan, Najran, and Sa'da.

2. *An air unit*: 50 Royal Canadian Air Force soldiers using Caribou, Otter, and H-19 helicopter aircraft. They were deployed in San'a, Jizan, and Najran.

3. *Civilians*: 28 international staff and 20 local employees.

These UNYOM personnel were to be stationed at Jizan and Najran in Saudi Arabia and at Sa'da, San'a, Rawdha, and Hodaidah in the Yemen. Varying numbers of headquarters personnel were stationed at San'a, with liaison officers in Jeddah and Cairo.

Their mandate from the secretary-general was to observe, certify, and report. Enforcement of the disengagement was to be the responsibility of Egypt and Saudi Arabia. UNYOM personnel were to patrol north of the Yemeni border in Saudi Arabia (to check for arms traffic) in three sectors: the west, using jeeps based in Jizan; the center, in a very mountainous region, requiring fixed wing aircraft for higher altitudes and helicopters for lower ones; and the east, using jeeps based in Najran. UNYOM was also to monitor Egyptian troop withdrawals from their posts at the San'a airport and at the Hodaidah seaport on the Red Sea and its airport. These last two assignments would require light observation aircraft and helicopters and about seventy personnel, including crews. The US government was to provide logistical help on a reimbursable basis. Von Horn had instructed UNYOM to take precautions to avoid combat; on June 18 his own plane, traveling from San'a to Najran, was hit by sniper fire from the ground. There were no casualties and only minor damage.

Von Horn's skepticism over the small size of UNYOM and its total inadequacy (as he saw it) to fulfill even so passive a mission as that mandated by the United Nations increased as time went on. His candor and pessimism became an issue between him and the UN Secretariat. The Canadian government, hearing of Von Horn's dire predictions, underwent a cabinet split over the safety of its personnel in the mission. The Ministry of Defense in Ottawa, citing Von Horn's comments, opposed Canadian participation in UNYOM. It doubted the political premise expressed in Secretariat and US circles that the governments of Egypt and Saudi Arabia needed only a face-saver to begin disengagement. It cited the Egyptian ambassador to Canada as saying that Egypt would not withdraw troops if doing so would endanger the Yemeni republic. The ministry therefore sought Canada's withdrawal from UNYOM. However, the Ministry of External Affairs favored Canadian participation and prevailed in the end, with discreet support from Washington.

Von Horn's quarrel with the secretary-general was aggravated when Ralph Bunche told Von Horn that his request that Major David be made chief of operations could not be accepted and that—for policy (not personal) reasons, namely keeping UNYOM out of Great Power politics—David should be withdrawn from UNYOM. A compromise was reached whereby David was retained but not made a stand-in for Von Horn. The US government and various delegations at the United Nations felt that Von Horn had gone much too far in his outbursts, which had gained wide currency. His demands for more personnel and equipment became strident and were ignored. There seems little doubt from Von Horn's own memoir on this subject[2] that he had gone too far and had lost his credibility in New York, as well as the full support of the Secretariat.

Nevertheless, Von Horn had some real justification for his pessimism over the UNYOM mission and his concern for the safety and good health of his team. He had been appointed to an almost unachievable task in view of what was discovered to be Egypt's intent to rotate troops rather than withdraw them, and given his mission's lean logistical support in a country where ordinary sanitary facilities and almost everything else had to be imported by air. Headquarters in New York refused an enlargement of the UNYOM force for budgetary reasons. In fact, Von Horn's analysis was basically correct: the UNYOM task was not only a risky business, but also a fig leaf. It could not cover everything it was called on to verify, and it could enforce nothing.

Yet, in retrospect, UNYOM did a remarkable job. It served a useful purpose in keeping the disputants concerned for their own image at the United Nations. Despite natural obstacles of terrain and ground-fire risks, it closely verified Saudi compliance or noncompliance regarding aid to the royalists. Despite, and even because of, blatant Egyptian noncompliance, UNYOM observers went to great lengths to record troop withdrawals and replacements. The record made it clear that the entire exercise was cynically exploited by the Nasser government.

Nasser presented one face to Bunker, Badeau, and Kennedy, explaining every troop rotation as caused by Faisal's overt or covert renewal of arms shipments to the royalists. To the United States, he avoided any suggestion that his pledge of ultimate full withdrawal was conditioned on the general survivability of the YAR. But to former prime minister John Diefenbaker of Canada he stated that he had never promised to withdraw troops from the Yemen, only to reduce them, and then only if the Saudis made it possible; for if Saudi aid continued, YAR authority would collapse and that was unacceptable. He estimated to Diefenbaker that it would take three years before all Egyptian troops could be withdrawn. Diefenbaker reported all of this to the US Department of State at a high level.

On the front line of persuasion in both Cairo and Jeddah, Badeau and I could only do our best with the argument that both sides had made a formal commitment to the United Nations, and that it was on the basis of that commitment that UNYOM was deployed by the secretary-general. Nasser's officers in the Yemen did not dissimulate. With frankness and unanimity, the various commanding generals in the Yemen and in Cairo informed Von Horn and Chargé Robert Stookey that the overriding Egyptian objective was survival of the YAR, and that troop withdrawals would never be such as to jeopardize that survival.

Faisal had freely admitted, when I had sought an interview with him on May 29 (nine days before the US considered the disengagement to be fully in force), that in view of Egyptian bombings and troop rotations, he had resumed aid to the royalists after a voluntary cutoff on April 28. A single shipment to the royalists of ammunition, a few rifles, and a few vehicles had been made May 27. What otherwise could he say to "the people"?

I asked, "What people?" He replied that he meant the people of Saudi Arabia. I said there were other people to consider: those of the United States, the United Nations, and the world. A resumption of aid to the royalists would be used by Nasser to justify the thesis that the Saudi government had never stopped aid to the royalists and that Egypt was therefore justified in taking military action against Saudi targets. Faisal responded, "Let them do it!" I rejoined that, speaking as an old personal friend, Faisal's position so far had been far above that of his opponent. He should not lower it, but should restore the ban, especially now that observers would be in place in a few days.

Faisal accepted my advice as "coming from a friend," but he could not be sure that the shipment had not already crossed into the Yemen. (It later developed that this shipment had gone through and included 2,000 rifles.) If not, he would stop it through Prince Sultan, who was about to arrive at his office. Deputy Saqqaf had been present throughout this session with Faisal. As Faisal had not consulted him regarding the resumption of shipments, Saqqaf had been assuring me that the ban was in force. His advice to Faisal not to make the shipment had been rejected. Saqqaf sent word to Faisal via Emir Khalid ibn Abd al-Aziz and Sultan that he wished to resign, but his resignation was rejected.

THE ARRIVAL OF HARDSURFACE

On July 10, on the roof of the Ministry of Foreign Affairs, Saqqaf and I witnessed the arrival of the first of six US F-100Ds for Operation Hardsurface—the promised US military presence. It made a low pass over the city—there were no high-rises in 1963 Jeddah—and Saqqaf became quite excited. I told him there was no cause for worry, and he responded that on the contrary he wanted the pilot to be ordered to "break the sound barrier" to get the citizens out to see that Saudi Arabia was now in possession of its skies. He asked me to get in touch with the commander of the unit at once to order the pilot to "wake up" and "thrill" the populace. I declined, pointing out that this could smash windows and do other damage and that, in any case, it was difficult for me at this point to effect changes in pilots' arrival conduct, which was superb airmanship, and that I was sure the public would see that a friend with the latest in state-of-the-art military hardware had come to help.

The political and public-relations impact of the air unit had been the subject of much advance planning. By early June the advance party had worked out with the embassy and the Saudi military command recommendations for joint activity on the air unit's arrival. The Saudi military favored a prompt "training demonstration" on the Red Sea coast, which would signal to Egypt the presence of US airpower. The six F-100Ds would arrive in early morning, accompanied by one or two C-130s, which would land at the civil airport—the city's only effective airport—for static display to the citizenry. Royal Saudi Air Force F-86s piloted by Saudis would arrive at about the same time to prepare for an air show one day later. That show proceeded on schedule, on July 11, and was successful, getting Hardsurface off to an excellent start. Saudi pilots performed well in formations, doing pull-ups and rolls, and were given front "billing," ahead of USAF air refueling and high-level sonic "booms."

The Hardsurface unit was small and was based 800 airline miles away, in Dhahran. Interception of intruding Egyptian military aircraft would not be easy, especially if confined to the Asir province to the south. There were contingency plans nonetheless, providing a series of steps that could deter aggressive Egyptian behavior. These included picketing destroyers in the Red Sea, augmenting the air squadron, and creating a naval screen along the Yemeni border. I pointed out to the Department of State that if Egyptian attacks should nevertheless continue, the Saudis would surely seek a vigorous US response, as Bunker had assured Faisal they would do. I proposed that the Department of Defense review rules of engagement for the appropriateness of existing plans for the defense of Saudi Arabia, making sure that its phases offered *progressive* deterrence. A USAF photo reconnaissance of Saudi supply routes to Yemen would also be useful in evaluating the performance of disengagement, since the United States had tied the continued presence of Hardsurface to UNYOM's certification that Saudi supply trains to the royalists had ceased. It was clear that the Joint Chiefs of Staff had set aside adequate resources to augment the deterrence, whenever so ordered by the president. The air squadron was by no means the only deterrent. The commander in chief, Eastern Atlantic and the Mediterranean, saw to it that US destroyer visits to Saudi Arabia (mainly Jeddah) occurred at fairly regular intervals of six weeks.[3]

One slip in an otherwise smooth record of execution of plans occurred on July 16. I was in Ta'if for an appointment with Faisal at his summer office and residence and was accompanied by a representative from CINCNELM (commander in chief, North Atlantic and Mediterranean), Captain Penfold. There we encountered Defense Minister Emir Sultan, to whom Penfold mentioned the air training show to take place over Ta'if in a few minutes, about which we were assured that Sultan had been fully informed. He had not. Startled, Sultan reached for a phone and gave hurried orders that the Ta'if antiaircraft unit be informed that *friendly* military aircraft were approaching, namely, F-86s and F-100s. They would perform a series of formations, including air-refueling of the F-100s from a KB-50. Sultan's warning was barely in time to forestall a barrage of friendly fire against friendly aircraft conducting joint exercises to impress a friendly population.

The exercises continued, and training progressed. I recall that only seven Saudi fighter pilots had received combat training, while some thirty had received F-86 flight training. Maintenance was weak, but enthusiasm was high. The Saudis took to flying, and our instructors found them to be without nerves. They loved parachute jumping. There were just too few Saudis to match the Egyptians. At sea, the USMTM had very few sailors to train—perhaps eighty Saudis in uniform and only a few light coastal patrol craft. However, as stated, we were to step up the US naval presence for reasons of deterrence rather than training. We recommended and the White House agreed to a visit by more than one destroyer at a time, namely, a carrier task force, for October 30. It was to consist of the USS *Essex*, escorted by destroyers and submarines. Its arrival was to be a landmark date in the later diplomatic struggle to keep disengagement in operation.

The air unit promised by Ellsworth Bunker on behalf of President Kennedy in April 1963 was now in place, along with US Navy and Green Beret activities promised by Kennedy to Faisal in October 1962 during the prince's Washington visit. The Joint Chiefs of Staff had operational command over *general* Hardsurface flight patterns, but it was clear that rules of engagement, if any existed, were under the direct purview of the president.

As it happens, draft rules of engagement had existed from the beginning of May 1963. Subject to clearance or revision, they provided that if Egyptian aircraft were intercepted over Saudi territory, the information would go to the Joint Chiefs under the highest precedence. They would direct appropriate action after a decision by the president. The Pentagon had recommended rules for pilots to follow in the event repeated Egyptian intercessions occurred,and no decision for action had yet been made either by the Chiefs, the Department of Defense, or the White House.

On July 16 two Hardsurface introductory missions were flown: (1) Jeddah to Riyadh (for refueling), thence to al-Salayyil and Bisha in the south, but well north of the Yemen; (2) Jeddah–Bisha–Khamis Mushayt–Qahmah al-Mudhaylit–Jeddah, which brought the fighters much closer to the Yemen, and, by including Khamis Mushayt, into an Egyptian bombing target area. The flights were completed without incident, and we had reason to know they were noted by Egyptian pilots in flight. Deterrence thus *appeared* to be working.

I found that our flight patterns restricted our missions to the Asir area to not less than 100 miles north of the Yemeni border. This I protested, as the pattern of flying at such a great distance from the border would be noted by the Egyptian command in San'a and interpreted as opening the way for Egyptian bombing raids on Jizan, Khamis Mushayt, and other Saudi areas farther south. I suggested lowering the limit to five or ten miles, but my message elicited reduction only to forty. The boundary was very irregular. Given the US policy of not violating Yemeni airspace, and thereby avoiding any US acts of hostile intrusion against a republic we had officially recognized, I did not argue with the decision. But in agreement with Captain Penfold, we mapped out a week ahead a series of irregular and unpredictable fighter reconnaissance "training" flights up and down the Red Sea coastal area and to not less than forty miles north of the Yemeni border. As Egypt also conducted flights over Red Sea areas north of Jeddah, this area could not be neglected. Given the small number of qualified Saudi jet fighter pilots, the "training" aspects were to become saturated within a month or two, whereupon Penfold asked me for guidance. I could only reiterate "keep up training—the essence is deterrence."

Back in Washington, the chairman of the Joint Chiefs of Staff, Air Force General Curtis LeMay, had strongly opposed Operation Hardsurface and by the end of July sought to withdraw it, even though it had just begun. He saw no real mission for it but believed, rather, that it was tying up elements with a much higher priority for service elsewhere.

Therefore, all things considered, by late July I felt it was timely to ask for consultation in Washington with the highest authorities, and Washington agreed. I left Jeddah in the charge of Nicholas G. Thacher, my very able deputy chief of mission, and was gone until August 30, except for one return visit.

When I called on President Kennedy at the end of July, he was accompanied for our discussion by White House assistant Robert W. Komer, whose primary duties included the monitoring of all White House correspondence relating to the Yemen crisis (which Kennedy privately nicknamed "Komer's War"). Our talk centered on the rules of engagement of Operation Hardsurface, which the president had not yet approved. At one point in the conversation Kennedy referred to the undesirability of risking aerial combat with the Egyptian air force. I said I would like to contest the point, and Kennedy immediately became very attentive. Realizing as I did that John Badeau, not I, was his ambassador to Egypt, I nevertheless noted that I had served a few years in Egypt during the Suez crisis and believed I knew Nasser a little. To me, he was a brinksman who would test U.S. firmness to see how far he could go. His pilots could defy U.S. interception, ignore it, or take hostile action, after which Nasser could maintain that they were simply protecting themselves in shooting at our aircraft and that they were in Saudi skies doing their duty to interdict royalist supplies. I urged we not tie the hands of our pilots.

Kennedy at once agreed that our pilots would have the right of self-defense. However, if it became a matter of using force, he wanted first to be given the opportunity to make the decision. Beyond this, no promulgation of the rules of engagement took place, to my knowledge. In retrospect, it might have been useful, but it would have been hard to make it fully effective with so small a squadron, and I concluded that Kennedy would have preferred not to formalize what Nasser could construe as an ultimatum, then publicly defy while observing it privately.

This was my second and last meeting with Kennedy, and I came away from it impressed with the sincerity of his interest and with his desire to keep his hand directly on the helm of the crisis.

NASSER TESTS US RESOLVE

Earlier, the UNYOM liaison officer in Jeddah, acting in what he considered to be the overall interest of the mission and in disregard of the strict terms of the UNYOM mandate, had begun occasionally passing to me or to an embassy officer the substance of UNYOM findings regarding charges by Egypt concerning supplies to the royalists and Saudi countercharges. In one of these exchanges the embassy learned of a Saudi charge of Egyptian use of poison gas against Najran. This was a particularly serious matter and was imparted to us in the strictest confidence. Official reports from UNYOM were going directly and, in principle, exclusively, to the UN Secretariat in New York. An UNYOM investigation, however, found no evidence of such an attack in Najran itself. By Secretariat orders, UNYOM could not visit royalist camps and therefore could not verify whether there had been an attack anywhere other than in Najran.[4]

By July 23 UN observers in Jizan, Najran, Sa'da, and Hodaidah reported no sign of Saudi aid coming into the Yemen but confirmed Egyptian troop rotations rather than withdrawal. Three days later they reported that there had been a withdrawal of two thousand Egyptian soldiers on July 20, making a net total decrease in the Yemen of 2,500 men (10 percent of the total Egyptian force.) A disturbing bit of information reached Chargé Thacher in Jeddah that was relevant to my consultations in Washington. On July 31 the UN liaison officer in Jeddah privately stated that, by his mandate from New York, he was not authorized to make an independent check on Egyptian withdrawals, but must await an invitation by Egyptian authorities; however, regarding the Saudis, observers were supposed, on their own volition, to keep close track of border traffic heading into royalist areas. This one-sidedness was somewhat corrected by Von Horn, who tightened observation of Egyptian forces.

For a while compliance by the disputants seemed to improve. By mid-August 1963 UNYOM had certified the withdrawal of 5,300 Egyptian troops, plus 850 seen but not counted. The *net* withdrawal accepted by the secretary-general was 4,550 to 4,750—that is, after deducting 1,400 to 1,600 replacements. Replacements by air or sea were not fully measurable because Egyptian commanders refused UNYOM access to the port at Hodaidah, but they were deemed "large."[5] The total number of Egyptian troops staying in Yemen was not really known. UNYOM's counts were estimates, but well into the withdrawals and rotation of forces, Egyptian Marshal Abd al-Hakim Amr, chief of staff of Egypt's forces, stated that the approximate number was 30,000 men.

From Chargé Thacher in Jeddah, instructions were thus urgently sought from Washington in late July to permit flights of Hardsurface fighters close to the demilitarized zone, so that they would be seen in the Najran border area. Egyptian fighter-bombers had just attacked the Najran area at Qalima. Prince Sultan had made a bitter representation to Thacher regarding US inactivity in the face of this provocation. Washington authorized CINCNELM to instruct its air force commander, and pass to Thacher for the Saudi government, that on a one-time basis F-100s should proceed as soon as possible to the northern limits of the agreed 20-kilometer demilitarized zone. Any further flights that far south would need to be specifically authorized. Meanwhile, the United States made strong representations to Cairo, and it urged the Saudi government to notify the UN secretary-general of the incident. The Saudis were to be notified that we would be taking further steps, the nature of which would be imparted shortly.

The one-time restriction on the flight was soon rescinded, and Washington authorized CINCNELM to schedule five consecutive flights, August 4 through 8, provided the aircraft remained at least forty miles from the Yemeni border (as distinct from the DMZ). Further flights south had to be on a periodic basis, according to Hardsurface standing instructions. In Cairo, US chargé William O. Boswell made his representation regarding the Najran bombings (which were denied in the Cairo press), stating that the supposed gains by Egypt were in no way commensurate with the damage Egypt suffered in Western eyes, public and official. Boswell recalled to the Egyptian government that Nasser had given his personal assurances to President Kennedy that he would honor the withdrawal agreement. He asked for a public explanation by the Egyptian government.

In San'a, Chargé Blalock, on instructions, called on Egyptian commander al-Qadi to register concern. Qadi denied having authorized the bombing, saying that his own instructions were clear: no bombing inside Saudi territory. He had no evidence to prove or disprove the US charges, but speculated that it could have been a case of an inexperienced pilot. Blalock pointed out that the bombing occurred 40 kilometers north of the border and asked how such a degree of navigational error could be explained. Qadi had no explanation, but the Egyptian position continued to be that its bombings were confined to Yemen and were defensive.

My consultation with the president in Washington had coincided with an extensive policy review. Hardsurface had been deployed for six weeks, and stock was being taken in the Department of State of the future of disengagement and of the prospects for reducing US involvement. Interdepartmental meetings were frequent, and in mid-August, to my astonishment, the Department of Defense called a meeting with State to consider the time for a full withdrawal of Hardsurface. I then learned, for the first time, that Defense had planned the air unit's deployment to last only thirty days or, at a maximum, sixty days. The thirty days had already passed and sixty would come up in mid-September.

A Department of State message went out to Chargé Thacher in Jeddah, who responded with the recommendation that since Secretary of Defense Robert McNamara planned to invite the Saudi minister of defense, Prince Sultan, to Washington as his guest, it would be best to await the prince's acceptance of such an invitation before "redeploying," that is, removing Hardsurface. There were pros and cons to be weighed before a final decision was made on withdrawal of the air unit and before discussing the matter with the Saudis.

Reasons for Retaining Hardsurface in Saudi Arabia

1. It had helped stop Saudi aid to the royalists. Would such aid now be resumed? It was a military backup for US policy and was a commitment to Faisal by Bunker. It had been the clincher in getting Faisal to accept the disengagement agreement.

2. It had already deterred the Egyptian air force from deep air penetration.

3. It could be augmented if Egyptian attacks were resumed.

4. UNYOM had certified a *net* Egyptian troop withdrawal of three thousand; not impressive, but helpful.

Reasons against Retaining Hardsurface in Saudi Arabia

1. Hardsurface, as constituted, could not remove the Egyptian threat entirely, and the longer it remained, the less credible it would be in the eyes of the Egyptians and the Saudis. If bombings should recur well inside Saudi Arabia, the United States would face humiliation or be obliged to take combat measures against Egypt, thus widening, rather than narrowing, polarization in the Arab world. It could quickly negate the president's diplomacy with Nasser in favor of a resort to force.

2. Of lesser importance but not to be ignored was the expense of deploying Hardsurface (which was being paid for by the United States) and Defense's alleged need for the air unit for a peaceful demonstration exercise in India.

3. Of considerable importance was the prospect that the longer the air unit remained in Saudi Arabia, the more the Saudi government would come to regard it as its own and seek for it a combat and even a reprisal role against border violations. If refused, Saudi opinion could turn sharply against the United States. In addition, firing upon Egyptian planes or other Egyptian forces, except in self-defense or in the defense of Saudi Arabia against serious and determined assault, was not consistent with US policy in the area. Any order in a contrary direction was the prerogative of President Kennedy, who had not yet approved the rules of engagement and who clearly wished first to exhaust all diplomatic remedies and avoid closer Egyptian reliance on Soviet support. Thus, the continued presence of the air unit, in itself, could be deleterious, creating Saudi demands on its use that would be inconsistent with US Cold War strategy.

As the result of an August 16 session with the Joint Chiefs of Staff, the thirty-day limitation on deployment, giving due regard to all the above factors, was extended to sixty days. Should a further extension be required, the Joint Chiefs would plan the rotation or replacement of the present force. By mid-September, I was to advise them on prospects for immediate redeployment.

At a second meeting on August 19, I testified alone to the Joint Chiefs. With the participation of Assistant Secretary Phillips Talbot, we all agreed in principle to implement an air defense survey mission in early September that would develop requirements, concepts, and procedures for air defense operations and long-range training programs. It would operate in conjunction with USMTM. It was decided to defer McNamara's invitation to Prince Sultan until just prior to the eventual withdrawal of Hardsurface, the visit to take place a few weeks after the unit's withdrawal.[6]

The month of August 1963 was a sensitive one. Just as Saqqaf in May and June had been caught in the middle attempting to ensure that supplies to the royalists had ceased even before formal entry of disengagement went into effect so that Hardsurface could be deployed, he was now hard at work seeking to prove Saudi willingness to cooperate fully with Von Horn. If Von Horn agreed, Saudi Arabia would participate in effectively monitoring all camel and vehicle traffic into the north of Yemen. Saqqaf assured me that Saudi area commanders were directed to strengthen border patrols, capture violators, and try them for treason. He was particularly concerned over private smuggling. UNYOM welcomed Saudi cooperation to ensure registration with it of all cargoes, to determine whether arms and ammunition were involved, or only food and nonlethal supplies.

On August 7 and 8, UNYOM verified tracks from Saudi Arabia crossing into Yemen and the unloading of a large quantity of 120 mm mortar ammunition. When I returned to Jeddah for a few days from consultations in Washington, I raised this matter with Saqqaf on August 10. He knew of it and had voiced his objections to Princes Sultan and Faisal. He was told the shipment was not authorized and believed it was private smuggling. I was instructed nevertheless to formally protest to the Saudi government and did so, emphasizing the bad image it gave to both Faisal and ourselves. Faisal thereupon ordered Brigadier General Marzuk al-Turki to investigate border control conditions. He reported tracks of a convoy coming to the Saudi border village of Sharura. On August 12 the Egyptian Air Force bombed a border village in Saudi Arabia, and both the United States and the UN Secretariat made strong protests to Cairo. Von Horn, after a reconnaissance trip, found that Egypt had a battalion-sized unit with armor and artillery three to five kilometers inside the YAR border. He complained to Egypt's General Qadi that this was well inside the demilitarized zone. Qadi responded that he would be unable to interdict royalist supplies if he was to withdraw from the DMZ. Von Horn then took after him for refusing to carry out an agreement signed by his own chief of state.

So went the seesaw of multilateral efforts to make the UNYOM and UN Secretariat in New York as effective as possible in the disengagement process. The process improved, and Von Horn did his best to get the "bugs" out. The vehicles for so-called enforcement were therefore the United Nations and US embassies in Cairo and Jeddah. These were vehicles for embarrassment of the violator, made useful through reports by the secretary-general to the Security Council or by direct representations to either head of state from President Kennedy via his ambassadors. Of the two systems, public reporting in the Security Council was the more effective in most cases.

While the observers generally credited the Saudi government with officially complying with the disengagement program but not checking smugglers, they found Egypt not even making a move to pull back from the demilitarized zone or to withdraw troops from the Yemen in substantial *net* numbers. Smuggling was indeed a factor and some of it most probably was beyond Saudi control. However, in mid-August UNYOM intercepted near Abu Arish three Saudi civilian five-ton trucks loaded with small arms, ammunition, and mortar shells of Belgian, American, and Jordanian origin. The royalist training camp that had been in Jizan was moved (pursuant to the disengagement agreement) far out of that city to Ta'if, in the mountains above Mecca. An UNYOM patrol in Jizan discovered at al-Kuba in the DMZ 47 mm guns being sent to the royalists by Jordan. In Najran, UNYOM found two trucks loaded with ammunition and food, two tankers, and eighteen armed civilians, as well as eight camels and six donkeys loaded with ammunition proceeding from Najran to nearby Nahouga, both in Saudi Arabia but in the demilitarized zone. Such shipments, even if minor and not condoned by the Saudi government, nonetheless offered useful excuses for Egyptian commanders to continue bombing and to dismiss US protests.

UNYOM BEGINS TO UNRAVEL

In the middle of the general frustration of the UN mission, Von Horn resigned on August 21, via an angry letter to U Thant demanding an increase of personnel by two divisions. He had become an embarrassment to the secretary-general, and Major General Rikhye was assigned to replace him temporarily. The reasons for at least some of his dissatisfactions were shared by Major David, who also sought to be relieved but under pressure agreed to remain until October 23. UNYOM observers were increasingly discouraged, questioning their mission's usefulness, and morale seemed low.

Von Horn was popular among his UNYOM troops and with the Arabs. He came to have second thoughts about leaving UNYOM and sought to rescind his resignation. The secretary-general refused to withdraw his acceptance. Major David's services were uniformly applauded, but he was personally loyal to Von Horn and critical of the New York headquarters for foot-dragging, second-guessing, and obliging UNYOM outposts to scrounge for food. New York seemed oblivious to living conditions that were especially poor in Hodaidah, Jizan, Najran, and Sa'da. In San'a they were only a trifle better. Pay inequalities were irritating, transport was in short supply, and almost no time off was possible because of the staff shortage.

As the year wore on, this became an issue between the governments of the national contingents and the secretary-general. These governments became increasingly impatient to withdraw their nationals from UNYOM.[7] To compound U Thant's problems, Egypt, which had agreed to pay its 50 percent of UNYOM bimonthly costs, had failed by the end of August to confirm or deposit its obligations for July and August. As a result, the Saudi government was withholding funds at the end of August until Egypt acted. Thus, the second two months (to November 4) were not covered by deposits.

General Rikhye made a quick inspection of UNYOM. Some of the US embassies in the area, having heard Von Horn's complaints, listened with attention to Rikhye's explanations and rebuttals. Rikhye closed the Jizan station, as it was three hours' drive from the border, and he replaced it with small bases at Maidi and Haradh in Yemen, bulldozing an airstrip. Hodaidah was cut in personnel since Egyptian forces were not allowing UNYOM to board ships and make a head count. Rikhye explained that in New York the secretary-general regarded the UNYOM mission as political rather than military, something, he said, Von Horn never understood.

He accepted Saudi proposals for the joint manning of border patrols, where the Saudis would stop and search convoys. Money to the royalists could not be stopped, and therefore neither could the influx of arms and ammunition, despite good faith efforts by Faisal. Rikhye reported that Egyptian commander Qadi had said that he could not cut his total forces below 25,000 and still hold five principal cities in the Yemen. He would make no further withdrawals until YAR forces were strong enough to take over defense; they were, at the time, being "slaughtered" by the royalists whenever they met. As a consequence, Egyptian forces were bearing the brunt, and their losses had been great. Qadi told Rikhye that these losses were so high that Egypt could face mutiny or a coup in the absence of a victory.

Rikhye believed that UNYOM in its original form should be discontinued by November 4, the end of a two-month financing period, and patrols on the border stopped and replaced by occasional visits by officer observers. As matters stood, UNYOM had no peacekeeping role beyond observing, certifying, and reporting. Of enforcement powers it had none. This was left up to the disputant parties.

In his report of September 4, 1963, U Thant took issue, without naming Von Horn, with reports of low morale and inadequate supplies, transport, and facilities. This evaluation resulted from reports by Colonel Branko Pavlovic, Von Horn's successor, and General Rikhye. U Thant reported Egyptian withdrawals of troops to be 13,000, he downgraded to "lesser numbers" the picture on replacements, and said that assistance to the royalists had been reduced; he affirmed, however, that "such traffic certainly had not ended."[8] He stated that he had oral assurances from both governments that they would defray the expenses of UNYOM for the two months starting September 4, 1963. Von Horn denounced the report to our chargé in Beirut, Evan M. Wilson, and turned to the ever-eager Lebanese press to carry on his dispute with the secretary-general. It was embarrassing to U Thant, but after a time it faded in importance.

The summer of 1963 had seen two months of joint funding of the observer mission by Saudi Arabia and by Egypt. The arrangement seemed to be working, but not perfectly: It saw a complete stoppage of *officially* sanctioned military assistance to the royalists by Saudi Arabia, but some continuation of cross-border smuggling. It saw vigorous, repetitive training of Saudi pilots through Hardsurface and a sharp decline but not a complete stoppage of Egyptian bombing. It saw a net drawdown of Egyptian troops in the Yemen, and a rising popular discontent there over the size and intrusiveness of the Egyptian military and political presence.

The sprouting of a grassroots Yemeni desire to take back full control of its internal and external affairs was dramatized that summer by a conference of heads of principal Yemeni tribes, held at Umran. The early Egyptian reaction to this gathering, to which Egyptian personnel had not been invited, was divided. The Egyptian military held that its forces should continue working with Abd Allah al-Sallal and other Yemeni leaders whose political lives depended on Egypt's presence and power, and that Egyptian forces should stay in the Yemen as long as necessary to achieve military victory. Outside the military, others had a different reaction. They saw military victory as unlikely and wanted the Yemeni republic, once it was secured against defeat by the royalists, to be broadened to ensure durability by consensus of the leading tribes.[9]

Cairo's instructions to force commanders were to allow the government of the YAR to explore means of strengthening and broadening its base of popular (tribal) support. The wider that base, the sooner Egypt could reduce its hemorrhage of lives and national treasure. Increasingly, Nasser showed a desire to reduce Egypt's commitment but not to write off the YAR entirely and by no means to accept a political or military defeat. Indications of this policy had appeared rather early in 1963 and showed a skillful calibration by Nasser of his priorities and of the image of Egypt that he wished to project in his Arab neighborhood. He was beset by limitations and did not possess wide options.

Faisal and Saudi Arabia at this political and economic stage sought only quiet and security. Since Faisal's fiscal reforms, the kingdom had money, but it badly needed time and peace in which to spend it well. Development had not even begun, and everything could be jeopardized by an aggressive Egypt poised at the back door of the kingdom and avowedly hostile to the Saudi leadership. Faisal felt his country caught by Egypt's enveloping military presence from north, west, and south. Hardsurface was temporary and not fully effective. The kingdom was inherently insecure. The limitations built into US policy objectives were of time, distance, and competing problems, notably Vietnam. Kennedy wanted to avoid all-out Saudi-Egyptian warfare, which could damage Saudi Arabia immeasurably and draw the United States out of its policy of seeking a tolerable relationship with Nasser. A military confrontation with Egypt would lead to anti-American turmoil throughout most of the Arab world, and the United States would undoubtedly fight Egypt, in the final analysis, to prevent Saudi Arabia from becoming an Egyptian satellite.

In late August 1963, I was instructed to deliver a letter and an oral message from President Kennedy to Faisal, to wit:

1. The disengagement agreement, although hampered by the occasional failure of the parties to honor it, had been successful in preventing large-scale Egyptian air raids or deep penetrations such as had previously hit the southern communities of Jizan, Khamis Mushayt, and Abha.

2. The United Nations had certified a net withdrawal of a considerable number of Egyptian troops since the agreement went formally into effect (July 4, 1963.)[10]

3. The United States had contributed materially to the start of disengagement by bringing the parties to agreement on its terms and by putting pressure on Egypt to make withdrawals. By introducing US forces into Saudi Arabia, it had helped prevent major Saudi-Egyptian confrontations.

4. The United States was gratified at the prompt Saudi undertaking to suspend aid to the royalists and to continue financial support of the UNYOM. The United States remained concerned about smuggling, as this could severely damage Saudi Arabia's international reputation and could shift the blame for any failure of the disengagement process from the Egyptian to the Saudi government.

5. A reduction of hostilities in the Yemen would remove the basic reason for an Egyptian military presence and would speed withdrawals.

6. President Kennedy urged strict compliance by all parties with the disengagement agreement and cooperation with the United Nations, to which the world looked for an assessment of performance by the parties.

7. Disengagement alone could not resolve the Yemeni conflict. Direct talks between representatives of Egypt and Saudi Arabia, as proposed by the United States, would offer an opening. Saudi Arabia had cited Egyptian propaganda attacks as justifying Saudi rejection of such talks, but the

Saudi government permitted royalists to use Mecca Radio. This was inconsistent with the Saudi undertaking to suspend help to the royalists and to leave the Yemenis to themselves.

8. The United States would welcome the suggestions of the Saudi government on how to achieve detente.

Faisal's answer was pointed and terse: Detente would come when Nasser got out of the Yemen.

Faisal now began a campaign to hold me responsible for this result, alleging that my assurances (in Bunker's presence) that the United States could induce Nasser to live up to his word had tipped the scale; he had accepted disengagement based on my promise. This was quite inaccurate, but I decided at once to let him give me the heat, as the alternative pointed toward a failure by the White House to demonstrate the necessary leverage with Nasser.

Our embassy efforts in this critical period, and those of the US embassy in Cairo, centered on helping UNYOM and Hardsurface, encouraging communication between Faisal and Nasser via trusted subordinates, and achieving acceptance by both Faisal and Nasser of a truly Yemeni solution—that is, in whatever form might be freely chosen by Yemeni leaders. It was thought that Nasser's acceptance of a political rather than military solution was possible, and, since a military solution was patently impossible, Saudi Arabia could accept an independent nonroyalist Yemen, as Riyadh had a geographical and long-term financial advantage in the contest for a friendly Yemen. This advantage already had begun to outweigh Egypt's temporary military advantage, and involvement was increasingly burdensome to Cairo. It would thus appear to be in both the Saudi and Egyptian interest to encourage the establishment, by tribal consensus, of a broadened Yemeni government.[11] The house of Hamid al-Din could not be returned to power, nor was such a return desirable, but some of its adherents could join a coalition. Any political solution would expedite a departure of Egyptian troops from a country increasingly restive under foreign rule.

The makings of any international compromise depended on (1) the sufficient unhappiness of both parties with their current situation, and (2) the presence and capability of a mediating agency that could produce a formula whereby neither party appeared to have been defeated and both could validly claim some gain. The ideal agency, whether mediator or conciliator, would need to be the most prestigious available and would have at least the *image* of impartiality. This usually meant the United Nations, because of its standing mandates to work for the peaceful settlement of disputes. Secondarily, it often meant the United States as the foremost power on the UN Security Council.

We felt in embassy Jeddah as well as Cairo that we had at last a thesis fully agreed upon with the Department of State that would carry weight with our two respective chiefs of state. In Cairo, on October 7, 1963, Ambassador Badeau had a thorough review of the situation with President Nasser. He invited Nasser's reflections on the Umran conference of tribal chiefs and on contacts proceeding between the government of the YAR and certain opposition elements. Egypt, Badeau acknowledged, had made considerable sacrifices in the Yemen and now entertained a concern that these not have been expended in vain. However—and here he bore in very strongly—the US government felt that Egypt's prestige and honor could be maintained if an independent and broadly based Yemeni government emerged from the current strife. The United States would help such a government in its economic development—an appeal to a known desire by Nasser to turn over this burden to the United States. Forcefully Badeau asserted that the US government found Egypt quite deficient in matching troop withdrawals with the cessation of Saudi aid to the royalists. The UN secretary-general, seeing no success in UNYOM, now intended to cut back the observer mission and might wish to terminate it altogether on November 4.

Badeau strongly urged that Egypt tell the secretary-general that UNYOM had served a useful purpose and recommend that he extend its mandate from November 4, 1963, to January 4, 1964; he also urged that Egypt continue to support UNYOM financially. The United States, for its part, would continue to press the Saudi government to maintain its financial support (although this had become increasingly difficult in light of the Saudi view that UNYOM had been quite ineffective in bringing about Egyptian withdrawals).

I was instructed to make parallel representations to Faisal to ensure continued Saudi funding of UNYOM, pointing out that Nasser had agreed to UNYOM's renewal, and to give every chance to the Yemenis to form a broad-based government. If the Saudi government failed to renew the UNYOM mandate, there would be a strong possibility that the Yemeni government would call for a meeting of the UN Security Council, charging that the Saudis were arming dissidents in the Yemen and urging that a UN presence be established in that country to report on Saudi infiltration and interference that threatened the peace. Faisal was to be urged, as a minimum, not to disrupt the process of political reconciliation and the development of a consensus in a reconstituted government of the Yemen. Should Faisal press for a clear statement regarding whether we would withdraw the USAF squadron if his government resumed aid to the royalists, I was to say that the final decision was for President Kennedy to make, but that I expected the unit would be withdrawn.

I presented my points to Faisal on October 6, accompanied by Rodger Davies, who was visiting from his position as director of Near Eastern Affairs at State. I elaborated to Faisal in another session after Davies had left, on October 12. It was the eve of the chiefs of mission conference (in Istanbul), chaired by Assistant Secretary Phillips Talbot, destined to be a strategy session on the dispute between Egypt and Saudi Arabia. James N. Cortada, US chargé in Taiz, was on consultation in Jeddah and Egypt, and was available, if needed, for an exchange of assessments with Faisal, supplementing my standing intelligence evaluations.

Both of my sessions with Faisal were rough. He insisted that the US government was responsible for disengagement and that he could not sit with arms folded while Nasser showed no intention of withdrawing forces. What would the United States do if disengagement failed because of Nasser's cheating and Saudi Arabia thus resumed aid to the royalists and was then attacked? If the United States had changed its policy, as he suspected it had, he needed to be so informed so that he could provide for the defense of his country. He stated that US intelligence on the Yemen was poor, rejected its findings, and brushed off our offer to bring Cortada into our discussions to provide a comparison of information. He said he was not interested in assessments based on what a US chargé d'affaires in San'a heard from Egyptians.

At this I became a little annoyed, and I reminded the prince that he and I had agreed to exchange frank appraisals on points of fact. Faisal appeared to calm down, but as he obviously did not want to hear Cortada's view, I did not press the matter. What was more important, I had begun to hear that Faisal had moved in his thinking away from restoration of a royalist regime in the Yemen and toward a readiness to accept any form of broadened government in that country that might be achieved by the Yemenis of their own free will *after* Egyptian troop withdrawals were complete. In this his views followed closely the developing concepts of U Thant, but he was not ready to admit this to me.

Following my return to Jeddah from our sessions in Istanbul, I received instructions on October 18 from President Kennedy to deliver an "oral" message to Faisal in response to the views he, Faisal, had given me on October 12. The president reaffirmed the abiding concern of the US government for the integrity of Saudi Arabia and its support of Faisal's leadership. For this reason disengagement must not be allowed to fail. US policy contained no "behind-the-scenes" element. Extraordinary representations had been made to Egypt. The US government, having recognized the Yemen Arab Republic, could not, however, be put in the position of aiding its overthrow, as Faisal, a leader with the highest sense of honor, would readily see. The US and Saudi governments must not be at cross-purposes in preserving the integrity of Saudi Arabia and UNYOM, which had contributed to stability and should be renewed.

This message did not satisfy Faisal nor did a follow-up that I sent on October 29, the day U Thant was to send his two-month report to the

Security Council that would state whether the parties accepted renewal of UNYOM. An answer came back within hours from Saqqaf in Riyadh that was somewhat blurred but appeared to ask for a timetable of Egyptian troop withdrawals as a condition of renewal of UNYOM. This was manifestly impossible in the hours remaining before renewal and seemed to presage a rejection; U Thant would have been obliged to state that Faisal, in effect, had rejected renewal of UNYOM by posing conditions in the form of questions that U Thant could not possibly answer. Egypt had accepted renewal. I therefore headed for Riyadh in a borrowed USAF C-130, which would stand by in Riyadh to fly me to Dhahran, the nearest communication point for coded messages to Washington and New York.

Hard-pressed by Charles W. Yost, one of the US ambassadorial delegates to the United Nations, U Thant had agreed to postpone the typesetting of his report by a day, to 4 P.M. on October 29 for publication on October 30. U Thant agreed with Yost that once Faisal's demands were in print, they would be very hard for the prince to retract. Once UNYOM was out, the civil war in the Yemen could escalate and expand. Meanwhile, I was instructed to inform Faisal that in addition to Nasser's public commitment to withdraw 6,000 troops, the Egyptian leader, under great pressure, had promised withdrawal of another 5,000 by the end of 1963.

On October 30, I had a three-hour landmark session with the prince, with Saqqaf taking notes. I urged that Faisal at once clarify to U Thant his unconditional acceptance of renewal of UNYOM so that an amendment could be incorporated in the secretary-general's already drafted report to the Security Council. I said that at present the secretary-general found the situation too ambiguous to handle. Egypt had accepted UNYOM's renewal, but Saudi Arabia had not, and U Thant could only consider the prince's apparent demand for a timetable of Egyptian troop withdrawals to be a condition impossible to carry out in the time available. It therefore constituted a rejection of U Thant's recommendation that UNYOM be renewed.

Unknown to us as we met, U Thant had in fact already initiated steps to disband the observer mission. The US delegation to the United Nations reported on October 30 that UNYOM's removal was already well under way, by order of Ralph Bunche. A ship was due in Hodaidah on November 2 to pick up vehicles and equipment. The United Nations had asked the US government for the loan of a C-130 cargo plane to lift 100 Yugoslav troops from Najran to Cairo. Bunche had pointed out that the secretary-general wanted to shift the mission in the Yemen from a military to a political presence (apparently on Ambassador Spinelli's recommendation) and to post high-level Secretariat officials in Jizan and Najran and in San'a.

I recommended that the prince channel his fully justified dissatisfaction over Egyptian disengagement to us, the United States, not to U Thant, because President Kennedy was right now exerting great pressure on Nasser to live up to his agreement. Kennedy could only carry out the pledge he had made to Faisal if the Saudi government continued to refrain from military aid to the royalists. I reminded the prince that he had asked me whether I trusted Nasser to carry out the disengagement agreement and I had replied that I trusted President Kennedy to exert his full leverage with Nasser to get him to carry out his promises. It was on this basis that Faisal had agreed to Bunker's proposals; Faisal had since then reiterated to me many times his own trust in the president and in the US government. It was therefore not appropriate to ask the United States for a "guarantee," which connoted a degree of distrust.

Faisal responded that he was pained to find that his friends, the Americans, were blaming him for the collapse of UNYOM, whose continuation he had not rejected. He had been consulting with his Council of Ministers on various alternatives.[12] Finally he stated that he desired a night to weigh the matter and asked if I could remain. I did, of course, at a hotel where Saqqaf and I had a long talk. He was hopeful of positive results and would see Faisal early the next morning, when he would propose categoric renewal of UNYOM for two months—or as a fallback, one month—during which Faisal would delegate to him the mission of considering, along with me, ways to make disengagement more effective.

The next morning, October 31, on my arrival for resumption of talks at the Red Sea Palace, Saqqaf met me with relief on his face. He said Faisal had agreed to a categoric prolongation of UNYOM, and a cable to that effect was now being sent to New York. Separately, a draft letter was being prepared to look over with me.

I met at once with Faisal, Saqqaf attending. The prince had heard a summary on the BBC of U Thant's long report to the Security Council on October 28 regarding termination of UNYOM in favor of a civilian UN presence. Faisal made no comment to me on its extensive provisions. He produced a draft "oral" message, in English, to President Kennedy that required my concurrence. It would say that I agreed that the United States would be somewhat more forthcoming than in the past as to what it was actually doing to induce Egypt to comply with its disengagement pledge. (I had supplied no details.) The message would state (a) that I promised that the United States would take steps and use pressure to obtain an expeditious Egyptian withdrawal of its forces in Yemen; (b) that I concurred that renewal of UNYOM should not lead to the same experience as during the preceding four months; and (c) that I concurred in an immediate opening of discussions with Saqqaf as to what might be possible for the US government to undertake in terms of pressure on Egypt to withdraw forces as speedily as possible. Saqqaf would pledge his fullest cooperation in implementing disengagement, including refraining from aid to the royalists and, in accord with the Bunker agreement, from giving permission to them to use Saudi Arabia as a base of operations.

This "oral" message had been prepared by Saqqaf, who promised that it would not be released. It was made clear I must countersign my approval now or a renewal of the UNYOM mandate would not occur. Looking closely at the English text, I substituted the word "toward" for "against" and "other party" for the "United Arab Republic" whenever these words were associated, and agreed to sign, as amended.

It was a gamble and a most irregular way of doing business. There was no time to refer to Washington to await editorial changes and then try to negotiate them. The stakes were high, and I knew President Kennedy's policy was to see UNYOM renewed. The policy permitted flexibility in application. This latest Saudi gambit bore the earmarks of a toning down by Saqqaf of somewhat tougher language by early drafters in the ministerial council. The clock was ticking, however, and I was not sure at the time whether any renewal notice from Faisal would reach U Thant in time.

Faisal readily accepted my editorial changes. I flew back to Jeddah with a two-month UNYOM renewal in my pocket and a text that Washington might not like in detail or form but could hardly say lay outside the parameters of active Kennedy policy. The first reaction by Washington to my report and to the text suggested something less than complete satisfaction with procedure and language but no disavowal of the action taken. A personal note from Assistant Secretary Talbot was warmly congratulatory. In New York, Secretary-General U Thant received the urgent telegram from Saqqaf, approved by Faisal, renewing Saudi support of UNYOM for two more months. The report was amended on October 31 to restore UNYOM for another two months in approximately its original form and size and to cancel the secretary-general's measures for withdrawal of the mission.[13]

In retrospect, I concluded that Faisal had been under pressure from hawkish members of the Saud family to pin down the United States or abandon disengagement. He was probably not fully aware of the tough representations made by Ambassador Badeau to Nasser and was trying to test the degree to which he would endanger the US protective relationship through renewal of aid to the royalists. I had been able to tell the prince that Nasser had been swayed by US pressures enough to pledge withdrawal of 11,000 troops by the end of 1963. In any case, what Faisal required of me was no more than putting in writing what I was already doing, and I felt then that he was extricating himself from an impasse with his family and advisors.

My return to Jeddah coincided with an afternoon reception aboard the carrier USS *Essex*, escorted by several types of war vessels. The visit had been scheduled six months earlier, during the Bunker mission, as an expression of US solidarity and determination to support the integrity of Saudi Arabia. The Saudi guests included the minister of defense, Prince Sultan; Prince Mish'al ibn Abd al-Aziz, governor of Jeddah; a variety of officials from the Saudi press; and a selection of leading Saudi business-men. They were treated to a show of drone targeting, depth charge firing, and other naval exercises, and to light refreshments. It was something totally new to the populace and was made the more relaxing by virtue of a partial leak that had occurred over my just-completed session with Faisal. The diplomatic episode was now public property and was inter-preted as having staved off open warfare between Egypt and Saudi Arabia. The Saudis, though, are not given to excesses of panic or exuberance, and its press was controlled by general guidance. I do not recall that it ever mentioned the crisis, although the naval visit was well covered. A local businessman financed a dinner for all of the crews who could be spared ashore; well over one hundred men enjoyed a fine meal, fraterni-zation with Saudi officers, and a change of scene.

Just before his death three weeks later, Kennedy had considerably stiffened his attitude toward Nasser's noncompliance with his disengage-ment undertaking and sent him the strongest message on record, setting a tone for the future. Kennedy informed Nasser that the United States would not stand idly by if he were to carry hostilities into Saudi Arabia. Further, the United States would not consider granting the additional economic aid Egypt had requested until the Yemen situation improved, inasmuch as the occupation of the Yemen constituted a drain on Egyp-tian resources and was contrary to the disengagement agreements under-taken by Cairo. Washington asserted that Saudi aid to the royalists had ceased months prior, and Egypt's failure to live up to its agreement on withdrawals could not be justified.

Kennedy had made the determination, after my October 31 session with Faisal, that the Hardsurface unit should be withdrawn by the end of January 1964. Much of the tone of Kennedy's letter informing Faisal of this decision emanated, I feel sure, from the exceptionally sharp reluctance of Faisal, in October 1963, to promise renewal of UNYOM despite the presence of Hardsurface. Additionally, Faisal's demand to me of October 31 contained an element of finality. If Nasser did not now comply during the two months from November 4, 1963, to January 4, 1964, Faisal would find it hard to renew UNYOM again. The result for Kennedy had to be a decision (pushed hard by JCS chief General LeMay) that Hardsurface would leave, with the verbal assurance to Faisal that it could return in greater force if Nasser launched a serious military offen-sive on Saudi Arabia. Another factor in determining the end of Hard-surface was the developing conclusion in U Thant's and Kennedy's offices that the principal Yemeni tribal leaders were groping for a consensus that could lead to reconciliation with the opposition, and to political cooperation with the United Nations in the search for a new ruling coalition. This would render the Egyptian presence in the Yemen irrelevant and oblige Cairo to leave (or be charged in the UN Security Council with aggression).

UNYOM could not succeed as a means of expediting disengagement. This was attested by the UN secretary-general's reports and its mandate. Perhaps, if the parties agreed (as U Thant hoped), it could be transformed into a political advisory body, assisting the YAR in its search for intertribal consensus. Kennedy and U Thant were therefore on the same general track. Washington was concerned about preserving the peace and Saudi stability while this transformation was being effected. As previously mentioned, moreover, Nasser had signaled that he might cooperate in order to lighten for Egypt the burdens of his unpopular and expensive war.

Whether Nasser also bore in mind, by this time, the strategic vulnerability of Egypt cannot be confirmed—Egypt's Nile dam could be hit from the Hejaz by a mercenary pilot in a leased bomber aircraft. What is sure is that the highest levels of the Saudi government had such a measure under advisement, but only as an unlikely last resort. For the immediate future it was rejected. Before Hardsurface, Saqqaf had volunteered this to me and one of his country's delegates to the United Nations; having in mind still-fresh Egyptian air raids, he pointed out to a US delegate that Saudi Arabia could hurt Egypt more in one bombing run on Aswan than Egypt could inflict on Saudi Arabia in months of air attacks.

This had been very much in my mind as I struggled with Faisal to maintain the disengagement process. Much to our relief, we now had a mandate valid from November 4, 1963, to January 4, 1964. It proved to be the last renewal for which I had to struggle, and for which I could be held primarily responsible by Faisal, either as Kennedy's spokesman or on my own account of twenty years' association with the prince.

KENNEDY'S DEATH AND THE RESHAPING OF UNYOM

President Kennedy's assassination on November 22, 1963, inevitably led to reevaluations of the ties between the White House and Saudi Arabia. President Lyndon B. Johnson, in acknowledging Faisal's message of condolence, reaffirmed in strong terms US support for Faisal and for the kingdom.

The relationship between Faisal and President Kennedy was unique in the experience of both leaders. In their extensive correspondence, much attention was given to style and to preserving the touch of the special personal regard that sprang from their October 1962 meeting in Washington. Kennedy had attempted to win both confidence and restraint from Faisal. In the West and the East, little regard was shown for Saudi Arabia, where the extravagances of King Saud during the previous ten years were remembered far more than Faisal's reforms. Had Nasser sought to invade Saudi Arabia following his botched air drop of February 1963, Faisal would have had, in my view, no real help from any quarter other than the United States.

Even there he could see rescue imperiled. Since the USAF Second Air Division had been expelled by the Saudi government from command of Dhahran Airfield, US public interest in Saudi Arabia had indeed flagged. Vietnam preoccupied the White House, Defense, and State; congressional interest was usually negative or nonexistent. With great effort I was able just once in my tour of four years as ambassador to obtain a visit to Saudi Arabia from Capitol Hill. Senator Bourke B. Hickenlooper of Iowa, a most thoughtful and considerate man, came on Thanksgiving Day 1963; after our dinner he and I flew to Riyadh to visit Faisal for a courtesy call and *tour d'horizon*. No substantive exchange occurred, but the gesture was much appreciated by the prince. Still, it was essentially President Kennedy who had kept attuned to what was now a twenty-year US commitment to the territorial integrity and political independence of Saudi Arabia.

Earlier in November in New York, U Thant had decided to appoint Italian ambassador Pier Spinelli, then director of the UN European Office in Geneva, as his special representative and head of UNYOM, to work for a coalition government in the Yemen. U Thant was urging that this work be financed from UN contingency funds (and thus avoid a formal meeting of the Security Council). It would be far less costly than the deployment of UNYOM.

Spinelli arrived on duty November 9 in the Yemen, relieving Lieutenant General Prem Singh Gyani, who returned to his regular post as commander of the UN Emergency Force in Gaza and Sinai. Colonel Pavlovic became chief of staff. UNYOM had to be partially rebuilt as a number of observers had left the area by October 31, when U Thant started to disband the organization because of the apparent lack of Saudi support. By January 1964, twenty-one observers were in place, hailing from Denmark, Ghana, India, Italy, The Netherlands, Norway, Pakistan, Sweden, and Yugoslavia. In his January 2, 1964, report to the Security Council,[14] as in his October 28, 1963, report, U Thant asserted that no arms or ammunition were verified by UN observers as crossing from Saudi Arabia. He credited the liaison work by Saudi soldiers, moving with UN observers from one crossing of the sand tracks to another, as evidence of Saudi good faith. Upon request by a UN observer, these Saudi officers would do what the observer was not empowered to do: stop the convoy and inspect its contents. However, the secretary-general reported *prima facie* evidence that Saudi Arabian authorities were "providing some forms of encouragement to the Royalists."

Saqqaf had correctly predicted, when he called on me in November to express condolences on Kennedy's death, that Faisal would renew financing of UNYOM after January 2. U Thant had requested renewal for six months to give Spinelli time to work for a political settlement in the Yemen. Faisal renewed for two months, however, until the beginning of March 1964. The royalists had built up their supplies, probably via Baihan, an area bordering conservative, British-protected south Arabian sheikhdoms. There UNYOM had no mandate to operate, as the area was not considered part of the Bunker agreement. In his March 3, 1964, report to the Security Council,[15] U Thant included mention of this route and "extensive and coordinated operations" designed to cut roads in the Yemen from San'a to Hodaidah, Taiz, Ma'rib, and Sa'da. The crucially important San'a-Hodaidah road was blocked for a week. However, the far north, where incidents of bombing had reoccurred in late fall of 1963, was quiet.

In early 1964, more than 4,000 Egyptian troops arrived in the Yemen, and more than 1,000 departed—a large discrepancy considering the 11,000 withdrawal figure publicly promised by Nasser under US pressure in late October 1963. It is clear that US pressure had failed to shake Nasser's position on troop rotations, which now showed a reported net increase of 1,000 to 2,000 men. No Egyptian overflights of Saudi territory were reported, however. Spinelli had taken up with Egyptian authorities the "unfortunate impression" created by the increase of Egyptian forces. He was told that the decrease of forces was suspended because of heavy royalist attacks, and that the phased disengagement of Egyptian troops would be resumed when reasonably secure conditions existed in the Yemen.

Around the end of February 1964, I was visited at my office by an old Arab friend from the 1940s, my earliest days in Jeddah. Sheikh Muhammad Alireza was a prosperous international businessman of a renowned commercial family and the older brother of Ali Alireza, later to become Saudi ambassador to the United States. He was also a friend of Faisal's. Sheikh Muhammad asked to see me in private and proceeded to read to me a letter in Faisal's own hand, addressing him as "brother"—a term of respect that touched the sheikh deeply—urging him to accept appointment as the Saudi ambassador to Egypt. Faisal gave him no special instructions, but made no bones about the sensitivity and difficulties of the job. Sheikh Muhammad wished to have a good relationship with US ambassador Badeau. I said this presented no problem and that I would write a letter of introduction. I cautioned him about security. Nasser's special police were ubiquitous and dutifully "bugged" diplomatic residences as best they could.

Alireza's appointment was a sign that Faisal was ready for the restoration of relations with Egypt and improved diplomatic communication. Sheikh Muhammad's unique capabilities were flawless English, sophistication combined with utter loyalty, and an exceptionally wide international circle of friends. He was to be an alter ego for Faisal in Cairo.

RESTORATION OF THE EGYPTIAN-SAUDI DIALOGUE

The process for which the United States and the UN secretary-general had been working—direct negotiations between Egypt and Saudi Arabia at a high official level—had at last become possible. In his March 3 report to the UN Security Council, U Thant noted that the implementation of disengagement remained disappointing, but that one encouraging sign on the horizon was the improvement in relations between Saudi Arabia and Egypt that had emerged from a conference of Arab heads of state on January 13.[16] The secretary-general reported that for some time both he and his special representative, Spinelli, had been urging the two parties to start in this direction and that the presidents of Algeria and Iraq had agreed to act as joint mediators. A Saudi Arabian delegation had met with this mission and had subsequently issued a communiqué stating that it welcomed the resumption of political relations with Egypt, provided that a meeting be held in Riyadh, to be attended also by the two mediating presidents, relating mainly to problems connected with the resumption of diplomatic ties. The secretary-general expressed his hope that the result would include progress toward disengagement, which, he regretted, was lacking, mainly because of Egypt's failure to undertake a genuine withdrawal of troops and thus foster political progress and stability in the Yemen. U Thant also announced that the parties had agreed to the extension of UNYOM for another two months, to May 4.

It was clear that U Thant and Spinelli had settled in their minds on a different game plan than had been possible when Von Horn led UNYOM; this active and imaginative new UN team would replace the US government and its ambassadors, which had been serving as the needed mediator. All this was greeted in Washington, Cairo, and Jeddah with a sense of relief. The United States had played an essential role in preventing a direct trial of military strength between the parties. And UNYOM's renewal, supplementing UN/Arab diplomacy, was temporarily useful as a sheet anchor of stability in reopening Egyptian-Saudi relations as they cautiously moved toward resumption of full diplomatic ties.

It was also clear that Faisal and Nasser, for the time being, were refraining from steps that would interfere with their new efforts at bilateral diplomacy and that this factor had more weight than US representations. On the merits of the case, Faisal could have been justified in restoring aid to the royalists. By the secretary-general's reports, he had complied while

Nasser had blatantly violated disengagement. Furthermore, Nasser's air force was reported to be dropping poison gas canisters on Yemeni villages.

The meeting in Riyadh was held without Saudi consultation with us. To those of us at the embassy, the change was most welcome. While we naturally were most curious as to the state of play, we were relieved that the United States was at the point where it did not have to expend heavy verbal ammunition with Faisal to preserve nonbelligerence. Nasser was not going to war right now with Saudi Arabia, and Spinelli was doing a most competent job in encouraging a broader-based government in the YAR. U Thant's reports to the Security Council noted no signs of any Egyptian air or ground attacks on Saudi targets. The secretary-general also noted a shift of blame for royalist attacks on the Baihan region— previously used to justify net imports of troops into the Yemen from Egypt.

The Egyptian troops on the ground continued to be rotated, not withdrawn, and were holding key points and strategic paths. Otherwise, they were inactive at their outposts, even though being sniped at. However, as earlier indicated, UNYOM personnel were quietly investigating their alleged use of poison gas on Yemeni villages in the royalist area. Canisters of the gas had been picked up and tested in the United States. The gas was lacrimogenic, and could be fatal if used in high enough concentrations. The secretary-general was informed, but did not wish to publish the information. Instead, he is reported to have charged Nasser in a strong personal letter. So far as I know, this apparently experimental use of the gas was never stated publicly. Its most inhumane employment, as reported to me, was against a northern Yemeni village on a market day when alleys and squares were loaded with people.

The coinciding in December 1963 of US notification of withdrawal of Hardsurface by the end of January with a call by Nasser for a meeting of Arab heads of state in Cairo was fortuitous and by no means planned. The latter overshadowed the former, and the shock of Kennedy's assassination blunted the impact of the air unit's withdrawal. We had given Faisal advance warning that the air unit's presence in his country was not permanent, and we had allowed for no further discussion of its tenure when the time came. That being the case, the Saudi government owed us no report on Faisal-Nasser discussions in Cairo or elsewhere, nor on other meetings, and I received none. I had the mixed sensation of frustrated curiosity and relief at the lifting of this burden. The US role in the Yemen dispute was now sharply diminished.

Quite willingly, both Egypt and Saudi Arabia renewed UNYOM's financing for the two months from July 4 to September 4, 1964. In his July 4 report to the Security Council, U Thant recommended this renewal to keep order, but stated that if real progress toward disengagement was not achieved during these two months, he would recommend UNYOM be shut down. Meaningful withdrawals of Egyptian troops were to be the touchstone. Since net withdrawals of significance had not been recorded after six weeks, U Thant checked with both parties on August 19 and ascertained their nonobjection to UNYOM's termination. Thus ended a seven-month extension of UNYOM without the guardianship of Hard-surface. Both Nasser and Faisal were now, so to speak, investing in each other and in their image at the United Nations.

The year 1963 was a critical milestone in the tightening of US security bonds with Saudi Arabia. It was the year of Kennedy, Faisal, and Nasser, a testing of strong wills, but also the year of Ellsworth Bunker's successful March–April mission. Under great stress, the unusually cordial personal relationship established earlier between Crown Prince Faisal and President Kennedy was maintained.

Kennedy was determined to shield Saudi Arabia's territorial integrity and independence. To strengthen the Faisal regime from overthrow, he encouraged much-needed political, social, and fiscal reforms and was prepared to confront threats from abroad, including covert measures within the kingdom. The small USAF fighter unit Kennedy authorized to conduct "training" flights in the sensitive area just north of the Yemen border was a symbol of vital US interest. Though it could not be 100 percent effective in preventing intrusions, it was a warning that did not go unheeded.

Nineteen sixty-three was also the year for preserving a degree of US civility, if not cordiality, toward Nasser, in contrast to the six years of chill during the Eisenhower administration. Kennedy recognized Nasser as the foremost leader in the contemporary Arab world and set out to change the image of the United States from one hostile to Arab progress and strength to that of a friendly interest in material Arab advance. Setting aside differences in ideology, Kennedy sought to find areas of agreement with Nasser and to develop them. He particularly backed economic assistance in the face of mounting congressional opposition.

Several factors changed the scenario of the dragged-out Egyptian-Saudi clash over the Yemen, lifting the centrality of US mediation and shifting the major burden toward the United Nations and then to the disputants themselves. One was the impact and timing of the death of President Kennedy. Another factor was Pier Spinelli. Almost imperceptibly, his mission, closely consulting US mission chiefs in Cairo, Taiz, and Jeddah, moved into tight liaison with U Thant in New York. Determined, patient, and statesmanlike, Spinelli traveled the area, debriefed his UNYOM personnel, met the leading Yemenis of various persuasions, and shared his impressions with the three US mission chiefs before making his reports to the secretary-general. Badeau, Cortada, and I shared all our information with Spinelli in utter frankness. It was a refreshing experience after a year of tension.

Spinelli was the man of the hour for his boss, U Thant. As one important result, U Thant began to take initiatives instead of waiting for consensus or the discharge of marginal formalities. An example was his direct message to Faisal urging a renewal of UNYOM for six months to allow time for Spinelli to engineer a broader-based government of the Yemen and to keep the lid on disengagement between Egypt and Saudi Arabia while this was going on.

A third factor was Nasser's summoning of all Arab heads of state to meet with him in Cairo in January 1964. The basis of the gathering was Israel's reported plan to divert Jordan River waters. Nasser's summons was a transparent device to extricate himself from the corner into which he had strayed by virtue of his expensive and self-defeating adventure in the Yemen. He needed to reinject new life into his image as an Arab nationalist and as a champion of Arab rights. This was particularly important to him following the failure of his 1963 unity talks with the governments of Syria and Iraq. The Israeli diversion, as I saw it, was already an old story in the early 1950s, which had been dealt with vigorously but unsuccessfully in 1954 and 1955 by Eric Johnston, President Eisenhower's special emissary on Jordan River waters. The problem had been quiescent since the Johnston mission had failed when an Arab League political committee rejected its recommendations. Nasser had now revived the "threat" as imminent, citing unverifiable reports that Israel was about to divert the entire upper Jordan to its own use. This call to arms included Faisal, who, under Arab circumstances, could hardly refuse to attend. His acceptance offered a unique opportunity for a one-on-one Egyptian-Saudi bilateral.

Although Nasser's move to extricate himself from isolation was smart, it was also a risky gamble in the course of which he could have stumbled out of a small but divisive (and expensive) struggle in the Yemen into a full-sized Arab-Israeli war. He was skirting the precipice, but he counted on his charisma, on Arab nationalism, and on anti-Israel fervor to submerge criticism of his fiasco on the Arabian Peninsula and restore his own pan-Arab leadership.

According to reports, as Faisal walked to the door of the January meeting place in Cairo, a waiting Nasser, smiling broadly, had declared in a loud voice, "I expected to see you carrying a machine gun!" As this anecdote suggests, Faisal and Nasser had had a meaningful acquaintance.

During a private meeting in late July 1963, Faisal and I had discussed Nasser. He described the man he had known as a friend. He spoke of Nasser's resentment of the patronizing manner in which his father, a postman in Assiut, had been treated by wealthy landowners. Nasser, he said, had acquired some hangups from this boyhood experience, which was at least partially responsible for his behavior and his aggressiveness in seeking Egyptian hegemony over a wide area. I had the impression that under better circumstances Faisal could renew relations with Nasser. At the time, however, he had no alternative but to keep him at a distance. Faisal urged that the United States completely cut off all economic assistance to Egypt, whereupon, he asserted, Nasser would have to leave the Yemen and abandon (or be expelled from) his position as president of Egypt. I responded that it was most unlikely the United States would find this step useful in its overall Arab policy in the Cold War context or that such a move would have the result Faisal predicted.

Perhaps because between us we had worn out this topic, Faisal had changed the subject and expressed his deep admiration for the United States, saying, "After Allah, we trust the United States." He was totally sincere, I believe. Then he suddenly indicated a desire to reverse King Saud's 1962 action in terminating the US joint command at Dhahran Airfield, declaring, "Get rid of Nasser and you are welcome back in." In effect, he was expressing the wish that Nasser, as an impediment to closer US-Saudi relations, be removed by terminating US-Egyptian relations. It was quite unrealistic, and he knew it, but, as I reported to Washington, it voiced his exasperation that the politics of Arab unity were blocking a tighter Saudi-US security bond.

9

THE DEPOSING OF KING SAUD:
FAISAL'S ACCESSION

Unique in the history of Saudi Arabia as a kingdom—as distinct from the house of Saud in the nineteenth century—the deposing of King Saud and the immediate accession of Faisal to the throne stood alone as an example of a forced transfer of power that occurred without violence or direct threat of military action. This drama reached its climax in November 1964.

Faisal had been operating as de facto king since October 1962, on the basis of the delegation of full powers to him by his ailing half-brother, King Saud. During 1963 Faisal had added greatly to his reputation for judgment and leadership in both the domestic and foreign fields. His public following was demonstrably great, and the collegium (as I call it) of elder princes and the *ulema* were solidly with him and ready to support him as the head of state. Faisal's authority thus gave sanction to the drastic budgetary restriction on royal emoluments and to a shrinking of Saud's discretionary purse, which Saud had treated as a cornucopia open to his whims. The purse strings were now controlled by the will and the planning of a group selected and headed by Faisal.

Saud returned to Saudi Arabia in the summer of 1963 from extended medical treatment in Europe. Irritated over these developments and reportedly jealous of Faisal's popularity, Saud was stirred into action by some of his sons. Eager for the prestige of high office, they prodded him to reassert his royal will and to give evidence that the authority he had delegated could be recalled at any time. Active opposition to the king's reassertion of authority was grouped around the Al Fahd or "Sudairi Seven." Prince Fahd bin Abd al-Aziz, minister of the interior, was at the center of the action in this confrontation. Other members of the Sudairi Seven were Prince Sultan, minister of defense and civil aviation; his deputy, Prince Nayif; Prince Salman, emir of Riyadh; and Princes Turki, Ahmad, and Abd al-Rahman. By December 1963, a confrontation had developed.

In November 1963 as an opening gun, King Saud summoned all tribal leaders to meet him in Riyadh. After his return from Europe, he had toured the Eastern Province, where his popularity was the highest, augmenting his visit with the traditional royal largesse that accompanied these gatherings. Now Saud was about to go on a visit to the Hejaz. Welcoming arches and other decorations had been erected in Jeddah to celebrate his coming. The erection of these arches had been a routine part of Saud's travels in the kingdom since the late 1940s, well before he became king. It always seemed an unnecessary extravagance, since the king was traveling in his own country. This time the arches and large photos were abruptly removed from their emplacements in Jeddah and Mecca.

The king was shaken. Fearing the worst, he moved quickly to the city of Ha'il, just south of the great Nefud sands of northern Nejd, but his apparent hope of gaining tribal support was not realized. Then, suddenly, the Royal Guard arsenal at Riyadh was taken over by the National Guard, commanded by Emir Abd Allah ibn Abd al-Aziz.

On December 14, King Saud returned to Riyadh, attracting little attention. He held an audience with tribal leaders at Qasr al-Hukm. That evening he collected those of his extensive family then present in Riyadh and put them in the Nasiriyya Palace complex, deploying the Royal Guard on the two most conspicuous sides of the outer palace wall.[1] An inside wall was knocked down to give camping space to the *Khawiyya* (the Brotherhood, a traditional, personal bodyguard of senior emirs) and miscellaneous Bedouin leaders. Altogether, about five hundred people were encamped. It was speculated that this very public move was prompted by the king's sons, who assembled on December 15 and 16 from many quarters in response to rumors of attempts to assassinate their father.

Feeling secure in his palace, the king now sent a message to Faisal demanding the resignation of the Council of Ministers, but offering Faisal permission to continue as president of a new council that could not include Fahd or Sultan. The king also demanded a more active role for himself in the new government.

Faisal refused the king's demand, pointing out that to follow them would be interpreted by the public as an action taken under duress. He attempted an interview with the king but was rebuffed. Faisal kept his cool and even notified the king's mother (a "queen mother" of great prestige) that he had nothing against her son, and that if Saud would name those alleged to be plotting against him, they would be dealt with.

The first move toward conciliation was taken by the grand mufti, Sheikh Muhammad bin Ibrahim Al al-Sheikh, of the same Wahhabi family line as Faisal on his maternal side. With the solid independence of his position as head of the *ulema* and of his family lineage, the sheikh listened to the king's complaint, to wit: he was being "plotted against"; he was being mistreated and slighted; he was prevented from visiting his people; he was therefore justified, under the *sharia*, to defend himself by calling out the Royal Guard. The mufti warned the king that if he took action leading to bloodshed, the *ulema* would withdraw their pledge of loyalty. This warning was repeated to the king two days later when he received the *ulema* at another audience at Qasr al-Hukm. Saud was jolted by the revelation that support by the *ulema* could be so quickly lost. He withdrew the Royal Guard, which was restive in any case after four days and nights at their posts without knowing their objective and after having lost their arsenal to the National Guard.

Meanwhile, Faisal was informed by his half-brother Abd Allah ibn Abd al-Aziz and by Emir Sultan that he could count on the complete loyalty of the National Guard, the regular army, and the air force. (There was, as yet, no real navy.) Thus, Faisal had, as indispensable assets, the promised loyalty and obedience of the armed forces. Power was still in his hands, but the challenge to limit or withdraw it continued. Faisal was now being pressured by his supporters, as was the king by his sons and his entourage. Faisal was attempting to restrain his brothers and leave the king with ceremonial title and duties, while retaining all substantive powers for himself. Saud, in seeking first to invalidate those powers, and then later to recover them for himself, succeeded only in precipitating a showdown in which he could only lose.

One gambit led him to think he had won. As king, he had received Egyptian president Nasser's December call for the January 1964 Cairo conference of Arab heads of state to confront Israel. He accepted, attended, apparently expressed no substantive views, and was most courteously treated by Nasser, with whom he exchanged the customary effusive telegrams of regard on his departure. Faisal also attended. While Saud's trip to Cairo was under the agreed rubric of ceremonial powers, it may well have encouraged him—along with the egging on of his sons—to again try for a bigger bite of power.

By mid-March 1964 a new Faisal-Saud confrontation was under way. After several days of camping in the desert, Saud sent Faisal an "ultimatum" demanding that the Council of Ministers be rearranged to include some of the king's sons and others he would select; he also demanded that the king's privy purse be increased. Faisal was reported to have been given five days to comply "or there would be no sixth day." When no action by Faisal resulted, the king threatened to proclaim the changes himself. His sons put out leaflets warning the citizenry of a conspiracy against the king. The National Guard was put on alert status. At the Nasiriyya Palace the Royal Guard spent the night inside, but not in public view. Fears began to develop in Riyadh that one or more of Saud's extremist sons might attempt assassinations, including that of Faisal.

Faisal countered by sending the king an ultimatum of his own in late March: either make a public announcement that he was giving up all governmental powers or abdicate and leave Saudi Arabia. The king did not accept the ultimatum and continued to insist that some of his sons receive cabinet posts and that he retain certain powers. Mediation was stepped up by the *ulema*, in particular by Emir Saud bin Jilewi, governor of the Eastern Province; his cousin Abd al-Aziz ibn Musa'ad bin Jilewi, emir of Ha'il; and Abd Allah ibn Abd al-Rahman, uncle of the king and of Faisal. The two emirs were rated as particularly useful mediators, being old friends and supporters of Saud but absolutely loyal to the Saud clan as a whole and not in favor of the king's insistence on the return of all his powers.

The war of ultimata continued for a few days, but a sign of the trend was the withdrawal of the Royal Guard from Nasiriyya Palace. In the end, it had refused to be involved in a showdown. The monarch, with some hundred or so family members and retainers, was therefore alone, though undoubtedly watched and guarded by the regular army commanded by Prince Sultan.

On March 24, the king made a last effort to divide Faisal's supporters, again demanding the resignation of the Council of Ministers and the formation of a cabinet of commoners under Faisal. The congress of elder princes, *ulema*, and senior sheikhs then gathered with Faisal and heard the story of his difficulties with Saud. After spelling them out, Faisal asked the conclave to deliberate on what should be done. He then left the meeting. The conclave weighed the problem for six hours, then met with Faisal again and recommended to him that the king abdicate and Faisal take his place as king. Faisal asked a modification to provide that Saud be shorn of his elaborate lifestyle and reign, not rule, but others argued persuasively that the people would never grasp the distinction between a king who ruled and one who only reigned.

A delegation made up from the collegium then called on the king on March 27, telling him that the Royal Guard must be placed under the Ministry of Defense; that the Khawiyya, inherited by Saud from King Ibn Saud, must go to the National Guard; the personal Khawiyya must go to the Ministry of the Interior; the Royal Diwan (chancery) must go to the presidency of the Council of Ministers, except for one secretary and two clerks; and the privy purse must be halved. The king capitulated on most points, but balked over the cutting of his privy purse.

Meanwhile, tensions rose as the senior princes sought to rush Faisal into taking the kingship, and rumors spread that Saud's sons planned an attack on Faisal's palace. The regular army and National Guard were mobilized. Faisal, with difficulty, calmed the princes. The Royal Guard went to its barracks, except for a few who refused to leave Saud. Emir Saud bin Jilewi, who had been in Riyadh, returned to Dammam, characteristically downplaying events and telling his American friends that this had been a small family affair about which too much had been made.

On March 27 and 28, Faisal issued orders carrying out the changes that the delegation had demanded of the king. This became Royal Decree no. 2, carried on Radio Mecca on March 30, which stripped the king of *all* powers and authority; it was signed by Deputy Prime Minister Khalid ibn Abd al-Aziz and approved by Faisal. It cited a *fatwa* of March 29 signed by twelve leading members of the *ulema*, stating that since the "health and the current circumstances" of the king rendered him unable to undertake the duties of state, they had decided that the law on general welfare required that Faisal assume all affairs of state, foreign and domestic, in the king's absence or presence, without reference to the king. Note was also taken of the unanimous decision of those of the royal family present that Faisal assume the king's powers, thus making permanent the delegation of powers that Saud had reaffirmed two years earlier, on March 15, 1962.

The imprimatur of the *ulema* was essential to the "constitutionality" of this shift of royal powers, but the power of the collegium of senior princes was of utmost importance. The princes had strongly favored a forced abdication, but Faisal would not agree. Most Arabs appear to have applauded Faisal's restraint. To Faisal personally, retaining Saud as titular king with no powers other than ceremonial allowed him to honor his pledge of fealty to Saud made in 1953 before his father.

THE ACCESSION OF FAISAL

Some months later, on August 29, 1964, a reliable report asserted that King Saud was gravely ill, but that this "illness" was the result of the government's closure on August 22 of all of his palaces in Jeddah and the Eastern Province for the "inventorying" of royal property, to guard

against theft and unauthorized sales. The action was actually more drastic than this. The doors to palace buildings were locked and sealed with
wax, the electricity was cut off, and the main gates were secured with
ropes. Even more significant was that discharged employees were given
written recommendations for employment elsewhere in the Saudi government. Nasiriyya, the palace complex in Riyadh, was not affected.

On the same day as the report on the king's poor health, I had the
opportunity to ask prince Faisal about it. Faisal replied that Saud's health
seemed good, even improved since his "retirement." Faisal then flew to
Alexandria for a summit with Nasser, and I flew to Washington, where I
was scheduled to chair a selection board for the promotion of senior
officers, a two-month assignment. Considering the proclivity of Arab
news reporters to manufacture scenarios around the movements of diplomatic officials, I was later glad to be well removed from any possible
charge of influencing what was to follow.

During the last week of October 1964, our embassy in Jeddah began
hearing rumors that, among the huge extension of several thousand
princes, the senior princes of the royal family intended to force the
abdication of Saud. We heard that leading members of the *ulema* were
gathering in Riyadh and that prominent royal princes were already
there to greet Faisal on his expected arrival by car from Jeddah. An
impeccable source close to the family told an embassy officer that he was
convinced the *ulema* had assembled to draft a new *fatwa* deposing Saud
from kingship and replacing him with Faisal. When asked by US chargé
Thacher about the timing, the source pointed out Saud's attempts to
reassert his authority as monarch and also that, inasmuch as Cairo's Voice
of the Arabs had for the last several months ceased attacking the royal
family, it was a good moment to force Saud out. Before, a demonstration
of solidarity by the family had been imperative in order to avoid a general
Arab conclusion that Nasser had toppled a Saudi king. But now there was
no need to leave him in the kingship. The source concluded that Saud
would try to block the move of the princes and *ulema* but would not be
able to rally the needed popular or military support.

Faisal's car and his retinue stopped some 180 kilometers short of
Riyadh and camped at Dawadimi to await the outcome of events. Faisal
told his brothers, "I shall have nothing whatever to do with your project
of deposition. I await here what shall happen, and can only say that I shall
not continue to lead the state unless I have the authority."[2] On November
1, Faisal entered Riyadh and proceeded to the villa of his brother Prince
Khalid ibn Abd al-Aziz.

The needed authority to rule came only after a brief but sharp trial of
strength between Saud, aided by his eldest son Prince Muhammad, and
the senior princes, sons of founding king Ibn Saud, plus leaders of the
ulema. King Saud and Prince Muhammad had focused on two probable

sources of support, knowing that the power centers of elder princes were against them. The first center lay with eastern tribal chiefs, and here Saud adopted the time-honored procedure of holding his outdoor *majlis* at a particular rock near but outside the old city of Riyadh. It was an historic spot, long used to facilitate direct Bedouin contact with the person of the ruler, the royal receipt of petitions, and the royal distribution of largesse in the form of scattering coins. All this was considered an act of sovereignty, used by King Ibn Saud, and in good times would draw a large crowd of Bedouin, who would give a mass demonstration of allegiance. This time it brought relatively few and was considered a public-relations failure. Meanwhile, significant tribal leaders and leaders of the National Guard were reported to have joined the *ulema* and princes opposed to Saud. Among the princes, the prime movers were, again, the Sudairi Seven.[3]

The other source of support explored actively by Prince Muhammad was the Royal Guard at Nasiriyya Palace. Prince Muhammad seemed to have initial success in mobilizing a few hundred of the Royal Guard to resist any outside attempt to take over Nasiriyya, but when Muhammad tried to deploy the guard around the vast perimeter wall, disaffection arose as the guard began to realize that their opponents could be brothers or cousins. This, I was told, marked the turning point.

It was reported to me in confidence that King Saud, faced by opposition he could not match, particularly in the *ulema*, still refused to abdicate, contending that he was invested with his office by God and by his late father. At that point, according to a rumor that may never be substantiated, a very senior prince approached him with his hand on his sword— not customarily worn except at ceremonies—and said in so many words that he had always believed it would fall to his lot to be the one to dispose of Saud and that he was now ready to do so unless Saud abdicated at once. It was not necessary to carry out the threat.

The matter was settled on November 1, by Saud's deposition, announced on Radio Mecca on November 2. The deposition terms included sacrifice to the state of all Saud's palaces but one, Nasiriyya. Hundreds of paper flags, distributed by the municipalities, appeared in Riyadh and the Dhahran area carrying the legend "Faisal the Great."

All chiefs of the diplomatic corps at Jeddah were called to the Foreign Ministry at 2:15 P.M. on November 2 to hear the announcement that the Council of Ministers and Consultative Assembly, an appointive body largely made up of notables of Mecca, had met at 10:30 A.M. under the chairmanship of Prince Khalid ibn Abd al-Aziz to hear a letter of October 28 from members of the house of Saud, deposing King Saud and giving their oath of allegiance to Faisal as king and imam. This title referred to executive guardianship and defense of religious authority, as distinct from doctrinal leadership by the grand mufti and the *ulema*.

The announcement, by Minister of Information Jamil Hujailan, stated that ministers and members of the assembly had asked the *ulema* to examine this procedure from a legal standpoint. The *ulema* had produced a new *fatwa*, dated November 1. Having considered carefully their previous *fatwa* of March 29, they now stated, under the leadership of Sheikh Muhammad ibn Ibrahim, the grand mufti, that they had found convincing justification for deposing Saud. They therefore called on Faisal to accept their allegiance to him as legal king, on the understanding that he was required to keep faith in God, enforce Islamic doctrine on all matters, and oblige the people to abide by these.

The announcement then went on to relate that, immediately upon hearing this news of the "coronation" of Faisal,[4] joy prevailed and the citizenry gave their allegiance to him, led by the princes, ministers, *ulema*, army, police and national guard officers, and dignitaries. Faisal received their allegiance, standing throughout a three-hour ceremony, with the playing of martial music followed by expressions of praise for the new king.

President Johnson, on November 2, sent Faisal a congratulatory telegram in the Saudi style, extending warmest good wishes, anticipating continued friendship and cooperation, and ending by invoking God's blessing on Faisal and his country for a long and fruitful reign. The message was carried on Mecca Radio and widely appreciated. Later that same evening, Faisal broadcast a brief statement to his people, invoking divine guidance and promising continuity in his program of domestic reforms, cooperation in world efforts for peace and disarmament, collaboration with Arab states, and execution of the decisions of two Arab summit conferences. Radio Mecca broadcast a decree that the cabinet would remain unchanged, with Prince Khalid as deputy prime minister and Faisal remaining prime minister.

From the Eastern Province, observers sensed a cool preliminary reaction. King Saud, as their former viceroy, had been "their man." Faisal was associated with the Hejaz, of which he had been viceroy for a very long time.[5] This fact aroused concern that his interests would lie heavily in that region rather than in the area where most of the country's wealth was being earned. But such reactions did not represent more than a wave of sympathy for Saud, the "old man," who deserved better than "being kicked out." Tribal chiefs reacted with shrugs and the comment that "change is the will of Allah," and in any case Faisal had been de facto ruler for the last two years.

Of most importance was the general view that the procedure of deposition had been legal under *sharia*, and that it was therefore "constitutional," to use Western terminology. On November 3, a note from the Embassy of Saudi Arabia in Washington formally advised the Department of State of the action taken. To avoid further trouble, Saud and his active sons were kept under palace arrest in Nasiriyya for a short period. This forced but nonviolent transfer of power occurred at a time in the Middle East characterized more by power seizures[6] than by observance of ancient, *sharia*-based and *ulema*-sanctioned Arab precedent. A great weakness of power transfers in most Arab countries newly independent after World War II had been their lack of "legitimacy." Such a lack is usually compensated for by the use of force, where public protest is actively expressed or expected.

In the eleven years Faisal was to rule, the reasonable expectations of his subjects and of their recognized leaders, private or governmental, were well satisfied. His reign was respectful of religious opinion and values. His lineage for the position of king was the best, being derived from the two interdependent pillars of the realm: the family of Al al-Sheikh (Abd al-Wahhab) and the clan of the Sauds—the religious and political pillars of the state.

In debate and in executive performance Faisal knew no peers in the doctrine of Hanbalite law and in national educational development in the modern context. His Turkish-born queen, Iffat, assisted him greatly in the expansion and reform of female education. The solidity of the kingdom and of Faisal's leadership was demonstrated not only by material progress but also by the orderly and progressive guardianship of the two holiest places of Islam, Mecca and Medina.

One instance may suffice here to highlight the manner in which Faisal effectively wielded power, combining his lineage and intelligence to mix progress with religion. A delegation of about 150 *ulema* and citizens from Buraida, a town north of Riyadh famous at that time for its insularity and ultraconservatism, came to call on Faisal to protest national plans for a local system of girls' schools. Faisal received them with courtesy, heard them out, and engaged them in conversation on Islamic theology and observances. He demonstrated by his comments a detailed knowledge of the weaknesses of some of the group's religious leaders. With this introduction to the matter at hand, he gave his ruling: the families who protested need not send their daughters to the school, but those who wanted this education for their girls, particularly in the essentials of science, geology, mathematics, geography, and so forth, would not be barred from sending them. The school would be built, and it was. Within a year, another Buraida delegation called on Faisal to petition for a second girls' school.

Saud, in contrast, originally a generous man of buoyant disposition, particularly before he became ill, simply did not have the mental training or discipline for the rapid changes of the political and economic landscape of the Middle East. The *ulema* were particularly put off by Saud's alleged alcoholism in later life. Most of his brothers had been scandalized by the publicity surrounding the 1958 incident of the million dollar check allegedly drawn to pay for the assassination of Nasser, and they had learned to be concerned over the caliber of some of his closest advisors. These included several of his sons considered dangerously irresponsible and a nonfamily member, a favorite and manager of Saud's fleet of sedans, who had risen to become custodian of Saud's privy purse.

It became apparent to the princes and senior *ulema* that not only was the immediate choice of ruler involved, but also and acutely the question of succession by primogeniture. If Saud were to remain king, his sons would do everything possible to ensure that one of them be named crown prince. None was considered to be qualified; some were deeply distrusted. Should Faisal's health be irreparably weakened, Saud would certainly return to full kingship and thus be able, by law, to revoke all the powers delegated to Faisal. Deposing Saud would break this legal chain. A successor to Faisal was therefore selected—Emir Khalid.

The choice of this fourth son of the founding king seems to have been based on several factors. Though not a full blood brother, Khalid was an old and trusted friend of Faisal. He had accompanied Faisal to the United States in 1943 and 1945 and had observed Faisal's diplomacy aimed at ensuring the international status and security of the realm. He was not as deeply experienced in foreign affairs as he was in the domestic tribal scene, where he had real depth. He therefore supplemented Faisal's rule in a vital sphere. Faisal, nonetheless, encouraged him to preside as deputy prime minister in cabinet meetings to broaden his perspectives. He was a man of steady judgment and impeccable character, utterly without pretense.

Did Faisal break his vow to his father? It could be argued that he did. But I conclude that he tried hard to carry it out and in the end had virtually no choice but to behave as he did, permitting deposition to take its course. To have held out again for a titular Saud kingship without substantive rule would have brought the realm into confusion and financial mismanagement.[7]

Although it was certainly in the interest of the US-Saudi security partnership that Faisal become king, I can certify, firsthand, whatever others may say, that this accession was 100 percent Saudi, completely free of any US or other foreign influence. Saudi Arabia's ancient system of decision by consensus with full participation of religious authority operated then, and in today's more complex environment continues to be the touchstone of stability. That President Johnson's congratulatory message came only after Faisal's formal accession to kingship reflected careful avoidance by Washington of any implication of US intrusion into Saudi internal politics. Washington and the embassy in Jeddah had been of one mind that any earlier message of congratulation, while the power struggle was still on, would be potentially damaging and unwelcome on both sides.

One of Cairo's most noted editorial writers looked forward to the expected Saudi stability even before the deposition. On April 4, 1964, in the aftermath of the *fatwa* of March 29, Mustafa Amin described the power shift in Saudi Arabia as the outcome of a battle between arch conservatism, as represented by Saud, and moderate conservatism, as represented by Faisal, who, Amin said, had shown his statesmanlike qualities. Considering the erstwhile hostility of Cairo's controlled press toward Faisal and the Sauds, this editorial represented an overture of peace by Nasser and a clear indication that the Egyptian president did not wish to exploit the power struggle in Riyadh; rather, he was interested in better relations.

Faisal was cut from the stamp of legendary kings, and assuredly earned an honorable place in history with his father. It was my privilege to deal with him on matters of high security to his realm, and I had as much of his friendship as our differing appraisals of current policy allowed. I came to respect him deeply, in spite of arguing with him exhaustively in innumerable sessions, sometimes for hours at a time. But we never argued in bitterness, for we shared a purpose in the realization of common values.

EPILOGUE

I departed my Saudi Arabia post in May 1965, some seven months after Faisal became king. Egyptian forces remained in the Yemen, but Egyptian-Saudi relations were for the most part tolerable, though at times tense. During 1964, Faisal and Nasser had at last been in tentative negotiating contact, each holding the other responsible, after a fashion, for maintaining disengagement. I say after a fashion because, despite Egypt's rotation of troops in lieu of withdrawals, the meaning of disengagement had altered. Nasser now eagerly wanted out of the Yemen but on terms that would not damage his prestige, which meant preventing the return to authority of the Hamid al-Din and the imamate. Considering the extent of Egyptian economic losses and casualties—variously estimated at around 5,000 dead—in the ill-starred Yemeni venture as a whole, this seemed obvious.

The year 1964 had been a relatively quiet one in Egyptian-Saudi relations. Nasser had readily agreed to a set of procedures to jointly encourage the formation of a consensus among the major political (tribal) forces in the Yemen. Whether any member of the Hamid al-Din family could be admitted to this congress of tribal leaders was a question but not the most important one facing the tribes—or Nasser or Faisal—as long as representation of the old ruling family did not bring with it the return of Badr and his elders or the imamate. At that moment the main concern of Yemeni leaders was to diplomatically effect an Egyptian exit.

The negotiations among the various tribes had limped along through 1964, punctuated by desultory clashes of YAR and royalist forces, often in the Baihan region and occasionally on the Saudi border and in Saudi villages near the smuggling supply routes. These latter attacks were not taken as constituting serious aggression against Saudi Arabia, but Nasser exploited them as deterrents to supply operations mounted from Saudi soil, with or without official sanction.

A crisis arose in August 1965, followed by a Faisal-Nasser meeting at which they signed what came to be known as the Jeddah Agreement, effectively establishing joint Egyptian-Saudi monitoring of disengagement in place of UNYOM. The year 1966, however, began with tension between the Egyptian and Saudi governments and a lapse in the Faisal-Nasser dialogue. There were reports of Egyptian troop concentrations near Haradh and vitriolic Egyptian radio campaigns against the Saudi regime.

The revival of the Faisal-Nasser dialogue became a basic objective of US diplomacy, but neither disputant was willing to travel to meet the other. Meanwhile, Mecca Radio began responding to Cairo's attacks. A Kuwaiti attempt at mediation, which Faisal had accepted but Nasser had not, never got fully into swing.

At the start of 1967 Egypt twice bombed Najran. No casualties resulted, and damage was minimal. The United States interpreted these as warnings to Saudi Arabia against encouraging large-scale operations by Yemeni royalists. At the same time, the bombings revealed Egyptian nervousness over the Saudi success in bringing loyalists and republican dissidents together in a single coalition. All told, what had been tolerable relations between Saudi Arabia and Egypt were now drifting in January 1967 toward a complete break. It would take the June 1967 Arab-Israeli war to push the situation in the Yemen toward conclusion.

After the virtual wipeout of Egypt's forces by Israel that June, Nasser saw that the only salvation for Egypt, and for his own position, lay in promoting unity, not subordination, of Arab states around an Egypt injured but still indispensable to Arab defense. At an August 1967 conference in Khartoum, Nasser shrewdly described to a rapt and fascinated Arab League audience the catastrophic dimensions of his battle losses at Israel's hands and emphatically assured Arab heads of state present that the days of Egypt's interference in the affairs of fellow Arabs had passed. The emphasis from now on would be to avoid serious disagreements between Arab brothers and rebuild the defenses of Egypt as the "front-line state" facing the common enemy. To this end, Egypt would require massive aid from all loyal Arab nationalists in rebuilding a respectable force. This assistance would require that Nasser write off Egypt's military presence in the Yemen and any further Egyptian military control over the composition of a Yemeni tribal consensus.

Nasser had sent word to Faisal proposing decisive talks pursuant to the Jeddah Agreement. In the absence of a Saudi response, Nasser accepted

the volunteer role of the Sudanese government as mediator to inaugu-
rate private talks with Faisal at Khartoum. Additionally, at a foreign
ministers' conference in Khartoum preparatory to the summit, the Yemen was fully discussed to the extent that an Egyptian proposal was made
to Saudi Arabia to revert to the Jeddah Agreement and to a three-power
committee of Morocco, Iraq, and the Sudan to monitor the disengagement. Nasser and Faisal had agreed to keep the Yemen off the conference
agenda; Faisal had guarded Nasser's dignity as his own. By agreement
they ignored the YAR delegation totally—which was upset at being excluded from the settlement procedure, as was the representative of the
Palestine Liberation Organization.

At Khartoum, Faisal pledged an enormous aid package to Egypt. Central to Faisal's thrust was establishment of Saudi Arabia's freedom to
modernize and develop without foreign interference. That route was
now open, and because of his country's vast potential, the Arab world as
a whole would be influenced not by "Arab socialism" or other of Nasser's
vehicles for centralization of power but by "Free World" and open market
example—so reasoned Faisal in a long telegram to President Johnson,
with whom he had enjoyed an excellent rapport.

Johnson was deeply disappointed, however, over what seemed to him
abandonment of an opportunity to initiate discussions for an Arab-Israeli
peace. The conference had bought off the hostility of negative Arab
forces but only by pledges against contact with Israel, or recognition of
any peace with Israel, for the indefinite future. Faisal considered this
secondary, but Johnson, facing powerful pro-Israeli forces in Washington, did not.

Thus Faisal emerged victorious in his long-standing resistance to an
Egyptian military presence in the Yemen. Ultimately, as reported by
Egyptian foreign minister Mahmoud Riad, the Yemen problem had been
solved in ninety minutes at a meeting hosted by Sudanese prime minister
Muhammad Ahmad Mahjoub and attended by Faisal, Minister of De-
fense Sultan, Nasser, and himself. Nasser had asked Faisal to provide
ships to hasten the Egyptian withdrawal, and Faisal had agreed. The last
Egyptian troops left the Yemen for home between December 15 and
December 31, 1967.

As my scheduled May 1965 departure had neared, Faisal showed his
gratitude for US assistance over the years not by words of thanks but by
asking me to request that the US government assume the position of
national manager of Saudi development contracts. The United States
would thus stand between him and all prospective contractors for military construction, studying and evaluating all major proposals and super-
vising their execution.

Before leaving for Washington and appointment as ambassador to

Turkey, I had one final duty that gave me special pleasure—that of signing an agreement, with royal counselor Rashad Fira'awn signing on behalf of Faisal, that named the US Corps of Engineers to this exceptional role in the long-term development programs of Saudi Arabia. Thus began a still-surviving multibillion-dollar Saudi relationship with the corps that has yielded substantial returns to the US taxpayer. This relationship also greatly augmented Saudi military readiness and proved its value in Operations Desert Shield and Desert Storm.

A Note for Those Who Read the End
of the Book First

Policies stemming from the wise recognition by Saudi and US leaders of their regard for each other and their common interests have undeniably strengthened both countries economically and politically. The Saudi nation is still in the process of formation; its structure is and will be unique. It is worthy of careful study by the West.

However Islam adapts to the future, its heart is in Saudi Arabia. Actions taken there will have influence beyond national borders.

US officials who have felt and shown respect for the Saudi people and been rewarded by their attempts at understanding and accord have not been in the habit of underestimating the resilience of the Saudis. No "colonial" relationship has existed or is likely to arise as long as such respect exists.

If at first one does not perceive the democratic spirit in Saudi Arabia, it is nonetheless there; Saudis and Americans share the feeling of "born free under God" in the deepest sense. In the harshness of the Saudi climate, and through rugged challenges in the past, only the toughest have survived. Now that better times have softened both our populations, we may need to be reminded of the not-so-long-ago circumstances that united us. "Ten successors of FDR . . . and four sons and inheritors of Ibn Saud . . . have seen to it that what was begun that day on the USS *Quincy* would develop and flourish."[1]

NOTES

(Some of the still unreleased documents drawn upon for this book may appear in volumes of the Department of State's *Foreign Relations of the United States* not available at the time of the author's research but subsequently published.)

PREFACE

1. ARAMCO, originally called the California Arabian Standard Oil Company (CASOC), was the operative arm of Standard Oil of California in the early period of exploration and development of the Saudi concession. It should be made clear that no US company any longer owns any of Saudi Arabia's oil and gas deposits or the concession to operate them. The kingdom now owns the company, created by Royal Decree November 8, 1988, and renamed SAUDI ARAMCO, and Saudis from the chairman on down operate it for the government. The United States, however, continues to have a favorable trade balance with Saudi Arabia and has been assured a supply of energy from the kingdom.

2. Saudi Arabia, while it has its dangerous ultras, has been reasonably well inoculated against what in the West is called radical "fundamentalism" by the fact that it has always been governed by one of the strictest schools of Sunni Islamic law. The law is applied faithfully, and strict observances of Islam's tenets are supplemented by modern legislation similar to executive orders, filtered through ministerial deliberation and the traditional practice of supreme consultation and consensus.

PROLOGUE: HISTORY IN THE MAKING

1. The king, founder of modern-day Saudi Arabia, is often referred to by an assortment of names. Before his death in 1953, he preferred to use his modified Bedouin nickname, Ibn Saud (son of the Sauds). At other times, he was addressed as King Abd al-Aziz or His Majesty Abd al-Aziz Al Saud, abbreviated versions of his full name. For our purposes, in this text, he is alternately referred to as King Abd al-Aziz and Ibn Saud.

2. ARAMCO veterans estimated he had thirty-seven sons.

3. The king's career in the unification of many powerful tribes was known to have been built on developing a network of family allegiances. This is not to imply, however, that bedroom diplomacy was Abd al-Aziz's principal vehicle of statecraft. With many temporary marriages in strategic tribal areas, he honored the tribes and assumed the responsibility for tribal peace (*sulh*), guaranteeing justice pursuant to Quranic law. The Quran sanctions a maximum of four wives at a time, provided they are treated equally. Divorce is a simple declaration by the husband, and if by the king it is far from a dishonor; in fact, the divorcee of a king bears a lifetime honor from the brief marriage, especially if a son has been born during the union. This can bring her wealth and an advantageous second marriage.

4. This Ikhwan is not to be confused with the political Ikhwan al-Muslimin of Egypt and other countries in the modern period.

5. The judiciary in the kingdom was by tradition independent of the ruler, a true separation of powers. These two pillars of government were designed to supplement one another, not to be fused into one unrestrained dictatorship.

1. TROUBLED US-BRITISH COOPERATION

1. *Foreign Relations of the United States, 1942* (hereafter *FRUS*), vol. 4, p. 562.

2. The trucial sheikhdoms were Abu Dhabi, Dubai, Sharja, Ajman, Umm al-Qaiwain, Fujaira, and Ras al-Khaima.

3. US Department of State, *Principal Officers of the Department of State and U.S. Chiefs of Mission, 1778–1988*, p. 96.

4. *FRUS, 1942*, vol. 4, p. 570.

5. Except for a brief air raid on October 19, 1940, conducted by an Italian bombing team out of Asmara, Eritrea, against the CASOC stabilizing plant on Jabal Dhahran, active warfare did not reach Saudi Arabia. The raid was a feat of Italian navigation and seemed to constitute a political warning rather than a serious menace. Fuel constraints limited attack time over the target and the bombs were light. Damage was estimated at a little more than one hundred dollars, and there was no repeat. British forces would eventually deprive Mussolini of his Eritrean and Ethiopian empires, and his skilled Italian labor in Eritrea would be hired by ARAMCO in 1945 and play a most successful role in constructing the Ras Tanura refinery.

6. Winston Churchill, "The Battle of Alamein," in *The Second World War: The Hinge of Fate* (Boston: Houghton Mifflin, 1950), pp. 586–603.

7. Philip C. McConnell, *The Hundred Men* (Peterborough, N.H.: Currier Press, 1985), pp. 64, 197, a personal memoir by a key member of the wartime CASOC team; and Theodore L. Lenzen, *Inside International Oil* (privately printed, 1972), p. 25. CASOC was the predecessor of ARAMCO. See also Preface, note 1, and pp. 31–33 below.

8. Public media in the United States have erroneously construed the term "Arabist" to infer a pro-Arab bias, especially in the Arab-Israeli dispute. Actually, the term means a scholar of Arabic language and civilization, with no such implication.

9. Faisal had been the earliest recorded Saudi diplomat-at-large. He was only fourteen when he represented his father on a visit to London at the end of World War I, but for a long time in the 1940s Faisal had been relatively inactive, letting Syrian-born Yusuf Yassin manage the day-to-day business of the ministry. It seemed at the time that Faisal saw Sheikh Yusuf and Sheikh Abd Allah Sulaiman competing for the ear of the king. He was too proud to enter this fray, but became centrally active at the United Nations from its founding in 1945 at San Francisco and later, during the Palestinian debates. See Gerald DeGaury, *Faisal, King of Saudi Arabia* (London: Arthur Barker, 1966), esp. chap. 3.

10. At Cairo, I met Jane Constance Smiley of the Office of Strategic Services. She later would become my wife.

11. The consulate was to be established at the site of the camp established by the California Arabian Standard Oil Company, CASOC, which would in September 1944 officially change its name to ARAMCO. This site was chosen because it was conveniently on the Cairo-Karachi air route and had available water.

12. *FRUS, 1944*, vol. 5, pp. 664, 661–70 (Berle quote on p. 664).

13. Ibid., pp. 6,7.

14. *FRUS, 1945*, vol. 8, p. 887.

15. This was the anticline where CASOC's discovery well number 7 was located.

16. *FRUS, 1945*, vol. 8, pp. 915, 918, 943–50.

17. *FRUS, 1945*, vol. 8.

18. *FRUS, 1942*, vol. 4, p. 567.

19. *FRUS, 1944*, vol. 5, pp. 6, 7.

20. *FRUS, 1943*, vol. 4, p. 857.

21. The Department of State later made this up to Moose by assigning him as chargé to Baghdad, a much larger post, and later by two ambassadorial appointments, namely Syria and the Sudan.

22. *FRUS, 1945*, vol. 7, pp. 846, 847.

23. *FRUS, 1944*, vol. 5, p. 759.

24. The misstep by Minister Jordan that may have been decisive in antagonizing Ibn Saud came about as follows: Jordan, ca. 1943/1944, was reported to have asked for a private audience to complain about the handling of British aid money by the Saudi finance minister, Sheikh Abd Allah Sulaiman al-Hamdan. Jordan had taken a powerful dislike to this most trusted of the king's advisors and ministers. The implication of Jordan's complaint was a suspicion of dishonesty. The king listened intently. When Jordan had finished, Ibn Saud thanked Jordan gravely for his warning, "as a friend." He pressed the buzzer beside his chair and told the attendant to have Sheikh Abd Allah come immediately. The minister arrived in short order and crouched on one knee before his sovereign in the time-honored Bedouin fashion. The king called on his minister to produce immediately in the *majlis*, in front of the monarch and his guest, one million riyals. Abd Allah raised no questions but left at once and within a short time sacks of 2,000 riyals began to arrive on the shoulders and backs of sweating bearers who placed them carefully where heavy floor beams could support them. On it went, until Abd Allah informed the king that a million riyals were present. The king then told Abd Allah he could leave. Turning to Jordan, he asked if he would like to count the money. Jordan declined. Very quietly the king then said, "I think I

have an honest finance minister." This incident was conveyed to the author by Minister Eddy, who had an excellent information network not confined to English speakers. The likely informant to Eddy was the king himself.

25. *FRUS, 1944*, vol. 5, pp. 766–73.

26. Ibid., p. 771.

27. *FRUS, 1945*, vol. 8, pp. 1019–20.

28. Ibid., pp. 1030–31.

29. *FRUS, 1943*, vol. 4, p. 885.

30. *FRUS, 1942*, vol. 4, pp. 562–66.

31. *FRUS, 1941*, vol. 3, pp. 643–49.

32. See K. S. Twitchell, *Saudi Arabia* (Princeton, N.J.: Princeton University Press, 1947), pp. 43, 169, 172.

33. Brown and Jackson's maps were so detailed and accurate that they were used in Operations Desert Shield and Desert Storm in 1990–1991.

34. There was at that time, from my observation, no such thing as a hotel anywhere in Saudi Arabia, unless you counted an ancient, uninhabitable fleabag in Jeddah called the "Palass."

35. *FRUS, 1943*, vol. 4, pp. 935–37 ff.

36. Lenzen, *International Oil*, p. 25; and *FRUS, 1943*, vol. 4, pp. 921–52.

2. EARLY PRESIDENTIAL ASSURANCES AND THE ARAB CALL TO UNITY

1. *FRUS, 1943*, vol. 4, pp. 845–46.

2. Ibid., pp. 852–54.

3. *Peace and War: U.S. Foreign Policy, 1931–1941* (Washington, D.C.: US Government Printing Office, 1943), pp. 111–12.

4. *FRUS, 1939*, vol. 4, pp. 824–31; also, *Principal Officers of the Department of State, 1778–1988*, p. 96.

5. SOCAL had acquired rights in Bahrain from Gulf Oil for $50,000 on December 21, 1928, after members of the Red Line Agreement had turned it down on the basis of unfavorable geological reports. However, SOCAL's Edward A. Skinner, master oil driller, assisted and advised by geologist Fred H. Davies, brought in oil in commercial quantities at Awali on June 1, 1932—on the first try—to the consternation and humiliation of British geologists. SOCAL men and others then cast their eyes westward across twenty miles of shallow gulf toward a similar anticline, visible as a double hillock and known locally as Dhahran ("two backs"). The scramble was on.

6. Prominent merchant families are split between Bahrain and the Eastern Province of Saudi Arabia. Even in this early period of primitive communications, by methods always a bit mysterious, all conceivable types of news traversed huge distances with consummate speed.

7. SOCAL, in 1932, hired as go-between and advisor for the negotiation period H. St. John B. Philby, a British and Saudi subject who was also a converted Muslim and an advisor to Ibn Saud. He was a truly great explorer, a prolific writer, and by no means pro-British in matters relating to the Middle East. He had the franchise for the sale of Ford automobiles in the kingdom, and he liked Americans.

8. The story of the historic encounter between Roosevelt and Ibn Saud has

been told in detail by William Eddy in his memorandum of the conversation printed in *Foreign Relations of the United States, 1945*, vol. 8, pp. 1–3 and 7–9, and in Eddy's personal account, *F.D.R. Meets Ibn Sa'ud*, published in 1954 by the American Friends of the Middle East (superseded by Amideast). Eddy also gave me an oral report after his return to the kingdom.

9. *FRUS, 1938*, vol. 2, p. 994; *FRUS, 1939*, vol. 4, p. 696.

10. Not all of his best interpreters were Saudi-born, the king said. With those not Saudi-born he felt less free to speak his mind.

11. *FRUS, 1943*, vol. 4, pp. 808–809. For an extensive discussion of the Philby £20 million "plan" and its background, see H. St. John Philby, *Arabian Jubilee* (London: Robert Hale, 1952), pp. 213–20.

12. *FRUS, 1945*, vol. 8, pp. 690–91.

13. Eddy, *F.D.R. Meets Ibn Sa'ud*. See also, *FRUS, 1945*, vol. 7, pp. 2–3 and 7–9.

14. Eddy, *F.D.R. Meets Ibn Sa'ud*, p. 37.

15. On this subject, see Harry S. Truman, *Memoirs* (New York: Doubleday, 1955), vol. 1, pp. 68–69, and vol. 2, chaps. 10–12; also *FRUS, 1947*, vol. 5, pp. 1011–15, for Truman's letter of January 24, 1947, to Ibn Saud.

16. Neither Iraq nor Jordan broke relations with the United States at this period in their history. Iraq conducted a pro-Western policy, and Jordan was not yet a sovereign state.

17. During this period, estimates of Saudi reserves rose dramatically, as did almost simultaneously those of Kuwait and its fabulous Burgan field. In 1946, Saudi reserves were believed to be around 3 billion barrels and Kuwaiti reserves at 4 billion. By 1958, Saudi reserves were estimated to be 50 billion barrels and those of Kuwait 62.2 billion barrels (Roy Lebkicher, George Rentz, and Max Steineke, *ARAMCO Handbook* [Houston: Arabian American Oil, 1960], p. 123). The 1995 report by what is now SAUDI ARAMCO puts Saudi Arabia's total reserves at 259 billion barrels of recoverable crude (*Saudi Aramco and Its World: Arabia and the Middle East*, rev. ed., Houston, 1995, p. 216).

18. In London, at Mansion House on May 29, 1941, British foreign secretary Anthony Eden had given an address inviting closer cultural, economic, and political ties among the Arab states, saying that his government would support such a move. Eden had wanted to ensure Arab neutrality, if not support, toward Britain, hard pressed by its 1940 defeat by Nazi ground forces in Europe. When I arrived in Egypt as vice consul in early 1944, I learned from Egyptian friends that Eden's promise had been discounted and that huge mobs had gathered in 1942 to demonstrate their backing for the Axis forces of Field Marshal Rommel at al-Alamein.

19. *FRUS, 1947*, vol. 5, pp. 738–41, emphasis added by the author.

20. See King Abd Allah's *Al-Takmilah* (My Memoirs Completed) (London and New York: Longman, 1978).

21. *FRUS, 1947*, vol. 5, pp. 742–48. Emir Abd Allah, being fully recognized as a sovereign by the British government, declared himself king of the Hashemite Kingdom of Jordan May 26, 1946.

22. The Egyptian Wafd Party, picking up on the theme of Arab collective interest, and anxious to be at the vanguard of any Arab movement toward unity, had earlier called for meetings to explore the founding of an Arab political group, the Arab League. From the US legation in Cairo, I further learned that

the atmosphere in the Arab East had been very distrustful of any plan for a league that would almost automatically fall under Cairo's chairmanship and control. Nonetheless, no Arab leader, including Ibn Saud, wished to be registered as against any form of Arab unity. It was the Arab Holy Grail. Therefore, even Saudi Arabia fielded a delegation to the Cairo meetings.

23. *FRUS, 1947*, vol. 5, pp. 752–59.

24. It was later determined that Ibn Saud wanted fifty warplanes and full equipment for two motorized divisions, an inventory far greater than the kingdom could have put to use for some time to come.

25. Truman, *Memoirs*, vol. 1, pp. 164–65.

26. Ibid., p. 69.

27. Ibid., vol. 2, p. 136.

28. Ibid., p. 135.

29. Ibid., pp. 223–24.

30. *FRUS, 1950*, vol. 5, pp. 1169–73, and *FRUS, 1951*, vol. 5, pp. 1066–67.

31. Harry S. Truman Library, Independence, Missouri, letter in translation dated March 3, 1952, signed "Abd al-Aziz."

32. From the Harry S. Truman Library, Independence, Missouri, Memorandum for the President, August 9, 1951, signed Dean Acheson.

33. *FRUS, 1951*, vol. 5, pp. 1066–67

3. COLD WAR AND REGIONAL PRESSURES

1. In the Department of State's home quarters, Dulles required a limitation on all recommendations for action to one single-spaced sheet, to which, however, supporting documentation could be annexed.

2. *FRUS, 1952–1954*, vol. 9, pt. 1, pp. 97–98.

3. Ibid., pt. 2, pp. 2516–18, records a meeting in New York between Dulles and Foreign Minister Faisal dated March 2, 1953.

4. Ibid., Crown Prince Saud–Secretary Dulles talks regarding application of President Truman's letter of October 31, 1950 (*FRUS, 1950*, vol. 5, p. 1190).

5. These were later to become the independent states of Kuwait, Bahrain, Qatar, and the United Arab Emirates.

6. Dispatch no. 74 from Dhahran, February 20, 1952 (780022/2 2052), cited in *FRUS, 1952–1954*, vol. 9, pt. 2, p. 2258.

7. 780.022/2 1452 telegram 444, cited in *FRUS, 1952–1954*, vol. 9, p. 2576.

8. In 1948, the United States and the United Kingdom had held discussions that centered on the feasibility of a median line in the Persian Gulf, where offshore oil was thought to be present (and proved to be abundant). 890F.6363/2 1948ff, cited in *FRUS, 1948*, vol. 5, pp. 17–19.

9. *FRUS, 1952–1954*, vol. 9, pt. 2, pp. 2471–72.

10. *FRUS, 1950*, vol. 5, pp. 1190–91.

11. *FRUS, 1952–1954*, vol. 9, p. 2482.

12. Ibid., doc. 1489, p. 2492.

13. Ibid., pp. 2498–2503.

14. *FRUS, 1952–1954*, vol. 9, pp. 2541–42, which is doc. 1517.

15. The agreement called upon a tribunal to decide two matters: (a) the location of the common frontier between Saudi Arabia and Abu Dhabi, and (b)

sovereignty in the area comprised within a circle whose center was in Buraimi village and whose circumference passed through the point of junction of latitude 24 degrees 25 minutes North and longitude 55 degrees 36 minutes East.

16. Oddly enough, there is another version of the cancellation of Point IV on the record: Sheikh Yusuf Yassin had expressed the exasperation of the Saudi regime over the slow pace of US economic grant aid. The essence of the assistance had been to transfer technology rather than pour concrete; Americans were not contracted to build or transfer infrastructure. Therefore, members of Point IV were few, but liveable quarters for American families in those days were nonexistent or had insufferable problems of sanitation in a Jeddah basically unchanged with the passage of centuries. The city was picturesque, but its charm was strictly visual. So the first order of business for an aid mission was to create family dwellings. Construction proceeded with painful slowness. Capable contractors and work crews were scarce, and materials, fittings, electrical tools, electric cable, tubing, and appliances were not available in the kingdom. Everything had to be imported, and water and sewage disposal systems had to be improvised over a fossilized coral plain with a shallow aquifer of saline invasion from the Red Sea. Water was critically scarce; after months, there was little to show of any economic assistance to Saudi Arabia, which was paying for this housing and expecting instant public works. It was a classic gap of understanding that many of us encountered then and later in traditional areas of the Middle East not yet on the threshold of development. Simply put, Saudi Arabia was a case of not being ready for Point IV.

Sheikh Yusuf had come to Ambassador Hare and launched a biting complaint, at the end of which he informed Hare that the Saudi government had decided not to "renew" Point IV. "Renewal" was not a question, because no time limit calling for it existed in the agreements; the meaning, however, was clear. The Saudi response came to my desk in State when I was director of Near East affairs in the Bureau of Near Eastern, South Asian, and African Affairs. I recommended to the bureau chief immediate compliance with Sheikh Yusuf's notification, without discussion. Ambassador Hare had no objection, and dismantlement of the program began within days. Subsequently, to our surprise, Sheikh Yusuf expressed to Hare his astonishment and concern over our haste. Hare replied that the sheikh's message had been categoric and clear. Washington had at once accepted his view that the program was not timely and would proceed without delay in packing up (which, however, took some time).

Years later, as ambassador, I was told by Chief of Staff Ibrahim al-Tassan that he and many others had registered concern over "the actions of some people" to abolish the US aid mission. They had kept their disapproval to themselves, but now wished to state their regret over the hasty severance of bonds with the United States.

17. The Saudi government had a strong case, prepared with consummate care by George S. Reutz of ARAMCO, a great scholar of Arabic. It was certified by Abd al-Rahman Azzam for presentation at the arbitration tribunal and printed as the 539-page *Memorial of the Government of Saudi Arabia*.

18. *FRUS, 1955–1957*, vol. 8, pp. 294–97.

19. *FRUS, 1955–1957*, vol. 13, doc. 203, p. 309.

20. *FRUS, 1955–1957*, vol. 13, p. 412.

21. Ibid., pp. 478–86.

22. Ibid., p. 486.

23. *FRUS, 1952–1954*, vol. 9, pt. 1, pp. 14–28.

24. PL 480 wheat was an instrument of US economic aid whereby the recipient government repaid in local currency, which could then be re-loaned to it on easy terms for as long as forty years.

25. *FRUS, 1958–1960*, vol. 12, p. 716.

26. In 1912–1913, al-Hasa was seized by Ibn Saud's forces. For photos, see F. S. Vidal, *The Oasis of al-Hasa* (Arabian American Oil Company, 1955), p. 83. See also H. St. J. B. Philby, *Arabia of the Wahhabis* (London: Constable, 1928; New York: Arno, 1977).

27. Ownership of KOC was 50 percent British Petroleum and 50 percent Gulf Oil (American).

28. Department of State Central files. Following is the text of the October 4, 1963, accord:

The Government of Iraq having taken note of the statement by the Government of Kuwait of 9 September 1963 which included the desire of Kuwait to work toward ending the agreement concluded with Britain at a suitable time, the two delegations agree to the following:

1. The Government of Iraq recognizes the independence and complete sovereignty of the State of Kuwait with boundaries as shown in the letter of the Iraqi Prime Minister dated 21 July 1932 and agreed to by the Ruler of Kuwait in his letter of 10 August 1932.

2. The two governments agree to work for firm brotherly relations spurred on by nationalism, mutual interest and aspiration for complete Arab unity.

3. The two governments are to work for cultural, commercial and economic cooperation as well as exchange of technical information. To achieve this, diplomatic relations on the ambassadorial level are to be established immediately.

4. SAUD BESIEGED

1. The United Arab Republic (UAR), founded when Egypt merged with Syria in February 1958, essentially reduced Syria from independence to the status of the "northern region" of the union, subordinate to Cairo.

2. Egyptian editor Muhammad Hasanein Heikal, in *The Cairo Papers*, published photos of three checks drawn on the Riyadh branch of the well-known Arab Bank, "payable to bearer" and totaling £1,900,000 sterling.

3. By tradition, Saudi Arabia, as host to the two holiest sites of Islam, permits construction only of mosques as places of worship on its soil.

4. See above, p. 69.

5. The king had insisted to his brothers that his eldest son, Prince Muhammad ibn Saud, the minister of defense, take over as prime minister in his absence. He only gave in and agreed to Faisal in the last hours, with no policy or personnel changes until his return.

6. Combined Second Air Division and USMTM personnel at the time numbered 1,400 officers and men. A USMTM strength of 250 was recommended to Washington for the postwithdrawal period.

7. Turaiqi, he said, favored Saudi Arabia's dealing with the Soviet and East European bloc, but cabinet changes were likely and Turaiqi was probably on the way out.

8. Tassan and I were old acquaintances from my earlier assignments to Dhahran and were on excellent terms. Advanced in years, he had attended a school of sabotage at Ismailia, Egypt, courtesy of the British, in World War I. There he had known Colonel T. E. Lawrence, whom, he made obvious, he did not consider "legendary." A "capable man in handling bags of gold" was the only characterization I could draw from him regarding the romanticized author of *The Seven Pillars of Wisdom*. In other words, Lawrence had been astute in buying Bedouin support for British sabotage of the Turkish-built Ma'an-to-Medina railway.

5. BUILDUP TO CONFRONTATION

1. Heikal had been an informal go-between in this manner since the Suez War of 1956. His utility was that of the "no-commitment" sounder-outer, but he could also carry US messages to Nasser, who often preferred informal channels.

2. In the Yemeni imamate, or theocratic kingdom, a Sayyid was a member of a privileged ruling class of Zaidis, said to be direct descendants of the Prophet. They wore a distinctive dress, featuring an embroidered skull cap held in place by a small turban.

3. See pp. 125–26.

4. To the warning by Vice President Sadat in Cairo, Ambassador Badeau had responded that it was fear of Egypt rather than of the Soviet Union that drove Faisal and King Hussein to assist the royalists.

5. From all that I could gather later, Abu Taleb could not believe that the Free Yemenis, knowing him personally as a friend, would allow him to be killed. Unfortunately, once the violence that was to come was unleashed, it was not the sort that knew him who mounted his head on a pike, along with those of some twenty other senior officials, atop the medieval walls of San'a on September 26, 1962.

6. The results of Richards's visits in 1957 were as follows:

> *Lebanon, Libya*: accepted without public reservation
> *Iraq*: favorable, but without public identification with the doctrine
> *Saudi Arabia*: partial support without specific mention of the doctrine
> *Jordan and the Sudan*: no reply to the invitation
> *Egypt, Syria, and the Yemen*: rejection

For more information, see Charles D. Cremeans, *The Arabs and the World: Nasser's Arab Nationalist Policy* (New York: Frederick A. Praeger, 1963).

7. Clark was greatly assisted by his brilliant houseboy and interpreter, a Yemeni of good family named Rashid Abdullah Abd al-Rahim, also known as Rashid Abdu, who was informally adopted by Clark and his wife and educated in the

United States with financial help from Imam Ahmad. Abdu became an outstanding surgeon and a US citizen and donated a collection of medical books and much medical advice to Yemen's new university.

8. See Richard H. Sanger, *The Arabian Peninsula* (Ithaca, N.Y.: Cornell University Press, 1954), pp. 235–79.

9. This account is based on the author's recollection of the incident as relayed to him in 1946 by Minister Eddy. For highly readable details, see Sanger, *Arabian Peninsula*, pp. 268–69.

10. Foreign diplomats in Saudi Arabia have traditionally been given great courtesy and freedom, although until recently they traveled in the interior only with permission (usually given) and lived in Jeddah. They are now in Riyadh, the traditional capital.

11. All pharmaceuticals, for example, were taken in this manner by the imam's officers and warehoused without refrigeration, where they quickly spoiled. No trucks could leave one town for another without a *fuqq al-hashab* (literally, open up the wood)—a written permit, costing a fee and signed by the imam, that permitted the wooden barrier to the town to be raised.

12. Yemeni Arabs depicted the Jewish exodus by aircraft as motivated by prophecy—that one day a great bird would carry the Jews of the Yemen to a reconstituted Israel and that when it came, they must go. Many left weeping at leaving their ancestral land.

13. The imam, in my second and last call on him in 1962, affirmed confidently (without any foundation whatever) that the United States would rebuild for him the Ma'rib Dam. This site lies east of San'a at the edge of the Empty Quarter. The original earth-filled structure, which my wife and I explored on foot, dates from about 500 B.C., with its final collapse estimated at about 500 A.D. For at least a thousand years it supplied irrigation needs for an extensive farming delta at the end of a deep and now barren valley near the ruins of the Temple of Balqis. Today it has been rebuilt by Turkish contractors, thanks to the generosity of the president of the United Arab Emirates, Sheikh Za'id ibn Sultan al-Nahayan, whose ancestors had migrated from Ma'rib east to Oman after the dam's collapse. Imam Ahmad's wish was thus fulfilled, but not until some twenty years after his own, and his oligarchy's, death.

14. Badr granted amnesty to all prisoners except murderers and released all sons of tribal sheikhs held as hostages by Imam Ahmad. He pardoned all political refugees abroad, saying they were free to return, and discharged the Zaraniq bodyguards of Imam Ahmad. The Zaraniq are people of the hot Red Sea coastal plain, dark and very rugged, ethnically distinct from Yemeni Arabs. They were widely detested as a "foreign element," loyal only to the imam.

6. YEMEN

1. One member of the Congress, Sultan al-Kirshi, had been a US legation employee whose double role was unknown to American personnel before the coup.

2. In 1934, under the overall command of his father, King Ibn Saud, Faisal had led a column of infantry over this plains region against the Yemeni forces of the

late imam Yahya, in an assertion of Saudi sovereignty over the Jizan-Abha plains and mountain region. In 1962, the Yemen's northern boundary was the only demarcated boundary of Saudi Arabia. All other Saudi boundaries were either recognized but undemarcated, as with Jordan and Iraq, or were claims in active or inactive dispute, as with the various sheikhdoms of the lower gulf, the Sultanate of Oman, the south Arabian British protectorates, and the colony of Aden.

3. Pakistani blue- and white-collar workers were in considerable demand in Saudi Arabia and provided hard currency remittances to their newly established homeland. It was in Pakistan's national interest to maintain a good relationship with the Saudi government.

4. I had been asked some time back to make a call on my diplomatic colleague from Mali, who, feeling that I might be of some help, related to me that his official residence in Riyadh had become a squalid camp of Muslim escapees from indentured domestic service in Mecca and elsewhere. Irate "owners" demanded of him their return to duty but were prevented from access by the diplomatic immunity of the Malian embassy. King Saud would never take action to correct this abuse of fellow believers, and the abuse was further compounded by the tradition that slavery of Muslims by Muslims was a grievous sin.

The young Malian chargé felt and hoped that I might have some influence with Saud, for his situation was becoming desperate. He had no adequate sanitary facilities nor budget for such a quantity of food, supplies, and services. I took note of his complaint with all sympathy but could only point to international pressures, and not with any expectation that if I spoke to King Saud he would do more than deny that slavery existed in his country, as he had already asserted on more than one occasion. Perhaps there was a fine distinction between indentured service and slavery, but when the Malian showed me samples of contracts, enforceable by Saudi courts, it seemed a parallel without a difference. I reported the situation fully to Washington.

5. Saqqaf was not the only courageous Saudi official who disagreed with Faisal's support for the royalists. Abd al-Aziz Mu'ammar, the Saudi ambassador to Switzerland, confided to me in Jeddah in December 1962 that he had urged Saud and Faisal to join the United States and the West in recognizing the YAR. At the time, King Saud and his entourage were in Switzerland, and Saud was making no apparent effort to keep in touch with his government.

6. In early November 1962, U Thant had begun a series of talks with Arab representatives to the United Nations, asking them to settle the conflict through direct mediation or through the Arab League. The United States welcomed U Thant's posture because it gave Washington time for its own demarches to various Arab capitals regarding President Kennedy's formula for disengagement.

7. It was clear that Saqqaf deeply believed in Faisal and understood him better than most. Like Abu Taleb during the Yemeni imamate, he placed his position and his future at risk to help steer the ship of state away from the reefs.

8. Sultan was a half brother to Faisal and one of the leaders of the "Sudairi Seven," the sons of King Ibn Saud by a Sudairi princess.

9. Others on the flight were the deputy chief of USMTM, Colonel J. R. Johnson; chief of the army section of USMTM, Colonel D. F. Munson; and other

USMTM officers: Major Harry Miller, Major Donald J. Peterson, Captain Carmen A. Marguglio, Military Attaché Major Clark Scott, and Sergeants Everett H. F. Steele and Richard R. Carabello.

10. My air force informant had expressed outrage in describing the drop. Thinking he was referring to the harm intended against the kingdom, I agreed; but then he made clear his reaction was that of a military instructor: "Who in God's name would pull off such a mess! We always insist that any drop be completed within a 100-foot radius or it's no good!"

11. Nasser's miscalculation recalled the 1954 atmosphere in the Sudan, two years before its independence, when Ismail al-Azhari, leader of the Sudanese Unity Party, answered a query of mine by asserting that "unity" by no means meant subjection to but merely closer relations with Egypt, not a structural hierarchy with Nasser as boss. Nasser, meanwhile, had never believed Azhari would be anything other than his instrument for annexation until 1956, when Sudanese independence was actually declared. This led Azhari to reveal his position as he had himself explained it to me. Nasser's instrument of intrigue and propaganda then turned on Azhari as enemy number one of Arab unity, and sought by every pressure, even to occupying and claiming a border area, to bring him down. This was shrugged off by the Sudanese, who waited until Nasser tired of the invasion and withdrew.

12. Such a direct relationship between a career officer and his president is rare, in my experience, and usually exceptional even with political appointees after their initial year of ambassadorial service.

7. THE 1963 BUNKER MISSION AND BEYOND

1. Bunker had been chairman of the American Sugar Refining Company before taking up diplomacy. For an account of his Dutch-Indonesian efforts, see Christopher J. McMullen, *Mediation of the West New Guinea Dispute, 1962: A Case Study* (Washington, D.C.: Institute for the Study of Diplomacy, Georgetown University, 1981).

2. Not to be confused with the eight points presented to Nasser.

3. I often reflected afterward that Faisal knew a great deal more English than his strict reliance on Arabic in diplomatic business would suggest. I believe he understood the discussion perfectly and could have compared notes afterward with Saqqaf. He had effected a face-saving improvement of terms and had signaled to Bunker (for Kennedy) that reforms and economic development were his business, not to be monitored by the United States with a carrot and stick.

4. The reader should also recall the bitter feelings toward Nasser of the French government over the loss of Algeria. There is an implication here that Faisal could have been considering an appeal to Paris for unconventional weaponry.

5. The Saudi Eastern Province was already served by an ARAMCO station, operating on US current and imaging.

6. Relations between the Sauds and the Yemen's Hamid al-Dins were never close, or even cordial, during my time in Arabia. Not only was the imamate of the Shiite persuasion—regarded by Sunni/Wahhabi Saudis as heretical—but the rule and mentality of Imam Ahmad was despotic and brutal, as contrasted with the Saudi tradition of first among equals, operating by consensus.

7. This was not a routine matter for Faisal, as ultraorthodox clerics in Saudi Arabia vigorously opposed any such system as radio or television that might detract from their control over Islamic principles and even result in women appearing on television screens. Faisal could face down these objectors because he was a devout Muslim of the best Wahhabi lineage. His mother was of the line of Al al-Sheikh, that is, of direct descendance from the eighteenth-century spiritual guide of the Hanbalite Sunni school of law in Saudi Arabia, Muhammad ibn Abd al-Wahhab. Faisal's father, Ibn Saud, for his part, was a direct descendent of Muhammad ibn Saud, eighteenth-century ally of Abd al-Wahhab. The television project was implemented fully by RCA Corporation a few years later. I was able to see a leading member of the Saudi religious fraternity give practical and sensible sermons to television viewers from Riyadh. Faisal seemed to have selected moderates of the *ulema* as first telecasters.

8. A Syrian coup d'état on March 8 had brought into power a new military government friendly to Arab unity but not willing to be subordinated to Cairo.

9. It was later revealed to me by Saqqaf that the Saudi interlocutor was Saudi ambassador to the United Kingdom Hafiz Wahba, who had obtained Faisal's permission to listen, but not comment, to the Egyptian official messenger, Hasan Sabri al-Khouli.

10. Bunker and Nasser had met once before, socially, in India, when Bunker was ambassador in New Delhi.

11. Bunker gave the silent treatment to certain questions raised by Nasser. For example, Nasser wanted dismantlement of four Saudi bases he claimed were being used for training royalists. Bunker did not respond but retained this for bargaining purposes.

12. Earlier, Saqqaf told me privately that this dialogue with Cairo was an ongoing but rather fruitless experiment, passively, rather than specifically, authorized by Faisal.

13. "Suspension" was dropped in favor of a final act of commitment.

14. The US Navy had encountered occasional Egyptian harassment in transiting the supposedly free and open Suez Canal on its way to a visit in Jeddah. The commanding officer of a US destroyer related to me that while in the canal he was overflown barely above mast-high altitude by bombers that opened their bomb bay doors as they passed overhead. No bombs were dropped, but the action was insulting. Out in the Gulf of Suez, an Egyptian destroyer had gone to general quarters on seeing another US destroyer pass by, going south, but had retracted that order when signaled to do so by the US commander, who started an immediate maneuver of defense. US-Egyptian relations may have worn some varnish of civility in the Cairo Foreign Ministry and in Nasser's office, but they resembled small-boy nose thumbing and taunts as far as the US Navy was concerned.

8. OPERATION HARDSURFACE AND THE UN OBSERVER MISSION IN YEMEN

1. Dhahran al-Janub ("Dhahran the South"), not to be confused with Dhahran, the oil center of the Eastern Province.

2. Carl Von Horn, *Soldiering for Peace* (New York: David McKay Co., 1966, 1967), chaps. 23–28.

3. Saudi officials and prominent citizens were entertained aboard ship, and US Navy personnel helped the embassy entertain crews ashore. Such activities, however, were not easy: there was no place for entertainment, and women were veiled; no liquor could be served, and no dance halls or dating existed. The photographing of "old things" was restricted out of shame and fear of bad publicity, the result of hypersensitivity to retarded economic development. We did what we could. Embassy wives prepared excellent meals for snorkeling and waterskiing picnics at Ubhur, an inlet of the Red Sea some twenty miles north-west of Jeddah. It offered magnificent opportunities for views of coral reefs and their unbelievably varied fish populations. Wealthy Arab merchants put on lavish mutton and lamb feasts that were attended by the entire crews along with most of the male business community of Jeddah.

4. Robert Stookey, then US chargé in San'a, has since maintained that Egypt "was sufficiently determined upon victory to employ gas massively and consistently as a means to terrorize and demoralize civil populations." Robert Wilson Stookey, "Political Change in Yemen" (Ph.D. diss., University of Texas at Austin, 1972), pp. 484–85.

5. Ibid., p. 484.

6. Despite the consensus arrived at during this meeting, at its conclusion General LeMay commented, "I just can't see why we cannot *tell* Nasser to get out of the Yemen!" It was an expression of frustration, not a query.

7. The Yugoslav government decided to withdraw its contingent on November 4, whereupon its reconnaissance company at Sa'da and Haradh withdrew and a larger element at Najran prepared to depart. For a brief summary of the circumstances leading to the deployment and ultimate withdrawal of UNYOM, see United Nations Department of Public Information, *The Blue Helmets: A Review of United Nations Peace-Keeping* (New York, 1985), pp. 188–97.

8. Report of the Secretary-General to the Security Council, September 4, 1963, doc. S/5412.

9. Rikhye was convinced that the only solution was a political one: to broaden the Yemeni republican regime to include antiroyalist tribes now opposed to the Egyptians; it might even include certain princes.

10. The formal UN certification date of July 4 was the peg for each subsequent two-month renewal of disengagement and funding of UNYOM. The United States, for purposes of deploying Hardsurface, considered disengagement operative on June 7.

11. In mid-October 1963, instructions came in from State reporting that it had notified the royalist chargé in Washington, Ahmad Zubara, that the US government was ready to lead a Free World drive for coordinated aid to a more broadly based government of the Yemen. The resulting funds would provide initial budgetary support contingent on the establishment of such a government and on Egyptian compliance with disengagement. Zubara was asked to transmit this notification to the royalist headquarters in the Yemen.

12. I learned later from Saqqaf that, at a meeting that same day with veteran counselors to his father, Faisal had put the question, "What would the United States do if disengagement failed?" Sheikh Hafiz Wahba had responded flatly that Faisal should not depend on British help, which would not be meaningful. Rashad Fira'awn was just back from France, where he had been checking for

Faisal on the possibility of French assistance and the feasibility of recruiting mercenary pilots and buying or leasing the latest French aircraft. He responded that the French were well disposed to assist in air defense, sales, and training and could be approached more specifically to determine how far they would go. Saqqaf, meanwhile, had consulted directly the British and French ambassadors in Jeddah and was told that both governments recommended that Saudi Arabia renew UNYOM.

13. Report of the Secretary-General to the Security Council, October 28, 1963, doc. 5447, with maps, and ADD. 1 and 2, dated, respectively, October 31 and November 11, 1963.

14. Report of the Secretary-General to the Security Council, doc. S/5501, 1964, pp. 5, 6.

15. UN docs. S/5572, S/5681 and ADD. 1.

16. See Hafiz Wahba, *Arabian Days* (London: Arthur Barker, 1964).

9. THE DEPOSING OF KING SAUD

1. Nasiriyya was an extravaganza, with an enormous carpeted *majlis* ringed with more than one hundred expensively upholstered and gilded chairs, with twenty or more huge chandeliers overhead. The air conditioning of the main building was said to equal that of the Pentagon. In an elaborate garden outside, a fountain with colored lighting spouted precious fresh water sixty feet into the air.

2. From another source I was later to learn that when the princes spoke alone to Faisal, urging him to cooperate, he again refused, invoking the oath he had sworn to his father of allegiance to Saud.

3. The success of the Sudairi Seven in group action had enormously increased their status and foreshadowed Sudairi rule for the future. The extended Sudairi clan, cousins of the Al Saud, had occupied particularly sensitive security positions in the realm since the accession of Ibn Saud.

4. Saudi Wahhabism rejects royal crowns and decorations, thrones, and the like.

5. King Ibn Saud in the 1930s had named Faisal viceroy of Hejaz, to please the people affected by his conquest of that area in the 1920s, and Crown Prince Saud emir of Nejd and the Eastern Province.

6. Egypt in 1952; Iraq in 1958, 1963, and 1968; Syria in 1949, 1953, and 1961.

7. A reliable source, in May 1964, told our Jeddah embassy that King Saud had transmitted nine tons of personal gold hoard abroad and arranged for its sale.

POSTSCRIPT

1. *Saudi Arabia*, vol. 12, no. 3 (Fall 1996), p. 2.

SELECT BIBLIOGRAPHY

The primary source for events in this book is the memory of the author as augmented by his personal archives and materials still unreleased at the time he conducted his research and writing. The presidential libraries of Presidents Eisenhower, Johnson, Kennedy, Roosevelt, and Truman were consulted. The *Foreign Relations of the United States* (*FRUS*) volumes then published were an invaluable source. All items in the book pertaining to Saudi Arabia, Kuwait, and Yemen have been consulted in the *FRUS* volumes for 1932, 1933, 1937, 1938, 1939, 1941–45, 1947–54, 1955–57, and 1958–60. Volumes subsequently published on the years 1961 and thereafter will no doubt provide equally useful material for scholars who wish to pursue the subject further. Other sources include the following:

DeGaury, Gerald. *Arabia Phoenix.* London: Harrap & Co., 1946.
Dickson, H. R. P. *The Arab of the Desert.* London: George Allen & Unwin, 1949.
———. *Kuwait and Her Neighbors.* London: George Allen & Unwin, 1956.
Dresch, Paul. *Tribes, Government and History in Yemen.* Oxford: Clarendon Press, 1993.
Eddy, William A. *F. D. R. Meets Ibn Saud.* New York: American Friends of the Middle East, 1954.
Facey, William. *The Story of the Eastern Province of Saudi Arabia.* London: Stacey International, 1994.
Hartshorn, J. E. *Oil Companies and Governments: An Account of the International Oil Industry in Its Political Environment.* London: Faber & Faber, 1962.
Hay, Sir Rupert. *The Persian Gulf.* Washington, D.C.: Middle East Institute, 1959.
Hickinbotham, Tom. *Aden.* London: Constable and Co., 1958.
Hitti, Philip K. *History of the Arabs.* London: Macmillan, 1943.
Ibn Razik, Salil. *History of the Imams and Seyyids of Oman.* London: Hakluyt Society, 1871.
Khadduri, Majid. *Socialist Iraq: A Study in Iraqi Politics since 1968.* Washington, D.C.: Middle East Institute, 1978.

Lenzen, Theodore L. *Inside International Oil.* Privately published, 1972.

McConnell, Philip C. *The Hundred Men.* Peterborough, N.H.: Currier Press, 1985.

McMullen, Christopher J. *Resolution of the Yemen Crisis, 1963: A Case Study in Mediation.* Washington, D.C.: Institute for the Study of Diplomacy, Georgetown University, 1980.

Momen, Moojan. *Shi'i Islam.* New Haven, Conn.: Yale University Press, 1985.

Mottahedeh, Roy. *The Mantle of the Prophet.* London: Pantheon, 1985.

Philby, St. John B. *Arabian Days.* London: Robert Hale, 1948.

Safran, Nadav. *Saudi Arabia: The Ceaseless Quest for Security.* Ithaca, N.Y., and London: Cornell University Press, 1985.

Sanger, Richard H. *The Arabian Peninsula.* Ithaca, N.Y.: Cornell University Press, 1954.

Schmidt, Dana Adams. *Yemen: The Unknown War.* New York: Holt, Rinehart and Winston, 1968.

Stookey, Robert W. "Political Change in Yemen." Ph.D. dissertation, University of Texas, Austin, 1972.

Twitchell, K. S. *Saudi Arabia.* Princeton, N.J.: Princeton University Press, 1947.

Wahba, Hafiz. *Arabian Days.* London: Arthur Barker, 1964.

Wilson, Sir Arnold T. *The Persian Gulf: A Historical Sketch from the Earliest Times to the Beginning of the Twentieth Century.* Oxford: Clarendon, 1928.

Winder, R. Bayly. *Saudi Arabia in the Nineteenth Century.* London: Macmillan; New York: St. Martin's Press, 1965.

Young, Arthur N. *Saudi Arabia: The Making of a Financial Giant.* New York: New York University Press, 1983.

In addition to the above works, also consulted were *Saudi Arabia*, a monthly magazine, and "Saudi Arabia," an official monthly newsletter, both published by the Information Office, Royal Embassy of Saudi Arabia, Washington, D.C. 20037.

INDEX

Page numbers in *italic* refer to photos.

273